Hushed Cries

Hushed Cries

Healing is Found in the Choices You Make

dorthea l. hughes

NEW YORK
NASHVILLE MELBOURNE

Hushed Cries
Healing is Found in the Choices You Make

Published in New York, New York, by Morgan James Publishing. Morgan James and The Entrepreneurial Publisher are trademarks of Morgan James, LLC.
www.MorganJamesPublishing.com

ISBN 978-1-68350-147-3 paperback
ISBN 978-1-68350-148-0 eBook
ISBN 978-1-68350-149-7 hardcover
Library of Congress Control Number: 2016910999

Cover Design by:
Rachel Lopez
www.r2cdesign.com

Interior Design by:
Bonnie Bushman
The Whole Caboodle Graphic Design

Life is about choices. Be careful what you say and do.
Like my great-grandfather John always said, "This is coming up again."

contents

My chOIce

I sat next to my father's bedside. Seeing him for the first time in three years, various thoughts filled my head—some good and some bad. Neither of us spoke. Instead, we listened to the unspoken conversations in our minds. Looking him over, I was amazed. In my mind, he had always seemed bigger than life, and now, lying in the bed watching television, he looked so small and weak. Where was the giant man who had created my nightmares and inspired my dreams?

When I first walked into his house, fear consumed me. How would he treat me? Would he scream and call me names? Could I dare to hope that I had been gone long enough for him to miss me? How could I be thirty-five and still feel terror at the thought of displeasing him? Self-consciously, I fingered my hair extensions and wondered if he would be angry with me for wearing them. I had also gained weight since he saw me last. He had always lauded my long, thick hair and chastised me for gaining weight. In that moment, I decided that if he said anything to hurt my feelings, I would walk out the door. I wouldn't turn back, and I wouldn't return—not even for his funeral.

Sitting in the silence, I glanced at my watch. Ten minutes had passed. He stared at the television, not even glancing in my direction. Perhaps we were each waiting for the other to speak. What could I say to him? How did I even get here? Glancing back at him, I surveyed his head of completely white hair. The enormous bed seemed to swallow his gaunt body.

I heard his wife chatting with my sisters in the next room. Every now and then, she would enter the room and offer me something to drink or eat and tell me how happy they were that I had come to visit. She behaved as if I had not been gone for the last three years, as if nothing had occurred that would make me walk out of Dad's life. *Did it happen like I perceived it? Or was I overreacting and just being difficult?*

The incident that had forced me to walk away screamed inside my head and anger rose up in my throat. Ironically, I lived only a few miles away from my father's house, and avoiding him in this small town had been difficult.

I wasn't wrong. I made a good decision three years ago.

Realizing I would need to use his phone when I was ready to go home, I surveyed the room. My insecurities spiked, reminding me of what had happened on that day that forced me out of his life. *What if we wind up arguing at the end of the visit? What if he kicks me out of his house before I can borrow a phone to call my husband?*

I might be forced to walk home and endure the cold, winter night. Sweat beaded upon my forehead, and I started to panic. Maybe I should make up an excuse to use the phone now. Maybe I should leave before anything could go wrong. On the other hand, if Dad didn't accept my excuse, I could anger him. I was just about to work up the nerve to ask for the phone to call my husband DeAnte, when my stomach rumbled. Sickness overwhelmed me. *I have to get out of here.*

In my home, I reigned as queen. There, my family loved and spoiled me. My home was my retreat—the place where I was in control of my life, of my emotions. *Why did I venture out of my sanctuary? What made me believe that I could handle this situation? If I leave now, I can probably still get home in time to watch* Law and Order: SVU.

When I left the house, DeAnte had been preparing dinner. *Have they eaten already?* I pictured myself enjoying my dinner of catfish, spaghetti, tossed salad, and garlic bread. My taste buds danced in my mouth. I didn't want to deal with the turmoil of my life tonight. I wanted to go home and watch other people deal with their lives.

I began rehearsing excuses to go home. I could easily say I needed to get home and get the children ready for bed, even though my husband always did that. I could say I had to go home and do my homework. I had been working on attaining a dual bachelor's degree from Franklin University in human resources and management. Everyone knew that Dad was big on schoolwork.

I looked over at him, preparing myself to speak, when a realization hit me: *He is going to die.* I realized that he would be dying sooner rather than later, and that I had to stop running from him. If I was ever going to deal with my past, it would have to be now. I also realized in that moment, that as much as I hated him, deep down, I loved him too. I wanted to spend as much time with him as possible if he would allow it. I realized that I missed him being in my life.

I still couldn't really believe that his cancer was back—that he had only nine months to live, at most. How could this be? Disbelief and regret played tug-of-war with my soul. Regret washed over me—regret for all the time wasted fighting and hating him, hating this man whom I loved more than anyone or anything. What would I do without him? Who would I turn to when I had a problem or needed unsolicited advice? Who would I hate enough to push me to do better for myself and my family? Who would fight the giants that I couldn't defeat? He had been the biggest monster in my life, someone who had tried to destroy me, mentally and physically—every day of my young childhood and most of my adult life. Nevertheless, he was Dad. How do I explain that the man I hated most in this world also held a part of my heart? Even though I hadn't spoken to him in years, I thought of him as a place of refuge. I always knew that he was there, that he was close, but that wouldn't be the case anymore.

As thoughts swirled through my head, a commercial flashed on the TV. Dad turned to me, smiled, and excitedly yelled, "The prodigal daughter has returned." While his joy warmed me, I did realize that gone was the strong voice that had once terrified me; this voice was now weaker. Before I could grasp the idea of the strength required for him to raise his voice, I saw him smile at me, and I dared to hope that it would be a good visit. My dad had the same effect on all of his children; we loved to see him smile.

It's difficult to understand how I could describe my father as a monster yet maintain an enormous desire to please him. Though I loved my mother and the rest of my family, I learned that it was not easy to make my mother happy, nor was it rewarding. I also learned at an early age that my brothers and sisters wished I had never been born. In truth, I was a Daddy's girl right from the beginning. He loved me more than anyone else in my life. My first memories of him are those of him protecting me or making sure I got whatever I wanted. Alternatively, my first memories of my mother are whippings and her locking me out of sight.

Many people say they don't remember most of their childhood, but unfortunately, I can't forget mine. Staring at my father's lopsided grin, my mind rushed into the past.

* * * * *

One of my earliest memories of my parents occurred in the spring of 1974. My mother was all about appearances, and nothing pleased her more than putting on a performance every Sunday morning at church. We arrived at church just in time for everyone to gush over how wonderful we looked, while she beamed with pride. Daddy hated to attend church with Momma, but he liked the compliments too, so he attended sporadically. When he came, he walked proudly behind us, basking in the compliments dished out to my mother. Like my mother, he enjoyed showboating. Both of my parents took pleasure in the fact that they could afford to dress their children better than all of the other families in the congregation.

My mother honored a routine every weekend in preparation for church. It began every Saturday morning with my brothers getting their hair cut by Mr. Flowers. Daddy had built my mother a beauty shop as an addition to their house. On Saturday mornings, my sisters laundered clothes in between getting their hair styled. After dinner, the boys gathered everyone's shoes so they could shine them, and the girls finished the day by ironing everyone's clothes for Sunday morning.

On Sunday morning, we got up early and ate breakfast before we left for church. We were all well-rehearsed for the parts we played during the performance. My brothers entered the church first—looking handsome in their little suits. My brothers, Jake, David, and Andre, walked single file followed by my sisters, Angel and Gina. My sisters had to be the perfect little ladies at all times. My mother and I always entered last. She wanted all eyes on her as she entered. As the grand finale, she would walk down the aisle behind me to the second row on the right side of the church where my brothers and sisters sat waiting.

My mind dredged up one particular Sunday. Sitting on my mother's lap, I began kicking the pew in front of me, which only made my mother scold me. Being a child, I soon forgot her instructions and began to kick the pew again, which earned me a quick slap to my leg. Hearing me cry out from the pain, Daddy snatched me off my mother's lap and loudly told her that she better not hit me again. Then, in a loud voice, he complained about the service being so long and said that I could kick the pew if wanted to, considering how much of his money my mother had given to the church. Because I had my father's consent, I kicked the pew repeatedly, and this time, no one said anything to me—not even my mother.

Following tradition, after church, we went to Dairy Queen for ice cream with my mother, my aunt, and her family. As a child, this was the best part of the day for me. On this day, Momma passed out all the ice cream treats, but she didn't give me or Daddy one. Before either of us could question her, she informed me that she didn't reward bad behavior and that I didn't deserve any ice cream. I cried and screamed that it wasn't fair. She told me to stop hollering, and that if I asked again, she would whip me. I quickly stopped yelling and wiped my eyes, but Daddy wouldn't let it go. He told her to go get me some ice cream. My mother refused. She ignored him and kept visiting with her sister and her brother-in-law. Growing angrier, Daddy scooped me up in his arms and marched to the stand. He ordered me a large vanilla crunch cone. I was scared of making my mother any angrier, but I was excited at the idea of having a *large* ice cream cone. I had never been allowed to have that much ice cream.

That day, I learned a very important lesson about Daddy. He would not stand for anyone to have something that his children could not have. I went back to the car with my cone and scooted in next to my mother. She called one of my aunt's many children over to the car, and before I could even lick my cone, my mother reached over and snatched it out of my hand, giving it to my cousin. Daddy was so mad, he knocked my cousin's ice cream out of her hand, just as she was taking a lick. The ice cream exploded everywhere in the car—all over her clothes, her face, and her hair.

My parents fought all the way home. Once we were home, all of us kids raced into the house and retreated to our rooms. We heard them fighting. I was scared and sad. Whenever my parents fought, I was scared Momma would hurt Daddy. She was always so mean to him. I didn't want her to hurt him because he wanted me to have ice cream. While my parents fought in their bedroom, I was left to the mercy of my brothers and sisters, who blamed me for ruining a day of family fun.

* * * * *

Frozen in the past, I flashed back to another scene. My fifteen-year-old sister, Angel, was in charge of giving me nightly baths. Once we were shut away from everyone behind the bathroom door, she taunted me, telling me how much she hated me and how she wished I had never been born. I hated bath time and often tried to get Momma to allow me to go to bed without a bath, making the excuse that I wasn't dirty. My protests and whining only seemed to frustrate her because she threatened me with whippings.

That night, my sister purposely ran a hot bath. When I put my hand in the water, it burnt me, so I told her it was too hot. She laughed and informed me that if I was old enough to know anything, she wouldn't have to give me a bath. As the water filled the tub, I heard my mother talking on the phone in the other room. My sister told me to get undressed and get in the water.

Taking a second look at the water, I cried out for my mother. "Shut up or you'll get us both in trouble," Angel yelled.

I ran for the door, but Angel grabbed me and threw me in the water. I flipped into the tub backwards and grabbed the wall with my right hand. As both of my feet submerged into the water, I realized that it was even hotter than I had originally thought. I let out a scream that would wake the dead, as my grandpa used to say. As my feet hit the bottom of the tub, I jumped back out of the tub, throwing water everywhere. Hearing the commotion, my mother dropped the phone and ran into the bathroom just in time to see my sister dragging me back to the tub to force me back into the scalding water. At the sight of my mother, I was relieved, believing she had come to save me. I immediately tried to tell her that the water was too hot. Cutting me off, she screamed, "I'm tired of all this nonsense. I'm trying to talk on the phone with my prayer partner!" She forced me back into the tub while murmuring about me being so spoiled.

Scared, I squirmed in her arms. I tried to get her to listen to me and believe that the water was too hot, but she lowered me into the tub despite my yells. I continued to flail wildly, causing her to lose her balance. She grabbed the side of the tub to brace her fall and her hand touched the water. She immediately grimaced and dropped me back into the tub. I let out another scream and fought my way out of the scalding water. Standing in the bathroom, I cried, secretly hoping that Momma would give Angel a whipping. My feet still stung. Momma put her hands on her hips and screamed, "Shut up that crying before I give you something to cry about!" Turning to Angel, she questioned, "Why is this water so hot?"

Donning her most innocent voice, Angel replied, "I didn't know it was hot, Momma. She must have turned the hot water up so I'd get into trouble."

"Well, let some of the water out, and let the cold water run. And hurry up. I'm tired of looking at her, so the sooner she gets her bath over with, the sooner she can go to bed."

With that being said, she calmly left us both in the bathroom. My sister started to laugh. I continued to cry. As my sister worked to get the stopper out, she continued to laugh. "That's what you get for trying to get me in trouble. Nobody cares what happens to you anyway, but if you try to get me in trouble again, I'll make your bath even hotter the next time."

Getting frustrated, I yelled, "Wait till Daddy gets home. He cares what happens to me. I'm gonna tell on you and you'll get a whipping for sure."

As quick as lightning, my mother appeared in the doorway. "Nobody's telling your daddy nothing. He don't need to be worried with mess. The hot water was just an accident, and I better not hear another word about it." Just as quick as she had appeared, she was gone. We heard her laughing again on the phone. Angel smiled at me.

After Angel fixed the water, she told me to get into the tub. I did, and the water was too cold, but when I complained, she told me to shut up. I sat in the tub and cried as Angel began to wash me. "Shut up that dang crying. Just because Gina got herself knocked up, I gotta take care of you little brats. I hate taking care of you, and I hate to hear your crying even more."

As she washed me, she ignored my whimpers, and I began to wonder if she was trying to take my skin off by scrubbing so hard. The more I cried, the harder she scrubbed, as if she enjoyed seeing me cry.

* * * * *

I remembered another time spending lunch with Daddy. During his lunch break, he would bring me treats. Lunchtime was really the only time I was able to spend with Daddy without having to share him with my brothers and sisters. I looked forward to lunchtime every day. October 14, 1974, was special because it was my fourth birthday. When I heard the sound of Daddy's jeep, I excitedly ran to the back door at lunchtime, but Momma told me to go sit down in the living room and watch *Sesame Street*. I heard Daddy coming in the back door, and when he came in, he called out to me. I jumped up to greet him, but Momma yelled for me to sit back down. Just as I turned my head back to watch the television, I heard Daddy come from the kitchen into the living room. He was bent over, steering something into the room. It was a shiny red tricycle with a basket and a bell on the handlebars. Red and white strings came out of the ends of the handles. Daddy was laughing as he entered the room, and I jumped up and ran to him, asking him if it was mine and if I could ride it. He put me on it and walked behind me, pushing me with his feet as I screamed with laughter.

Every day after that, I asked my mother if I could ride that tricycle, and every day she told me no, that she was busy. I even remember the day Daddy came in at lunch and asked me why I wasn't smiling. After telling him that Momma wouldn't let me ride my bike, he asked her why she hadn't taken me outside to ride my tricycle.

"I've got more important things to do than to sit outside while she rides around on that thing," she retorted.

"What important things? All you do is sit around on your butt all day and gossip with the church folk. I work all day every day to take care of you, so the least you can do is take my daughter outside and let her ride the tricycle."

"Okay. Okay. I promise. I'll try to make some time to let her ride," she pledged.

I remember the hope that flooded me when I heard Momma say those words. Momma never did find the time, though.

When Daddy came home and asked me if I had been riding my bike a week later, I told him no. That day, I rode the bike inside the house while Daddy ate his lunch. He even laughed when I bumped into my mother's new dining room table. Momma stood scowling and complaining that I was ruining her furniture, but Daddy seemed to delight in the fact that she was upset. As soon as Daddy went back to work that day, she yanked me off my tricycle and threw it down the basement stairs with a yell. "Don't even think about asking your daddy to ride that thing again, or else."

Daddy was my hero back then. Wonderful memories of him flooded my consciousness.

Shortly after Christmas, I woke up one morning and felt horrible. I told my mother that I felt sick, but she told me to go back to bed because she needed to get some things done before she opened the beauty shop. I tried to go back to bed, but sleep wouldn't come. After lying there for a while, I crawled out of bed and found Momma in the beauty shop.

"Momma, I still don't feel good," I whined.

Her customer smiled at me, turning to Momma. "Honey, we can reschedule if you need to take her to a doctor."

"Naw, she's fine. That child is spoiled rotten. She's just looking for attention. She's a hardheaded mess that won't listen to nobody but her daddy. Girl, she can't reach the age of twelve soon enough for me."

When I asked why she wanted me to turn twelve, she asked her customer to excuse her. She took me back into the main part of our house and whipped me, then sent me to my room and told me not to come back into the beauty shop. Hurt and confused by my mother's reaction to my being sick, I tried to lie back down, but my head continued to throb and my stomach danced the mamba. I began to feel the room start to spin, and I needed to get to the bathroom, so I crawled out of bed. I made it to the bathroom floor before I started throwing up and having diarrhea simultaneously. My retching must have been loud because my mother and her customer came in from the beauty shop to check on me. Momma put me in the tub to clean me up, and she took my temperature. I don't know what my temperature was, but the next thing I knew, she told her customer that she had to take me to the emergency room.

In the hospital, I saw the doctor speaking to my mother. After talking to the doctor, Momma came into my room and told me that I was sick enough to be admitted to the hospital, but not sick enough that I needed her to stay with me. "I gotta get back to the beauty shop. They're going to put you in a room, and then I'm going to go, but you better not embarrass me."

They quickly took me to my room and put me in a big metal crib. Reaching up, they pulled the sides down, and I began to cry hysterically. When I tried to pull the sides back up, my mother got embarrassed and told me to stop crying and let them do what they had to do so she could leave. The more I fought with them, the angrier she got. I watched while they placed plastic over the top of the metal crib and turned on a machine that was meant to help me breathe. The idea of them putting plastic over my head made me even more hysterical, so I began to fight again even harder. My mother, losing all patience with me, told them to stop fighting with me. I thought she was coming to my rescue, only to have her lift up the side rail, reach in, grab my leg, and pull me to her so she could beat my legs with the strap from her purse. When she was finished thrashing my legs, she pushed me back inside the metal crib and pulled the door down on me. She then informed the nurses that she had to go. "She'll be fine now," I heard her say as she exited my room. I don't know if it was from exhaustion or just knowing that my mother didn't care, but I stopped fighting long enough for them to get the tent properly placed over the metal crib. I lay there confused, wondering how she could act like she cared about me one minute but not the next.

After they left the room, I tried to lift the cage again, but it was locked. I cried again. Just as I reached the moment of exhaustion and accepted that no one cared about me, I heard Daddy in the hall, screaming my name. I heard the people in the hall reassuring him that I was all right—that I was just a little upset, but that they were doing everything they could to help me get better. I cried out for him so he could find me. When he entered the room, he made them let me out of the cage and told them not to put me back in that cage if they wanted to live. When they unlocked it, he reached in, pulled me out, and held me. He was crying just like me. He asked them if my momma had known they did this to me. They assured him that she had known and it was only so I could get better. He told them they had better get me better, but they better not put me back in that cage again. Again, Daddy had come to my rescue. He stayed with me as long as he could, but he had to get back to work. He left a pink dog with a flower in it on my nightstand and told me that the dog was there to protect me while he was away. He also left some candy. I was so glad that Daddy was Daddy. He always had a way of making me feel safe. Nobody loved me like Daddy.

As I glanced over at Daddy, the memories came in floods now, and I didn't stop them from overwhelming me. *I need to remember.* I sank deeper in the chair as I began to relive my past.

When spring of 1975 arrived, so did my older sister Gina and her son. Gina stayed only a short time, but her son, Jimmy, stayed with us for a while. Momma spoiled him. I didn't like him because Momma took everything that was mine and gave it to him. One Saturday, while Jimmy was at our house, my mother seemed to be in a particularly good mood. She let the boys out of most of their chores so they could play outside. Jimmy, who was a year older than me, told my mother that my sister hadn't given him anything for his birthday in January. Momma took him in her arms and hugged him and told him that was because *she* was supposed to give him his present. He was so excited and begged to know what it was. I wanted to know too. She had never given me a birthday present. She called my brothers over and whispered in their ears. As my brothers took off running back into the house, they looked back at me, laughing. When they emerged outside, they had my tricycle with them. My mother called Jimmy over to her and told him to get on and ride it. Jimmy began to laugh and run toward my bike. I cried and ran toward it as well. Jimmy tried to ride it, but I held onto the handlebars, screaming for him to get off. Jimmy and I began to scream at each other and cry out for the other one to let go, but neither of us did, which caused my mother to come over and snatch my hands off the tricycle.

Daddy came running out of the garage when he heard all the hollering. He immediately snatched Jimmy up by the arms and yelled at him to get off my tricycle. Mother slapped Daddy and yelled at him to get his hands off her grandson.

"Well, keep your grandson off the bike that I bought for my daughter," he yelled.

Before Momma could speak, he continued. "Why don't you ask Jimmy's granddaddy to buy him a bike? Better yet, you could ask his daddy to buy one for him if your daughter even knew who his daddy was."

The fight continued, and before we knew it, my parents were on the ground scuffling. All the kids were crying and begging them to stop fighting. When they realized they were fighting outside in front of the neighbors, they stopped fighting long enough to go into the house. Neither of them spoke to one another until later on that evening.

I guess Daddy realized he had gone too far. My mother explained to him that I was a little girl, and when I rode the bike, I spread my legs like a little boy. She didn't feel that was very ladylike, and he listened to her. She also said that she realized he had spent too much on the tricycle for it to sit under the stairs in the basement. Daddy pondered over her words: "We have so much. Why can't Jimmy share in our blessings? After all, he *is* family." I guess Daddy wanted to get out of the doghouse with Momma because he agreed with her. As tears ran down my face, I listened silently and let the realization sink in that I no longer had a tricycle.

For days to come, Jimmy teased me that he had a new tricycle. While everyone else moved on, I was still upset that Jimmy had my bike. One evening while Jimmy was teasing me, I decided I couldn't take it anymore. I told him that he couldn't color in my coloring book, which caused us to start shouting at one another. My mother was on the phone, as usual. My brothers told Jimmy to hit me and take my coloring books, so he did. When I ran into the kitchen crying, Jimmy and my brothers, David and Jake, followed behind me, each daring me to mention their name. My mother, angry at her phone call being interrupted, screamed for us to all be quiet. She asked my brothers what happened, and they told her that I wouldn't share my toys with Jimmy and that I was being selfish. My mother then made me go into the basement in the dark until she could finish her conversation on the phone and whip me. While I sat in the dark basement waiting for a whipping, my brothers and Jimmy opened the door and whispered down to me that the boogieman was going to get me. This only made me cry all the more.

As I sat there crying, I couldn't help but wonder why Momma loved Jimmy so much and hated me. I was her daughter. I was her baby. Jimmy was my sister's baby. As I sat in the dark wondering why, I heard Daddy's truck pull into the driveway. He had come home for dinner. As soon as he sat down, he asked where I was, and Angel told him that I was in the basement on punishment because I wouldn't share my toys with Jimmy.

Daddy jumped up from the table and opened the door to the basement and told me to come out of the basement. My mother, hearing Daddy shout down to me, got off the phone. Daddy and Momma began screaming at one another. She told him she had put me down there until she could get through with her phone call—it was important and couldn't wait. She told him that I was spoiled and didn't want to share my toys with Jimmy.

He yelled, "As hard as I work to take care of you and my kids, my daughter shouldn't have to share anything if she doesn't want to. Ruthie, you better not ever lock her in the basement if you want to see the light of day again."

She didn't take to being threatened by Daddy about how she chose to discipline me, and they began to fight again. Again, everyone blamed me for their fighting. Luckily, Daddy had to return to work, so their fight consisted of a few slaps back and forth. I felt bad that Momma and Daddy were fighting, but I was glad that he had come home and gotten me out of the basement. I was even happy that he had told her not to put me back down there.

* * * * *

As far back as I remember, I can't recall when my parents ever kissed one another or showed any affection for one another. For that matter, I cannot recall a time when I ever saw my mother express affection for any of us in that house. Daddy, on the other hand, kissed us on the cheek, tickled us, or hugged us. It was almost as if he was starving for affection, just like us. He never tired of giving us hugs and kisses.

Early in the fall of 1975, I remember coming home from kindergarten and going into our house only to hear Momma and Daddy screaming at each other. When I entered the kitchen, Daddy was sitting on top of the washer, and Momma was standing at the sink, washing dishes and throwing hurtful words over her shoulder at him.

I told them, "I'm home."

My mother just replied that I needed to go upstairs and change out of my school clothes. Daddy told me he was glad I was home and smiled at me. I noticed he had blood running down his arm. "Daddy what's wrong? Why you are bleeding?"

He told me to ask my mother. "She did it," he said.

I walked over to her in front of the sink and asked her what was wrong with Daddy. "Nothing he didn't deserve. Now, go change out of your school clothes like I told you to."

I cried. I wanted to know why she had to hurt him. I began to walk to Daddy, but he gently told me to go change my clothes. Scared for him to be alone with Momma, I asked him if he would be all right. He reassured me that he would be, and I went upstairs to change my clothes.

Before I could even get to the top of the stairs, I heard them fighting and screaming. She was upset at him for telling me that she had cut him, and he was upset because she had actually cut him. I ran upstairs to my room and hid in my closet under blankets and sheets.

After the shouts stopped, I heard Daddy's jeep leave. Momma called out to me to come to her. I was so scared, I couldn't move. She yelled that if I didn't come to her, she would beat me when she found me. I climbed further under the blankets and sheets. I heard her speaking on the phone. "I'm on the way. Yeah, I'm leaving him," she said.

I didn't want to leave Daddy, and after what she had done to him, I thought, *What if she cuts me too? Why did he leave me with her? Why did he have to always go back to work?* The next thing I knew, Momma was pulling me out of my hiding place. After she got me out, she became even angrier with me when she realized that I had not changed clothes like she told me to. When she asked me where my shoes were, I wouldn't tell her. I didn't want to leave Daddy.

"If you don't get your shoes on, I'm going to leave you too," she yelled.

"Fine. Leave me," I shouted. "I don't want to leave Daddy."

The thought of leaving Daddy to be with her scared me. She was the one who was mean to me. Daddy had never beaten me or even raised his voice to me.

Momma slapped me, grabbed my hand, and dragged me down the stairs, out the back door, down the alley, through another alley, and down the street to her friend Toya's house. As we made our way there, I switched between screaming, crying, and pleading with her to leave me at home with Daddy. I promised her that I would not tell anyone where she went if they asked me. She stopped running and just stared down at me. For a fleeting moment, I thought she would leave me there and allow me to return home to wait for Daddy to come home and rescue me, but then she told me she couldn't trust me and began dragging me again toward her friend's home. I was still screaming when Mrs. Toya opened the door. Mrs. Toya told me to stop giving my mother a hard time and led me to the back of her house to play with her kids. From the adjoining room, I heard Momma tell Mrs. Toya that it was a shame she couldn't leave me with my father since we deserved each other. Mrs. Toya giggled and whispered that I could still hear. "Aw, honey. She didn't mean it. That was just her frustration talking. Besides, a young girl belongs with her momma."

After that, Mrs. Toya and my mother left us to go to the school to pick up my brothers and sister. When she came back, immediately we all left. When I got into the backseat of the car, I immediately fell asleep. It was better to go to sleep and not think about the fact that we were leaving everything I valued the most behind—my daddy.

When I awoke again, we were in Kansas City at a hotel. This was the first hotel I remember ever staying in. My brothers and I followed my sister to our room. My mother had sent us ahead with Angel while she hid the car. I had to use the bathroom, so once we entered our room, I opened the first door that I saw. Only, that room didn't lead to the bathroom—it was the door to the adjoining room.

Peering in, I saw a man on top of a woman in bed, making noises. I was so shocked that I just stood there frozen. Somehow, I knew I should close the door, but my curiosity got the best of me. My brothers heard the noises on the other side of the door and came running up, which caused the couple to look up and see me in the door. When the woman screamed, I immediately closed the door. I didn't mean to stare, but I was curious. My brothers teased me about the whipping I was sure to get when Momma reached the room. Angel told me that if no one knocked on the door and told on me, she wouldn't tell on me because she knew it wasn't my fault. Surprised at her kindness, I relaxed. She began asking me questions. She wanted to know why I had opened the door. Then she asked me why I had watched those folks. She asked me if I had ever seen Momma and Daddy in their bedroom. Glad that someone was actually talking to me, I relaxed and answered her questions. I even giggled when I told her that I knew I should have looked away and closed the door, but I wanted to watch them. She giggled and told me she would have watched too. Just when I began to really relax and forget about what had happened, Momma arrived at the room, and my sister told on me. She told Momma that I didn't shut the door because I wanted to watch them in the bed.

"She's a nasty little girl, Momma," Angel screeched.

While Momma sat there silently, taking it all in, there was a knock at the door. It was the couple from the room next door. They came to apologize to my mother and me. They explained that they were newlyweds and apologized for what I had seen. Immediately after they left, Momma whipped me with a belt, screaming that she couldn't leave me alone for a minute.

We stayed there one night and moved on to Wichita, Kansas. Upon arrival at Momma's great-aunt's house, she informed us that she had to leave for a while, but that we would be all right if we minded her great-aunt. We were all a little scared because we didn't know the woman.

Before leaving, Momma told her aunt that it was okay to whip me if I gave her any problems and then proceeded to tell her how spoiled Daddy had made me. She made me sound as if I were an animal when she told her that I needed to be broken because she was never going back to my daddy. At the thought of never seeing Daddy again, I cried. My mother thought I was crying because she was leaving and told me to shut my mouth before she whipped me. She explained to all of us that she would be back in a couple of days. Panicked by what she had told her aunt, I told her that I had not been crying because she was leaving—I was crying because I wanted Daddy. I told her in front of her aunt that I wanted to go back home to Daddy. She was so enraged at my confession that she made my brothers go out and find some switches.

"She's going to need those switches for you. Now shut up that crying. We ain't going back to Daddy, so just get that outta your head."

As my mother walked out the door, I grabbed her and hugged her around the waist. I begged her not to leave me. She pushed me off, whipped my legs, and walked out the door as I lay on the floor crying. I looked over at the old woman sitting in the chair and cried that I wanted Daddy.

"Stop that hollering, child. You gonna make me have to get up from here, and trust me, you don't want me to get up."

Our great-great auntie had two grandchildren, Donna and Dalton, living in her home. Dalton played with my brothers, and Donna played with me. Donna didn't act or look like any girl I had seen before. She dressed just like her brother. She even wore sneakers. I, on the other hand, wore only dresses and didn't own a pair of sneakers. One day, Donna suggested that we switch shoes, and since I had never worn sneakers, I agreed. When she grew tired of playing with me, she joined the boys outside climbing a tree. I watched in amazement as she climbed the tree just like the boys. I had never done anything like that. Once she found a branch to sit and rest, she called for me to come up and join her. When I told her I didn't know how, she said that it was easy. She even bragged that she could do anything her brother did. I declined her invitation. Even though I wanted to follow her up the tree, I was scared both of Momma finding out and of falling, so I just stood around the bottom and waited for them to get down.

Momma rarely let me go outside, let alone do things that boys did. When the little girl came down from the tree, my brothers pointed out that my shoes were all dirty and scuffed. They told me I had better go tell the old lady what Donna had done to my shoes. Donna recognized where this was going and demanded that I return her shoes to her immediately. Jake and David told me not to give her shoes back until the old lady knew who had ruined mine. Again, Donna demanded that I return her shoes, but this time, she told me if I didn't give her shoes back to her, she would "whip my ass." I was so shocked that she said a cuss word that even though I was scared of getting a whipping from the old mean lady, I was more scared of Donna whipping me. She looked like she meant what she said. As I began to untie the sneakers and take them off in defeat, my brothers pleaded with me to keep them on, claiming that we would all get in trouble when Momma found out about my shoes.

I turned to look at my brothers. It was rare for them to speak to or about me nicely. While I was looking at them, Donna must have decided that I had had enough time to make up my mind, because she ran over and kicked me in the side. When I doubled over, she pulled my hair. I was both shocked and scared. I started to scream, and my brothers pulled her off me. Her brother jumped into the fight. It didn't take long for the old lady to yell at us from the house to stop all that fussing. Donna quickly kicked my shoes off and yelled to her grandmother. The old lady came to the door and asked what was going on. Donna immediately told her grandmother that I had been trying to be "fast" in playing with the boys, and that I had messed up my shoes. She further explained that I was lying and blaming her for the whole thing. My brothers and I began to all talk at once, trying to explain to the old lady that Donna was lying, but she wouldn't listen. Donna and Dalton told her that I had messed up my shoes, and when Donna refused to give me her shoes, I had picked a fight with her, taking her sneakers. I stood there in disbelief while I listened to Donna and Dalton lie to their grandmother.

I guess my brothers recognized that this was a battle we wouldn't win. When the old lady asked if they were just trying to protect me, she promised them that if they told the truth, they wouldn't get a whipping with me. They changed their story to match Donna and Dalton's story. I don't know how to describe what I felt in that moment. My brothers had lied to protect themselves. When I opened my mouth to explain again, David and Jake looked at me, pleading for me to take the whipping by myself.

As the old lady dealt my licks with her switch, I cried out in pain. I cried out for Daddy, who couldn't rescue me this time. I cried out for my brothers, who had lied to protect themselves. I cried out for my mother, who had given this mean old lady permission to whip me. I cried out for me because no one loved me enough to protect me.

Not only did I get a whipping, but the old lady wouldn't let me eat dinner that night or breakfast the next morning. After breakfast the next day, we were sent out to play, but no one would play with me. I thought since I had taken the whipping, they would be nice to me, but that wasn't the case.

Three days later, my mother and sister came back to the old lady's house. My great-great auntie quickly informed my mother that I was a liar and that she had whipped me. She bragged about how she wore my behind out. Before I could even explain, my mother told my brothers to go get her some fresh switches so she could whip me too. I tried to explain what really had happened, but all she could do was scream at me that she was going to give me what I had been needing, and that my daddy wasn't there to stop it.

"A mother doesn't like to whip her children, but it's something that has to be done," she said. Then, with a grin, she added, "But I'm going to enjoy whipping you because the whipping I'm about to give you is long overdue."

As she began to whip me, I ran from her, screaming, "Please don't whip me," but she caught me and pinned me between her legs. I pleaded with her, but she insisted she was giving me what I had long ago earned, telling me that it was Daddy's fault that I was getting this whipping. If I had listened to her and not to him, I would not be so bad, she said. With each word, came another lick. Just when I thought I would die if she hit me again, the phone rang and the mean old lady called out to Momma. I lay there on the floor, trying to catch my breath, both embarrassed and hurt by my undeserved whipping. I had been beaten three times within twenty-four hours for something that wasn't my fault. As I lay there on the floor, exhausted and looking up at my mother while she talked on the phone, I wondered why she hated me so much.

After she got off the phone, she spoke privately with her aunt. I listened quietly as I heard her explain. "Auntie, I have decided to go home." My auntie tried to reason with her. "Ruthie, are you sure that is what you want to do? You can leave the children with me. That way, if he is up to something, you won't have to worry about the children." Quietly I held my breath as my mind reeled. Were we really going home? *Oh please, Momma, don't leave us with this horrible woman. I want to go home and see Daddy!* Momma assured her auntie that we would all be all right. She turned around and came back to us and loudly announced she would be getting some sleep because we would be leaving for home in a few hours. Slowly I allowed myself to breathe. We were finally going home!

My heart leapt in my chest. Even though I was happy to be going home, I wondered what could have happened to Daddy to change Momma's mind. I hoped he was all right. I couldn't wait to get home and tell Daddy everything that had happened while we were gone. As I went to my assigned place to sleep, I lay there not caring about my bruises. I couldn't wait to get home and tell him everything. I lay there and thought about how angry he would be at everyone for how they had treated me. I played it over in my mind how I would tell him how my brothers had lied to save themselves, how Momma had beaten me this whole trip, and how that mean old lady had beaten me. I would tell him how Donna had beaten me up and ruined my shoes. Oh, I couldn't wait to get home and tell him how they wouldn't even let me eat. I imagined how he would fuss at Momma for all that had happened to me.

Most of all, I couldn't wait to get home to see Daddy. As I drifted off to sleep, I rehearsed how I would run up to Daddy when I first saw him and cover his face with kisses, and how I would promise to never leave him again.

I learned during the drive home that Daddy had broken his back at work. I did not know exactly what that meant, but I knew it wasn't good for Daddy. I could tell this just by the look Momma had on her face. I had never seen her look worried about Daddy.

Shortly after we got home, Daddy questioned us about where we had been and what happened. Even though I had promised not to tell about Mrs. Toya, I told him how Momma dragged me to her house, how her children laughed at me, and how I didn't even have shoes on my feet when we left home. Momma and Daddy argued over Momma dragging me down the street with no shoes. They argued over her family whipping me. Most importantly, they argued because she had left him.

Soon after that, we felt a calm that our house had never felt before. Daddy was happy, and Momma wasn't yelling or beating anyone. During the calm, Daddy was busy trying to heal and make Momma happy so she would love him again. I was so happy, loving both Daddy and Momma.

I used to rush home from school just so I could lie in the bed and tell Daddy how my day at school had gone. I was sad that he was in pain, but glad that he was home all day. Momma didn't whip me all the time anymore. She made us great lunches, and sometimes, she even looked in the room in between her beauty shop customers and smiled. When Momma smiled at us, I got a warm feeling in my stomach. I was so happy. I had Daddy every day, and Momma was being nice to Daddy and me.

Ever since I could remember, we had big family celebrations with Momma's brother and sister. We took turns going to Chicago, Illinois, or my uncle would bring his family to Kewanee, and we would meet up either at one of our homes or at the park. This summer was no different. Daddy was feeling better so he didn't mind when Momma insisted we participate. All of my family came together to laugh, eat, and enjoy each other. We played all day while the grownups talked. When the sun went down, my older cousins played hide-and-seek, and we younger cousins would catch fireflies and put them in Momma's canning jars. It was good times all summer long.

Little did I know that those were the last times we would all come together as a family. While we thought it was finally working out for Daddy and Momma, she was secretly planning to leave him. This time, she had no intention of returning, so she had planned her escape, down to every detail.

Momma never took us to the store with her—not even to buy shoes. She would trace our feet on paper and buy us shoes from the tracing. I should have been suspicious when one Saturday she canceled all her hair appointments and decided to go shopping for school and groceries. I was supposed to start first grade, and I was excited. My oldest brother, Andre, decided that he would stay behind and take care of Daddy so my mother could get all her shopping done. Daddy had been complaining of back pain all morning, but when my mother announced that she was going to the store, he got out of bed and found reasons to block her from leaving the house. As we drove away, Daddy stood on the porch and waved to us.

Momma drove a block and a half down the street and pulled into the Howards' driveway. She got out and told us to stay in the car. She told Angel to come and get her if Daddy followed her. I sat in the car patiently waiting for my mother to come out so we could go to the store. I had an uneasy feeling about leaving Daddy at home. Momma came back with bags and placed them in the back of her station wagon. She made several trips, then got back into the car, and we drove away. We drove about fifteen minutes before my brothers started questioning Momma about where we were going. She didn't answer. Instead, she just continued talking to my sister in the front seat with her. My brothers started to whisper that we must be leaving Daddy again because we were no longer in Kewanee.

Looking around, I realized that this was how the roads had looked when we went to see Momma's family. I tried not to interrupt Momma, but I began to panic. Why were we leaving Daddy again? Daddy was being good! I was being good! I couldn't even remember the last time Momma and Daddy had fought. How could she leave Daddy when his back hurt? Who would take care of him? As much as I tried not to, I cried, softly at first, but when the first tear fell, it was like a dam breaking. I couldn't stop. I began screaming that I wanted to go home with Daddy. I screamed at her as loud as I could.

"I don't want to go with you! I hate you. I wish you would just leave and never come back. I want my daddy!" I did not care how loud I screamed or what came out of my mouth. I wanted her to understand me. I didn't want to leave my daddy.

I realized she wasn't responding to my cries, and when I focused my eyes on her, I saw that she was ignoring me. I had to make her understand that I was serious. I don't know where the idea came from, but I couldn't stop myself. I wanted my daddy. Maybe if I caused her enough trouble, she would give in and let me return to Daddy. I cried even harder while trying to climb over my brothers to open the car door. My brothers yelled out to Momma that I was acting crazy, trying to open the door. She yelled, "Dorthea, stop it right now!" Finally, I had her attention. I knew I should stop, but I was hoping to make her so angry that she would just stop the car and put me out. I thought that if she put me out, I could go back home to Daddy.

When I felt the car stop moving, I stopped screaming and waited for her to tell me to get out and go back to Daddy, but those words never came. Instead, she took the shoulder strap off her purse, got out of the car, walked to the backseat, opened the door, reached in, and pulled me over the lap of my brother, and began to beat me right there on the side of the road. When her anger subsided, she stopped beating me, threw me back into the car, got in, and drove down the highway. Exhausted from my beating, I cried myself to sleep. When I awoke, we were in Chicago, Illinois, at someone's house, who gave Momma money and let us spend the night.

That night, while Momma handed me my pajamas, I begged her to let me go back and take care of Daddy. Every time I asked her this, she whipped me and told me that Daddy wasn't here to save me, so I needed to shut up.

My cousins at that house were nice to me. They saw how upset I was and took care of me as best as another child could. I got in the station wagon the next morning and got in the back so no one would tell Momma I was crying about Daddy again. I cried myself to sleep.

From there, we traveled to St. Louis, Missouri, to stay with more of Momma's cousins. These new family members scared me. They cussed, smoked, and drank. They even played cards for money. Momma would stay up all night with them. Who was this woman who smoked cigarettes, colored her face, and drank liquor? My mother did not smoke cigarettes—my mother went to church.

We slept in the front room of the house on the floor, so while we were supposed to be sleeping, we would peek out at her. I watched how she laughed and talked with the strange women and men who arrived every evening and stayed until morning. Everything about her changed. While we lived in her cousin's house, they had parties every night and gambled until dawn. Every night, someone was fighting over lost money, and some nights, we heard gunshots.

One night I awoke to loud laughing. As I lay in bed listening to the laughter coming from downstairs, I decided to go and see what was so funny. As I peeked at my momma with her friends, I heard her saying words that I had never heard come from her mouth. I sat mesmerized, listening to the sound of her laughter. I tried hard to remember her laughing this loudly with my daddy. I continued to watch her as a man walked up to her and said something in her ear. I do not know what he said, but she smiled at him and got up from where she sat and made him a drink. As she placed the drink in his hand and began to back away from him to rejoin her group of lady friends, he reached out and grabbed her rear end. I was so shocked that he had touched Momma's private parts that I must have let out a gasp, because one of the women noticed me and called me into the room with them. Hearing the ladies make comments as to how pretty I was, Momma turned and looked my way. I knew I should have just silently disappeared into the shadows, but there was a big part of me that wanted to see more of this momma who laughed and smiled with her new friends. Maybe this momma would love me, and I wanted her to love me.

Holding my breath, I walked into the room. I did not know what was going to happen to me when Momma realized that I had been watching her friends, but surprisingly, she called me over to her, embracing me as I came closer to her. Never had my mother embraced me before like this, and it felt wonderful. I liked this mother. I stood in her embrace, smiling at the women as I listened to her tell them my age. One of Momma's new friends commented about how sweet I was to want to be by my momma. I turned and smiled at this lady, but Momma quickly explained I was a daddy's girl, and unfortunately, my daddy had spoiled me rotten.

Momma's tone turned harsh, and before I could realize what was happening, she was using the same arms that had embraced me for her company to pin me against her while she applied pressure to the skin under my arm. I could feel her pinching me, but just as I was about to scream, I looked at her face and saw the look. I knew that look. It was the look that said, *Don't embarrass me, or it will be worse.* I tried to not scream, but the pressure was getting worse. I stood there listening as the women paid my momma compliments, and my eyes filled with tears. I couldn't exactly distinguish what they were saying, because the pain was excruciating, and all I could do was scream inside my head, *Momma, please stop!* Oh, why had I dared believe it would be okay to dare interrupt Momma's fun? I should have known she would not be happy with me. She finally stopped pinching me but did not allow me to move from her. I stood there wondering why I couldn't be like my brothers and sister and stay on her good side. Most importantly, why couldn't she love me like she loved them?

The conversation changed as the men started to flow back into the room. Momma turned to me with a smile on her face and told me to tell everyone good night. Just as I did what I was told, she turned and kissed me on the cheek and told me to get back to bed. It was so nice that I stood there for a second, wondering what had just happened. When I did not move as quickly as she wanted, the familiar face came back, and I darted toward the doorway. As I was walking up the stairs, I could hear the women teasing Momma that they had seen her pinching me and she should be ashamed of herself. Momma laughed before she explained. "Don't let that little girl fool you. Dorthea knows she did not have no business coming in here with grown folks."

One of the ladies replied, "Ruthie, when I saw your little girl's eyes fill with tears, I almost cried myself." The ladies teased her that she was too soft and sided with Momma. I could hear them all chiming in together that sometimes children had to be put in their places no matter where they were to make sure they understood who the boss was.

The next morning, Momma and her cousin woke us to the smell of breakfast being cooked. I dressed slowly, not wanting to see Momma—not because I was angry, but because I did not know if she was still angry with me. As I sat down to eat breakfast, I took special care not to do anything wrong that might cause Momma to focus on me. It didn't matter because once everyone was seated, Momma and her cousin began to laugh about what she had done to my arm. Momma asked to see my arm. When they saw the bruising on my arm, they began to talk about what had happened last night.

After Momma's cousin left and went to work, Angel wondered aloud to Momma why we were living with these people. Momma explained. "Your daddy doesn't know these cousins and would never look here for us, so we are safe here."

Angel replied," Momma, I didn't know we had family that lived like this."

Momma replied angrily," If you don't like the life I can provide, maybe you should go back and live with your daddy." Angel didn't say anything else. Even though I was young, that made sense because I didn't even know Momma knew people like this, and I didn't like the way my mother had changed. Even though she laughed more and appeared to be enjoying the company of her family, she did not seem to be any happier or treat us any better. Then one day Momma came home and said we had to leave immediately, that someone had spotted Daddy in the neighborhood.

We went to live with more of her cousins. These cousins had a big dog that peed and pooped all over the house. Momma knew Angel and I were scared of dogs, but she didn't care. The house smelled, and there were brown bugs everywhere.

"Momma, please pick me up!" I screamed while reaching my arms out to her and trying to climb up her body.

Over my screams, I could hear Angel screaming simultaneously, "Momma, please don't make us stay here. I'm scared!"

Momma just shoved me off her while screaming, "Shut up—you girls are embarrassing me." Momma may have said only a few words, but the look on her face said so much more. It was screaming, *Stop it right now—or else.* I dried my face as best I could on the arm of my jacket and tried not to look at the bugs wandering around visiting one another. When we first arrived, her cousin would put up the dog, but the longer we stayed, the longer they let the dog out around us.

At this house, they partied only on the weekends. I thought that meant that Momma would spend more time with us, but she spent every night with her new boyfriend. She would ride with him on his garbage route.

Again, we slept on the floor. I hated sleeping on the floor; it smelled like dog pee and poop. While we were on the floor, the brown bugs would climb on us. I cried myself to sleep every night. I just wanted to go home and sleep in my bed, where there were no brown bugs or big dogs in the house. I couldn't understand why Momma wanted to be here and not at home. Didn't she care that her children were scared?

One morning I awoke with a bitter taste in my mouth. Just as I began to wonder why, I felt something move in my mouth. I jumped up screaming, waking Angel and my brothers from their sleep. I was screaming and crying because I could feel it moving around in my mouth. My mouth began to fill with saliva because I didn't dare swallow. I continued to jump around and moan. Because they did not know what was wrong with me and I could not tell them, Angel began to get scared and began to scream, "What's wrong?" I could not answer her. My brothers laughed while I moaned and jumped all around. Momma's cousins woke up and came to see what was wrong, too. I did not know what to do, so I just opened my mouth and spit everything onto the floor. There were not one, but two brown bugs in my mouth. One just lay there, not moving, but one tried to escape but was unable to move quickly because it was trapped in my saliva. When I saw the evidence of what was in my mouth, I began to empty the contents of my stomach. This caused my brothers and sister to start screaming. I don't really know if they were screaming because of the bugs or the vomit that seemed to want to keep coming out of my belly.

Momma's cousins helped Angel clean everything up and instructed me to go back to bed, but I couldn't. I was scared another bug would get into my mouth, so I kept trying to get someone to talk to me. Momma's cousin kept hollering from the next room for me to be quiet and go to bed.

Eventually, I fell asleep, only to have Momma wake me up a few hours later when she arrived home. She was angry because everyone had told her what had happened, and she felt like I was disrespecting her cousin's home. I tried to tell her that I was scared, but she just kept getting madder and madder. The more I tried to explain, the more she threatened me, until she just reached over and smacked me. I couldn't understand why she was so angry with me.

After that night, Momma's cousin let her dog run free all over the house all the time. I was so scared. Angel said it was because they were mad at me, since I had made a "federal case" over the brown bugs. She also told me that Momma said the brown bugs were roaches. Even though she knew the dog walked freely in the home, Momma continued to leave us every night.

One morning, I woke up wet. At first I did not know why I was wet, so I smelled the liquid that was on my gown, and to my shock it smelled like dog pee. I screamed out in disgust, waking my brothers and sister. They quickly figured out the dog had peed on me while we lay sleeping and began to laugh. Momma's cousin came running from her room to see why I was crying again. This time, she told us that she couldn't keep getting woken up from all this nonsense, because she had to work. She was going to have to talk to Momma about when we were leaving her house.

Angel did her best to clean me up so we could all go back to sleep, but she warned me that I would probably get a whipping when Momma came home. Angel told me that she wished we could just go back home with Daddy. She told me that she didn't like how we were living either. When she was done talking to me, she let me lie beside her so I wouldn't be scared of the dog.

A few hours later, Angel woke me, telling me Momma was back and in the kitchen talking with her cousin. It sounded like they were arguing. All of us whispered that we hoped Momma would come out and tell us that we were going home, or at least leaving there. When Momma came out of the kitchen and walked toward us, I could tell by the look on her face that she was angry. She walked toward us, past my brothers and past my sister. She stopped short of me, reached down, tore the cover off, and began beating me with a belt. She beat me for disrespecting the only place we had to lay our heads. She screamed at me, saying that I was going to cause us to be homeless. With every swing of her arm that held the belt, I could feel the anger directed toward me. As the belt met with my skin, I felt pain in every part of my body. The belt never missed my skin—first my legs, but as I tried to avoid the belt, it began to land on other parts of my body—my back, my face, my arms. There was no part of my body that the belt felt was unreachable. My sister and brothers scrambled to get out of the way of the belt as Momma beat me. Running from her, I fell to the floor, but I quickly scrambled to my feet and tried to get away from the belt. However, my screams upset the dog, and he came running toward me. I tried to run to Momma as a shield from the dog, thinking she would protect me, but she just saw this as an opportunity to get hold of me while she whipped me. Trapped by the dog, I had to take her licks without running. After she got tired of hitting me, I lay back down on the floor and listened to her and her cousin laughing at me in the kitchen. They laughed about how the dog had scared me so bad I ran to my whipping.

My brothers and older sister lay there listening too. This time, they didn't laugh. I think we all knew the game had changed. This woman was not the momma that we had known. She drank, smoked, cussed, stayed out all night with a boyfriend, made us sleep in a house with roaches, and didn't care that a dog had peed on her child. We all knew this wasn't time for laughing at one another—this was time for all of us to be scared. From that day on, we didn't complain about the roaches or the dog. We stayed there for about two months.

One day, we came in from school and our cousin told us to go to the house next door where our mother was waiting for us. We went next door and found Momma with her boyfriend, Alex. He had given her the money for us to move into our own house, and they were already busy moving us in. Alex was nice to me. He always gave me candy or touched the top of my head when he saw me. I especially liked that whenever Momma was about to whip me, he'd grab her and start dancing, or tell her that he had to make a run and that she needed to ride with him. I couldn't tell if it was true or if he was trying to rescue me, but it worked, so I thanked him just the same.

I was so glad that he'd gotten us a house, so I ran up to Alex, jumped in his lap, gave him a kiss, and hugged him. My mother screamed at me to get down off him. She never said anything else, but I knew from the tone she used, that she wouldn't forget about it. She was definitely coming for me later. Alex immediately hollered at her. He told her that he was not that type of man, and if she thought so, he needed to be going. He told her that if she whipped me or did anything else, he wouldn't come back. He stormed out the door. Surprisingly, she didn't whip me. She just told me to go to bed. I didn't get any supper, but I didn't get a whipping.

The first night we were alone in the house, I was scared, but I shared a bed with Angel. I think she was scared too, because she didn't push me away when I cuddled up next to her. All through the night, we heard sirens, gunshots, and yelling. The next morning when Momma came home, she had to wake us for school—we had overslept, and none of us had gotten much sleep. I couldn't help but wonder who this woman was and where my momma had gone. How could a woman change so much? How could she leave her four children alone in this city at night just to go be with her boyfriend?

While we were getting ready, my sister spoke about it to Momma, saying that Momma didn't need to be leaving us alone at night. Momma snatched her up and told her that Alex was her man and that he wanted her with him at night. "I ain't got a job, and spending time with him is what it takes to get him to pay the bills."

"Well, if you're going to be leaving us every night, you could have left us in Kewanee with Daddy. At least we were safe there."

"Shut your mouth and get ready for school."

For the next couple of weeks, our routine consisted of Momma coming home every morning in time to rush us out of the house to school. We went to school each day and came home to find her and her boyfriend in bed asleep or sitting on the stoop talking with her cousin from next door. We did our homework while she cooked dinner. Then, Alex went home to his wife. After dinner, we bathed and went to bed, and she prepared to go to work with her boyfriend. She was never home with us at night except on the weekends, and on the weekends, she and her boyfriend hosted card parties.

After being in the neighborhood for a few weeks, we made friends with the children down the street. Sometimes, Momma allowed us to venture down the street to their houses and play, but mostly we stayed in front of the house where she could see us. One day, David brought a girl home to play with me named Baldy. Momma said Baldy liked David and was just using me to get into our house. I liked her. She would come over every day after school. She taught me all sorts of games.

One day while Baldy and I were about to leave and walk to her house, Alex came over and gave me an all-day sucker. When we reached Baldy's house, her friend Felicia called us over to her house to play. Felicia couldn't come to Baldy's house because she had to watch her little brother, Andy. I liked being with both Baldy and Felicia. They gushed over me. They told me I was pretty. When it was time for Momma to leave for the evening, she hollered down the street for me to come home. All three of my new friends walked me home. When I was halfway home, Andy asked me for a lick of my sucker, and I told him no. He cried. Baldy and Felicia tried to pacify him, but he continued to scream that he wanted my sucker. I just stood there feeling awkward. I knew he was littler than me, but I still didn't want to let someone else put their tongue on my sucker, so I continued to lick it and not share. Baldy and Felicia asked me if I would just let him have one lick, and I still replied no. Andy reached up and tried to grab it from me. Shocked, I slapped his hand. I stood there looking at all of them in disbelief. When I slapped his hand, he became angry and jumped on me. I pushed him off, but not before he had pulled my hair. I screamed in pain and slapped him across his face as hard as I could. Feeling panicked at what had just happened and fearing that they would all jump on me, I ran down the street hollering until I reached our front door. I tried to explain to my mother why I ran into the house screaming, but she wouldn't listen.

As Alex and Momma walked out the door, he noticed that my sucker was gone and asked me where it was. I tried to tell him what had happened, but Momma told me that they had to go. They walked down the steps to his truck. I went to my room and lay down. I was scared to look out the window. I was scared they would follow me home and get me back for what I had done to Andy. There were no adults to protect me in the house. Shortly after I lay down, my brothers told me that Baldy was downstairs and wanted to talk to me. Baldy had followed me home and explained to both of my brothers that it wasn't my fault. I sat up immediately and wanted to know if she had come to beat me up. They told me that she was there to say she was sorry. I stared back in disbelief. I was so glad she wasn't mad at me. I hurried downstairs to see my newfound friend. Baldy reassured me that neither she nor Felicia was mad at me. We played all evening until my older sister, Angel, came home and made us go into the house.

The next day at school, Baldy found me on the playground and invited me to go play on the Eagle's Nest until it was time for school to begin. The Eagle's Nest was shaped like half an egg upside down with triangular-shaped openings all over it that you could climb through. Once inside, you could simply meet with friends or climb to the top and hang upside down. Baldy instructed me to join her inside. When I stood up and looked around, I noticed Felicia and Andy were already there waiting for me. I started to turn around to climb back out, but Baldy reassured me that it was okay, so I walked to where they all stood among the other children. There were children everywhere, hanging upside down or climbing in and out of the play structure. It was hard to hear anything. When I reached them, Felicia asked me why I had slapped her brother. By the look on her face and the tone in her voice, I immediately got scared, and I knew this was a bad situation. Instead of answering, I tried to turn around and run, but Baldy and Felicia grabbed my arms. I tried to wrestle myself loose, but they threw me to the ground. When I saw Andy coming toward me, I kicked at him with my legs, but they grabbed my legs too. Through my tears, I saw someone give Andy a purse. I thought that was strange until he swung it at me. The purse was filled with something hard. I screamed in pain as he repeatedly hit me with the purse. As the rocks poured out of the purse from his frantic swinging, he grew tired of it. He fell to the ground and began biting me everywhere. I screamed with every bite. I screamed for Daddy, I screamed for Momma, I screamed for my brothers, and I screamed for the police. I had never experienced anything like this. I didn't know children could be this mean. When the bell rang, they left me lying in the dirt, crying and exhausted.

Jake was in the third grade, and our school did not have a third grade, so he had to wait daily at our school until a bus arrived to take him to his school. When the bell rang and all the kids ran into the school to start their day, he noticed me on the ground under the Eagle's Nest. He came and got me up, helping me into the school. He tried to find David so he could leave me with David and still catch his bus. Unfortunately, by the time he found David, he had missed his bus. We didn't know what to do. My clothes were all ripped, and my shirt barely clung to my body. My eyesight was blurry, and blood ran from my nose. Every time I swallowed, I tasted blood, and my mouth hurt. My brothers decided to take me home and show Momma what had happened to me. All the way home, we told each other that she would be so mad about what had happened to me that she would move back home to Daddy. We were so happy at the idea of moving back home that we never even considered she might not be happy with us when we arrived at the house. On the way home, we had to walk by housing projects, where a man offered to bring me into his house to clean me up. We almost accepted his offer until he told us that only I could come in and that my brothers had to wait outside.

Once we made it to the house, our hopes of moving home were quickly doused as Momma took one look at us and asked us what we were doing walking home. We explained to her what had happened, but she didn't care. She was angry that her card game had been interrupted. Alex came to our rescue, not letting Momma whip us for walking home and applauding my brothers for taking care of me. She made them go back to school. Alex took Jake to his school across town, and David and I walked back to our school. As David and I walked back to school, we walked in silence—neither of us knowing exactly what to say to each other. It was quite obvious Momma didn't care what happened to us.

When we arrived back at the school, we received a lecture from the principal about leaving the school. The principal explained to David that it was his job to protect me and sent him to his class, while telling me to go see the nurse before I returned to class. The school nurse treated my wounds, gave me clothes to change in to, and let me lie down in her office until I felt better, all the while muttering under her breath, "What type of momma would send her baby back to school looking like this?" I lay there, torn between wanting to tell her to stop talking about my momma like that and wondering the same thing.

A few days later, Baldy came to our house, wanting my brothers to come outside and play. I was hurt that my brothers would even think about going outside to play with them after they had hurt me so bad. When my brothers finished playing street ball with the neighborhood children, a few of them came and rested on our porch and talked. I still wouldn't go outside because I was scared they would get me again. I stood just inside the door and watched everyone talk and laugh with one another.

After a while, I grew tired of listening to them talk, and since everyone had gone home except mean ol' Baldy, I left the door to watch television. Before long, Jake came in and joined me, leaving David outside with Baldy. I thought maybe since it was just them outside, I could go outside with them and try to be friends again with Baldy. I wanted to be able to play outside with the other children without fear. I hesitantly went to the door and looked out at David with Baldy. Just as I began to open the door and walk out onto the porch, David saw me and screamed at me, "Leave us alone. Go back into the house! No one wants you out here."

I responded by telling him, "This is my momma's house, and I can come outside if I want to." They heard the shakiness in my voice and began to laugh at me. I was so embarrassed that Baldy had heard him yell at me. I screamed at Baldy, "You need to go home. This is my house!" David responded by informing me, "She is my girlfriend, and she can come over anytime she wants." They both laughed at me and called me names. I responded the only way I knew how, by closing the door and running back into the house away from them. I did not want them to see the tears of shame that were beginning to fall onto my face.

A little after dark, I looked outside on the porch to see what they were doing, but I didn't see either of them. I asked Jake where they were, but he didn't know either. As it grew even darker outside and there was still no sign of David, Jake began to grow worried as well. He began to look out the windows, and he even went outside and walked around the house, looking for David. When Jake reentered the house, he wondered aloud, "I wonder where David is? He knows he is not supposed to be out after dark. If Momma comes home and he isn't here, we'll all get into trouble."

We sat on the floor and continued to watch television, both of us taking turns looking out the windows and opening both the front and back doors during commercials, checking to see if we could see David approaching the house. When our television program ended and we did not have anything else to occupy our minds, we just sat and looked at each other. Every time we saw headlights approaching our driveway, we wondered if it was Momma. Jake looked out the window and said more to himself than to me, "Man, where is David? He better get back here before Momma gets home."

I did not say anything to him because I was thinking the same thing. Jake turned to me and asked, "Do you think I should go outside and look for him?"

I replied, "I don't know. If we go to find him and Momma comes, will we all get a whipping?"

"Dorthea, it does not make a difference if we are all gone or not. If Momma comes home and David is not here, she is gonna be so mad, we will all get a whipping anyway!"

"Well, if you go, then I'm coming with you!" I practically screamed. I was so upset, not knowing what to do, but knowing I was scared to stay at home by myself. We began to put on our jackets and shoes just as we heard someone running up the porch stairs. We both ran to look out the front window and saw David entering the front door. He entered the house all out of breath, quickly sitting down next to us on the floor. I heard him as he whispered into Jake's ear that if anyone asked, he had been in the house with us all evening. I wondered what he had done, but I knew from the looks on both his and Jake's faces that it wasn't good.

Jake and I were so glad that David was safe at home, so we continued to watch television, and neither of us said anything for the remainder of the evening. Shortly after my sister arrived home that evening, there was a knock on the door—it was Baldy's momma. We listened while she questioned Angel about when our momma would be home. She sounded angry and said she would be back. After she left, Angel called us all into the front room and wanted to know what had happened.

I sat there quietly while David told Angel how he had tricked Baldy to go out back with him and had beaten her up. He told Angel how he had asked Baldy to tell him how they had set me up. He told Baldy how much he hated me and was glad they had jumped me to get her to confide in him how they had planned my assault. When she had finished telling him her story, he asked her to go out back with him to make out in the shed. Once they were inside, he told her he was going to do to her the same as they had done to me. Apparently, he beat her up pretty bad, because her mother wanted justice.

When Momma came home the next morning, Angel told her what David had done. Momma called David downstairs and wanted to know why he had done such a thing. We all anxiously listened from the kitchen as he explained to Momma that as the new man of the house, it was his responsibility to protect us. Momma shocked us all by her response. She reached out and hugged him and told him she understood his thought process, but she explained that he was not to ever hit another girl as long as he lived. Just like that—no whipping, no hollering, and no threatening. Momma said she would talk to Baldy's mother. I suppose she did because that was the end of that.

We loved Saturday mornings because we would watch cartoons. We would get breakfast and sit around the television, covered in blankets and enjoying the freedom that watching cartoons provides for a child. This particular morning, my brothers allowed me to watch whatever I wanted while they crept back into the kitchen. At first, I wasn't interested because I was just glad that I could watch the cartoons of my choice for a change, but then curiosity got the better of me, and I decided to sneak into the kitchen and see what was more important than watching cartoons. I was surprised to find them standing over the stove, heating paper towels over the fire. They held them over the heat long enough to make the paper hard and crisp. Once the paper had cooled, they took pencils and wrote on it as if it were school paper. I asked them to let me try, but they frantically told me no and pushed me out of the kitchen. I returned to my cartoons, feeling left out once again.

By the time *Soul Train* had ended, my brothers were upstairs playing in their room, and Momma had returned from the trash route with her boyfriend. I was bored. The only thing on television was Westerns, and I was still scared of Baldy and her friends, so I didn't dare go outside to play. I decided to take a chance and make some writing paper as my brothers had done earlier. At first, the paper was doing just as it had for my brothers, but then the paper caught on fire, and not knowing what to do, I held the napkin as long as I could until it burnt my fingers, causing me to drop the napkin onto the floor. As the paper towel lay burning on the floor, I watched in amazement, wondering what to do. I ran to the sink and got a glass of water and poured it on the napkin, and this seemed to help, but I needed to get another glass of water to completely extinguish the fire. Once the fire was out, I was relieved until I saw the big black burn on the floor. My brothers, hearing the commotion, came running downstairs. They were shocked and stared in disbelief at the burn mark on the floor. I tried to wash it up, but no matter how much detergent I put on the floor, it didn't change the burn spot. Momma heard my brothers laughing and teasing me about what she was going to do to me when she woke up, so she came into the kitchen to see what we were all doing. My brothers immediately told on me.

She didn't even let me explain. She just grabbed my arm and started throwing me all around the room. She grabbed the broom out of the corner and cracked me over the head with it. Then she grabbed the skillet off the stove and slapped me, sending me flying to the floor. As I tried to run from her, I heard my brothers laughing. They were pretending it was a wrestling match and saying, "In this corner, we got Momma, and in this corner, we got our sister Dorthea."

Surely she would stop to make them stop tormenting me, but she was so focused on whipping me that she did not pay them any attention. I must have passed out from the pain because when I woke up, I was lying on the floor with my pants down to my ankles, and she had a chair on the side of me. She was preparing dinner. I reached down to my ankles to pull up my pants, but she saw me out of the corner of her eye. "Dorthea, don't you even think about moving. I am not finished with you yet."

I looked at her while trying to focus my eyes. I couldn't think clearly. I tried to remember what had happened to cause her to beat me. As I was trying to concentrate and remember, I felt a strange wetness in my mouth. The wetness had a bitter taste. I reached up and stuck my fingers in my mouth and saw the blood on my fingers. As I squirmed around, I could feel pain all over my body. My right forearm had a huge lump that not only screamed out in pain, but also felt hot to the touch. My legs were bruised, and my butt burned. I turned my body slightly over to examine my legs and buttocks and saw the red welts all over my arms and legs. They traveled all over my body, leaving a painful reminder to me that when Momma was angry, she could speak volumes without saying a word. I lay back on my back, careful not to cause myself any more pain than I had to, and remembered how the day had started so well before the incident had occurred that resulted with her beating me. I must have felt overwhelmed because I began to cry. As if hearing my tears made her angry, she came over and began whipping me again. She sat in the chair and whipped me until her arms got tired. Then she got up and returned to dinner. Until I fell asleep where I was, I lay there wondering how she could do this to me if she loved me.

When I awoke, she was in the living room on the couch taking a nap. I began to get up, and my brothers, who were sitting at the table eating their dinner, told me that Momma said for me to stay on the floor because she wasn't finished whipping me for almost burning the house down. When I cried, they laughed and asked me if I wanted to wake Momma up, so I continued to lie there sniffling, praying that she never woke up. I drifted off to sleep again. I awoke to the burning pain of the belt landing on my legs.

As I scrambled to clear my head and move so the belt did not find its intended target so easily, I realized Momma had woken up and was beating me again. I screamed out in pain, "Please, Momma, don't hit me no more. I promise I won't do it again. I am sorry!" I continued to plead with her to stop, but my cries fell on deaf ears. The hits hurt more so than before because the belt was aggravating wounds that were fresh. I felt like the belt was hitting my raw skin. Between blows, she screamed that I was going to make her late for when Alex came to get her to do the garbage route. She quit whipping me only when she heard his horn announcing his arrival.

After she left, I still lay on the floor crying. I was exhausted, but most importantly, Momma had not told me if I could get up. I did not want to do anything to cause myself to get another whipping from her. My brothers came downstairs and cleaned the kitchen. I asked them if I could get up and get dressed, but they told me that Momma hadn't said I could get up, so they advised me to stay there until she returned home in the morning. They laughed at me as I cried. They turned off the light and climbed the stairs to go to their rooms when I screamed for them to come back, begging them to turn the lights back on—I was scared of both the dark and the mice that lived in our house. They began to laugh at me and tormented me, telling me that I better not go to sleep because the mice would sneak up on me and bite me. I begged them to stay with me, but they told me that they were tired and going to bed. I begged them to leave the light on, but they told me they couldn't because then they would get in trouble. As they turned out the light and left me, I began screaming again. I screamed and screamed until my voice was hoarse, but no one came. As I cried myself to sleep, I wished for Daddy to come get me. If he was here, Momma wouldn't get to treat me like this.

Around midnight, Angel came home with her boyfriend. I tried to cry out to her not to turn on the light. I didn't want Danny to see me, but when I opened my mouth, my throat hurt, so only a low rasping sound escaped my lips. They both gasped when the light exposed me naked and bleeding on the floor. She sent her boyfriend home after he helped her carry me upstairs and put me in the tub. I heard them whispering something about Daddy. My sister, who had never been nice to me, came in and helped me wash and dry off. She even let me sleep in her boyfriend's jersey. This was the first time I ever remembered Angel being nice to me.

The next day, I drifted in and out of sleep until early afternoon when I heard my brothers snickering and trying to quietly pack. They didn't want to wake me. I asked my brothers, "What are you doing?" They wouldn't answer me. They just kept laughing at me. Thinking they might not have heard me, I asked them again, "What are you doing?" Growing frustrated, I tried to question them further, but I drifted back to sleep.

I woke again to them laughing and giggling, their suitcases packed and sitting neatly next to their beds. With a trembling voice, I asked them again, "Where are you guys going?" They stopped whispering and turned toward me. I thought they were going to answer my question, but they just stared at me for a quick moment and turned to each other and began to giggle between themselves. I tried to stay awake long enough to find out where they were going, but sleep would not let go of me. As the sleep took hold of me, I heard them laughing as they left the room.

Eventually, they came back into my sister's room and woke me up, teasing me that they were going someplace that I couldn't go, and I'd be so sorry for not going with them. David told Jake to stop teasing me because he didn't want me to go with them. After what seemed forever, Jake finally looked at me and began to speak to David. "It's too late. She won't have time to pack anyway," Jake said. They laughed at me and told me they were going back home with Daddy. He was sending a cab for them.

I don't know how it happened, but I was wide awake and moving out of that bed. I grabbed the closest clothes I could find. I didn't have time to pack, so I grabbed my book bag from school. I grabbed my pick-up sticks that Alex had just given me and some clean underwear, and then ran downstairs. My sister met me coming down the stairs in the kitchen and asked me what I was doing. I told her I was going home to live with Daddy. She cried and begged me to stay with her. I told her that I was scared of Momma and I was going home.

Momma saw me come into the living room with my book bag. She had her makeup on, and I smelled the liquor on her breath. Her nails were painted, and she was listening to music. Momma let out a long laugh before she spoke. Her eyes were fixed on me while she spoke. "Dorthea, are you leaving me too?"

Before I realized what I was doing, I quickly replied, "Yes!" I must have said it too hastily because she got that look in her eye.

"I thought you weren't going. I thought you wanted to stay with me."

"Why did you think that?"

"I told your brothers to wake you up over four hours ago. They said you didn't want to go."

"They didn't tell me anything. I just found out, so I just packed my bag."

"Well, you can't go. Your hair isn't combed, and you're not dressed properly."

"My hair don't look that bad, and Angel gave me a bath last night."

"Well, I think you should—"

A horn honked outside, and Jake yelled that it was the cab. Waiting on Momma to tell me it was okay to leave seemed as if it were an eternity. While Momma looked at me with a look we all knew too well, I waited for her to tell me that it was okay for me to leave her, okay to walk out that door, okay for me to return to Daddy. As I waited, my heart began to beat quickly. What if Momma did not let me go home? I felt my hands start to sweat. I began to fidget from side to side. My body began to sweat. I felt extremely hot, hotter than usual, so hot, in fact, that I thought I would pass out. I began to estimate if I could make it outside to the cab before she could catch me. I was scared to run to the door, but I couldn't stay there with her any longer. I just couldn't! Surely if I made it to the door and went outside, she would not whip me in public. Just as I was about to drop my things and run for the door, she began to speak in a calm, soft manner. "If I allow you all to return to live with your daddy, you have to promise you won't tell him where I live."

Quickly I replied to her, "I promise. I will not tell him anything. Momma, please, can I go?"

Jake screamed out, "Momma, we won't tell Daddy where you live! I don't ever want to come back to St. Louis ever again in my life."

"Okay, you can go!"

I screamed with happiness and quickly took off running out the door, hoping she wouldn't change her mind. I wanted to go back to Daddy so badly that I would have agreed to anything. I would have agreed to shave my head if she had asked me.

As I was walking out the door, my brother David announced that he wasn't going if I went. "I hate her, and I don't want to live with her," he wailed, "and if she's going, I can stay here and have Momma all to myself."

"Come on, David. Please come with us," Jake begged.

David laughed and snorted. "Naw. Ya'll go."

As I was running down the steps to get to the cab, I dropped my bag, and my pick-up sticks fell on the sidewalk. As I bent down to pick them up, Alex pulled up and saw the cab. Alex walked up the stairs to our porch and asked, "Where ya'll going?"

Jake did not answer him. He continued to run past him to the waiting cab.

"Momma is letting Jake and me go back and live with our daddy."

Alex ran halfway back down the sidewalk and hollered at the cab driver, "Don't you go nowhere. My name is Alex Tolton. Ask anybody who I am and they will tell you I ain't nobody to play with. I gotta go ask their momma something real quick. I mean it. Don't you move this car until I get back. It won't take me long. Man, please don't move this car!"

Alex turned away and ran back into the house. From the steps, I heard him ask, "Ruthie Ann, are you sure sending Dorthea back is the right thing to do, after all you've told me?"

I began to panic. What if she came outside and tried to stop me? Just as I had decided to leave my pick-up sticks and run for the cab, the door opened and Alex stood there, looking at me with tears in his eyes.

Alex reached into his pocket and gave me some money. "Be careful," he said.

I took his money, smiled at him, gave him a hug, and ran toward the cab. I was free—free from beatings, free from hurt, and, most importantly, free from a momma who acted like she hated me.

The cab only drove for about ten to fifteen minutes when it pulled to a stop. Daddy was standing by a blue Buick Electra 222. We were so happy to see him, and we got out of the cab and ran to him. We were all over him—hugging, kissing, and crying. At that moment, he was the greatest daddy in the world. He looked like a movie star smiling down at us. Daddy wore a long, black leather coat with a black cowboy hat. He sent us to his car as he paid the taxi driver. We watched him through the windows as if he would disappear if we lost sight of him. We were so focused on him that we didn't notice Mr. Johnnie Howard, Daddy's friend, or all the food in the backseat with us.

The backseat was filled with all sorts of goodies—desserts, Doritos, bread, sandwich meats, cheeses, pops, and candy bars. As my brother and I gushed over all the food, Daddy laughed. He asked us what else we wanted and said that there was nothing too good for his children. We had never eaten Doritos or Twinkies. Momma was from the South, and she believed black-eyed peas and cornbread was a meal. The only candy we were allowed to eat was peppermint or homemade peanut brittle that she would make once or twice a year—unless you counted the candy that Alex snuck us.

Daddy took us to his older brother's home in East St. Louis. My aunt made my brother and me something to eat while they all went into the next room and talked about what Daddy should do with us. My brother Jake was nine, and I was five—soon to be six, in a few days. The grown folks consisted of Daddy, his brother, his brother's wife, Mr. Johnnie Howard, and my older brother who was fourteen years of age.

My Uncle Andre and Aunt Grace tried to convince Daddy to either let them keep us or return us to our mother. They told him that he didn't know how to take care of children our age. Daddy argued that he was already taking care of his son Andre. Unwavering in their beliefs, they expressed their concerns with the way Daddy had raised Andre. My brother was allowed to have a checking account in his own name, allowed to drive the car, allowed to drink, and allowed to sit in on grown folks' conversations pertaining to his mother. They didn't like the way Daddy allowed Andre to believe he was grown, and they ridiculed Daddy's parenting skills.

They almost had him convinced to let them return us. I heard trembling in his voice as he asked who would tell us that we were going back to our momma. They told him to tell us that we were going to spend the night. He could leave in the middle of the night, and they would get in touch with my mother in the morning to return us. If my mother didn't want us, they would keep us, and he could visit us as much as he wanted. Mr. Johnnie Howard agreed with my uncle and aunt and told Daddy that it was the right thing to do for everybody involved.

My brother and I listened as the grown folks decided our future without even asking us what we wanted. We decided together to tell Daddy that we wanted him. We ran into the room, grabbed Daddy around the neck, and begged him not to take us back. He looked at us through tears and asked why. Neither my brother nor I spoke. We were hesitant to tell Daddy what we had been through. My aunt and uncle interjected themselves into our conversation with our father and told us either returning to our mother or living with them was for the best.

I turned to Daddy and screamed, "If you make us go back, she will beat me worse."

Daddy jumped up and asked what I meant by that.

"I can't show you Daddy because I would have to take off my clothes."

Aunt Grace took me into the bathroom and made me strip down to show her my body. She looked at me, cried out, and covered her mouth. Then she told me to get dressed and to stay in the bathroom. She stepped out of the bathroom, and I heard my Aunt Grace call my uncle to the outside of the bathroom door.

I heard her whispering, "She bruised all over, Andre. It's pretty bad. There are some fresh bruises and some old ones, and she's so skinny, her bones are poking out through her skin."

"Damn it. Are you sure? Let me see her back."

There was a knock on the door. He entered with my aunt and asked to see my back, arms, and legs. I saw the look of concern in his eyes. Why didn't my mother and father look at me like that? How could I understand that my uncle had to make a decision that would affect all of our lives? He couldn't force Daddy to send us back to my mother now, and he didn't want Daddy to get into trouble for getting revenge on our mother for beating me. He didn't believe my daddy should have us children alone either.

After my uncle and aunt stepped back out of the bathroom, they began whispering again, and I heard him tell his wife to hush.

"What are you going to tell Ace? If you tell your brother the condition of that gal, he gonna kill Ruthie Ann!"

"I don't know what Ruthie Ann was thinking when she did that to that gal."

"Andre, you can't tell Ace! You don't know what that man will do."

"We've got to tell him, and that's that! I don't know what Ace gonna do to Ruthie Ann, but he need to know what these children been going through!"

"Dorthea, put your clothes back on, sweetie, and come on back to the den."

I took my time coming out of the bathroom. When I got to the den, my brother was explaining that Momma used to whip me all the time and send me to bed with no dinner.

Tears ran down Daddy's face. Everyone was quiet while Jake told story after story of how I would get horrible whippings from my mom. The only time any adult spoke was to ask for another incident about my whippings. I saw the tears on each of their faces as I looked around the room. I went over and moved Daddy's arms so I could climb up and sit on his lap. He looked like he could use a hug. After my brother was done talking, they decided not to send us back to Momma, but now my aunt and uncle pleaded with Daddy to let them keep us.

He was so angry with the fact that Momma had mistreated us, specifically me. He stood up and began to pace in the den, and when he spoke his voice was loud.

"I don't know what's wrong with that woman, but I can fix it. There ain't nothing she can tell me to make me understand treating Dorthea like that!"

Uncle Andre tried to reason with his brother and calm him down.

"Ace, calm down! Now let's talk about this. Ruthie Ann has always had a firm hand when dealing with the children. I've believed her to love her children. For the life of me, I can't give you a reason for this, but I'm sure she must have her reasons."

"I know her reasons. She did it 'cause they my kids! It's obvious they don't fit into her new life with her new friends. If she didn't want them, she should have never took them with her. It's a good thing I came when I did. She would have probably killed Dorthea if I had not come when I did for my children. Maybe I ought to beat her and starve her so she can see how it feels, or better yet, I ought to just kill her!"

"Now Ace, you don't believe Ruthie was trying to kill them kids, and stop all this foolish talk in front of your children!"

My daddy and uncle began to argue with each other as to why and how this could have happened to me. I sat there and listened as their voices grew louder and louder. I watched as Uncle Andre began to pace back and forth as well. They would meet in the middle of the room and yell at each other. The conversation between them was so emotional, I thought a fight was on the verge of taking place.

"Now Ace, that don't make no sense. Ruthie Ann loves those kids! I admit, what happened to Dorthea shouldn't have happened, but you can't kill these children's momma because of it. You'll go to prison, and then what will happen to ya'll children?

"If you don't want the children to return to their momma, then let Grace and me raise them for you. They can stay here with us and our children. Grace don't mind. We have more than enough room, and you can see them anytime you want. Ace, what you know about raising children by yourself, especially a li'l gal?"

Daddy stopped pacing the floor and stared at both his brother and sister-in-law for a moment before he replied to their request to allow us to stay in their home and allow them to raise us.

"Can't nobody raise my children better than me, and what I don't know how to do, I'll pay somebody to do. I don't need nobody to take care of my children!"

My uncle began to protest, but Daddy stood up and began to put on his coat. Both my aunt and uncle did not want to give up on convincing Daddy to allow them to care for us in their home.

"Ace, why don't ya'll spend the night, and we can discuss this in the morning with a clearer head."

"No, I don't need no sleep. Ain't nothing gonna change my mind about this. Dorthea, Jake, Andre, Johnnie, get ya'll coats on!"

Mr. Johnnie tried to help Daddy's family reason with him, stating that we could all use some sleep before we hit the road.

Daddy yelled, "Unless you got another goddamn ride to get back to Kewanee, you had better get your coat on."

I was glad we were leaving. I didn't want them to get another chance to convince Daddy to let them keep us. I was young, but I could tell they had a way of talking to him that made him feel bad about himself. I believed the best place for us was with Daddy. I believed that we would be safe and secure with Daddy. We hugged and kissed our uncle and aunt good-bye and waved good-bye as we ran to claim our seats in the car.

For the next four hours, while Andre drove us home to Kewanee, Illinois, Daddy questioned us about everything we had done while we had been away from him. He wanted to know whom we had met, where we had stayed, and if Momma had a boyfriend. We told him everything, competing for his attention and trying to tell him the most. He was interested in hearing how Momma had changed by wearing pants and makeup, smoking and drinking liquor, cussing at us, and, most importantly, about her being gone every night with her boyfriend. He especially wanted to know more about her boyfriend. We told him how Alex spent the night at our house sometimes, and we told him how Alex's friends came over and played cards for money. He listened and asked a lot of questions. He was so interested in what we had to say—not like Momma, who never wanted to hear what we had to say or cared what we thought. That was our daddy—always concerned with what was going on in our lives. In between taking turns talking and sleeping, we ate all the way back home to Kewanee.

When we arrived home, Daddy told Andre to help me out of the car and into the house. As we entered the house, it felt different from what I remembered. It felt cold, empty, and lonely. As we took off our coats and adjusted to being in our new/old home, Daddy and Mr. Johnnie began to argue.

"You got what you went for, and now you need to concentrate on taking care of those children."

"I can't take care of these children by myself. I work both day and night. Ruthie Ann is their momma, and she gonna come home and help take care of these kids!"

I was shocked to hear that Daddy had planned on Momma coming home and being with us all along. I wanted to stay and listen to Mr. Johnnie and Daddy talk, but I was so sleepy that all I could do was think about that big bed in my room that longed for me as much as I longed for it. Climbing into bed, I realized I didn't have to sleep by the wall anymore because I had the entire bed to myself. No one would wake me every few hours to tell me to scoot over or tell me to share the covers. Most of all, no one would wake me at all, because I was alone. Ever since I could remember, I had shared this room. First, there were three of us—my older sister Gina on the outside, Angel on the inside, and me in the middle. When Gina moved out with her son, I shared it with Angel, who was promoted to the outside, but now it was all mine. I had a queen- sized bed all to myself. I thought I would enjoy having the bed to myself, but instead, I just felt lonely and scared. I tossed and turned all night, waking several times and wondering where I was. Were we at home? Had we really left Momma, Angel, and David behind? Just when the memories flooded my brain and I realized it was all real, I would fall back asleep.

I must have slept for only a few hours because it was morning and Daddy was hollering for us to get dressed and come downstairs. He had to take us to see a man who was going to make sure no one could take us from him again. When we arrived at the Henry County courthouse, he left Andre, Jake, and me sitting on a bench in the hallway while he went into an office and asked one of the nice women for help. When he came back to get us, we were taken into the judge's office to speak with him in private. The judge asked us to tell him everything that we had been doing while we were with our mother. When we finished, he instructed his secretary to take me to the restroom. I didn't think I had to go, but she insisted I try. I felt strange trying to go to the restroom while she stood there with the stall door open watching me. I felt embarrassed as I looked down at my holey underwear. After a few moments of me trying to go with no result, she told me it was okay. As I stood to pull up my clothes, she continued to stare. When I caught her eye, she just smiled and told me it was going to be okay.

When we returned to the judge's office, the judge thanked us for talking with him and instructed us to wait for Daddy in the hallway. As we were exiting the judge's office, I overheard the judge's secretary whisper to Daddy as she took her seat.

"Mr. Hughes, if you don't mind, I have some clothes that might fit your daughter. If you want them after this is over, I will give you my number and you can come get them tomorrow evening."

"I don't want your pity, and we don't need your hand-me-downs. I can buy my children anything they need!"

"Mr. Hughes, I did not mean to insult you. I just would like to help in any way I can. I just feel awful for what those children had to endure at the hands of their mother."

I guess Daddy realized the judge was watching this interaction because he quickly calmed down and replaced his angry tone with a much nicer, friendlier tone as he replied,

"Thank you."

When Daddy joined us, he told us that the judge had granted him his divorce and awarded him full custody of all his children, even David and Angel. He offered Daddy child support but warned him that if he granted it, Momma could seek visitation. Daddy turned down the child support but took all of the marital assets. With the knowledge that we would never have to leave Daddy again swimming in our minds, we began to squeal. We jumped all over Daddy, hugging him and planting kisses all over his face. He laughed and reassured us that nobody would ever take us from him again.

From the courthouse, we drove to the home of Daddy's girlfriend, Rochelle, and her mother in Rock Island, Illinois. She lived in a grand house filled with all sorts of pretty knickknacks. She smiled at us with a tight smile that did not seem friendly at all. She invited us in, but as we moved about her home, she watched our every move. She openly winced as we walked through her home. However, I could tell by the rise and fall of her voice as she continued to speak with my daddy that she was happy we were with him.

I told her that the little dolls and figurines that were everywhere throughout her home were pretty. Through tight lips she explained that they were very expensive and were not to be touched for any reason by little hands. Daddy continued to show us her home, and as we walked through her house, because I understood her message that we were not to touch her things, I held my breath, scared of bumping and breaking one of her beautiful pieces. Apparently, she did not trust us to be careful, because she immediately walked around and began removing some of the pieces out of harm's way.

She and her mother were so pretty, and they smelled so nice. After we were all seated and had introduced ourselves to one another, Rochelle told Daddy that he had some nice-looking children and asked him to go into her bedroom to talk. Rochelle's mother stayed in the kitchen with us children and fixed us food to eat. We spent the night at Rochelle's house, and sometime in the early morning, Daddy woke us up and told us to get dressed—we had to leave. I asked Daddy when we were coming back. He smiled and told me never. He said he could never be with a woman who didn't want to be bothered with his children. Apparently, she had told him in the privacy of her bedroom that we were cute and all, but she had raised her children and liked the freedom they had to party and come and go as they pleased. She felt Daddy needed to take us back to our mother. He spent the night, but woke up and took us out of her house.

Once we returned home, Daddy took us shopping. He explained the circumstances surrounding him bringing us shopping to the salesclerk.

"I just got my children back from their mother, and I will need seven days' worth of clothing for both my children."

"If you don't mind me asking, where is their mother?"

"She wanted to stay in the big city with the big lights. She didn't want to be their mother anymore. Look at them for yourself. She took my children and ran off, and while she had them, she beat my little girl and didn't feed her!"

The salesclerk cleared her throat and looked away, embarrassed at Daddy's candid blurt of information, before she turned to him and responded.

"I am shocked to hear that. I know of Mrs. Hughes personally. She always came in and purchased the most beautiful combinations of fabric to make her family clothing. She would always bring the children in to show us clerks the finished products of her work. Are you sure you need seven of everything? Surely they have some clothing. She made such beautiful outfits for the children."

"No, all they have are the clothes you see them wearing on their backs. I just left the judge, and the other clothing they had, I threw it away at the courthouse. I will need seven of everything. I don't know how to do laundry, and I don't know when I will find someone to help me take care of them."

The nice salesclerk looked as if she were fighting tears, and she turned and busily began to gather the clothing items I would need for seven days. She couldn't help us enough. The salesclerk finished gathering items for my brother quickly, and then she began to work on my needs. She came over to me and looked me up and down and quickly began to gather items for me as well.

I was so excited. Momma had never bought us this many clothes at a department store. "Daddy, can I help pick out my clothes? I don't want any dresses."

"I don't see why not. You aren't wearing a dress now."

"I know, but in the past, when we lived here, Momma always made me wear dresses, and I hated every one of them. The clothes she made me wear while we were gone from you, I didn't like them either. Those clothes were icky and looked like rags. I want to dress like the other girls I went to school with in St. Louis."

I waited to see what clothing items the salesclerk would pick for me. As she began to pile the items on the counter, I grew disappointed. The clothes looked like the same items Momma had made me wear before. Everywhere I looked, I saw lace and bows. Daddy must have noticed how sad and withdrawn I had become because he stopped the salesclerk and told her what she was picking out for me was all wrong.

"I don't want that type of clothes. She gonna need something else. She doesn't want dresses."

"Any little girl would want these items. She will look so pretty in these dresses. I assure you, once she tries them on, she will change her mind."

"No, she said she don't want them. Either you can get her some jeans, or I can find someone else to. It's up to you."

The salesclerk seemed shocked at how quick Daddy's temperament had changed toward her, but she removed the clothing items and began to select jeans and place them on the counter. As the items began to cover the counter, Daddy looked at me and saw the smile on my face returning.

"Are you sure this is what you want? Your mother never dressed you like this when you lived with me."

"Oh yes, Daddy! I hate dresses. I never want to wear a dress again as long as I live."

Later that day, Daddy enrolled us at Wethersfield Elementary School. While Andre filled out the paperwork, Daddy asked to speak with Mr. Wilson, the principal. After what seemed like forever, the principal called us into his office.

"Hello, Mr. Wilson. My name is Ace Hughes, and these are my children. I came here today to explain that I have custody of my children, and I don't want you to let their mother take them from this school for any reason. If she comes or calls the school, I want to be called. I work at Kewanee

Corporation, and my supervisor will get me to the phone right away if you call me."

"Mr. Hughes, we would need some sort of proof from the courts to honor such a request. If we do not have proof, we do not have the right to stop her from speaking with or collecting her children."

"I have the court papers from the judge. They were signed today. They grant me temporary custody, but in thirty days they will grant me permanent custody."

Mr. Wilson took the paperwork from Daddy and quickly read them. After he cleared his throat, he called his secretary into the office to review them. After she read them quietly, she excused herself to make copies for the school's protection.

"Mr. Hughes, we will do everything within our power to honor your wishes and keep your children safe." Mr. Wilson stood and extended his hand to Daddy. "Mr. Hughes, if either my secretary or I can be of any assistance helping the children adjust, please let us know." I guess this was a signal that the meeting was over because we all stood and exited the principal's office.

While we sat in the hallway waiting for the secretary to complete the copies needed for the elementary school, the high school, and the superintendent's office, I watched as the faces of the children came and went. Some faces I remembered, and some were new. I was excited to be back at home and ready to get back in school.

From day one at Wethersfield, I didn't fit in with the other little girls, who were dressed in pink dresses and pretty shoes. They had their hair fixed and looked like little princesses, while I, on the other hand, looked and dressed like a boy. I wore Wrangler blue jeans, button-down shirts, cowboy boots, and a blue jean jacket. The children who remembered me from kindergarten wondered why I was dressing like a boy. Some went so far as to ask questions, but most just made fun of me.

During our first recess break of the day, Monique joined me on the swing set. Even though last year we had fought every day over who would be first in the line, I was happy for the company. Neither of us said anything at first. We both just enjoyed the calmness of swinging. Then Monique turned to me and began to ask questions.

"When did you come back, and why are you dressed like a boy? My momma said your momma said she would never come back here and live with your father."

"Jake and I missed my daddy, so we came back to live with him. I'm not dressed like a boy. I don't like wearing dresses, so my daddy said I don't have to wear them anymore."

"Oh, well, I'll see you later."

Just like that, just as quickly as she had come, she was gone. Monique went back over to the other children and played. I wanted to join them, but before I could manage enough courage to go join them, my mind begin to reel, and I began to lose myself in thoughts. I was afraid to go over to the large group of children. What if they did not want me to play with them? What if they didn't like me? The sound of our teacher blowing her whistle brought me back to reality. I jumped out of the swing, landed on my feet, and quickly ran off to line up with my classmates.

As I approached them, I could hear Monique telling a group of children where she stood in line that I looked like a boy. They all laughed at me as I approached the line. I let everyone cut in front of me, trying to put as much distance between them and me as possible. I did not want to hear their laughter. As I stood in the hallway, placing my jacket into my locker, I witnessed Monique go to another group of classmates and begin to tell them how much I looked like a boy. I heard them begin to laugh as I quickly walked into my classroom and sat quietly at my desk, waiting for my teacher to enter the room and begin our lessons.

After everyone had found their seats, my teacher made an announcement to the class. "Dorthea's father is a single parent and doing the best he can to try to raise a girl. Not everyone here is the same. That is what makes each one of special and unique. I like that we are all different. If we were all the same, the world would be a boring place to live." When she finished explaining my appearance, she turned to the board and began to teach our class.

I guess she believed she was doing the right thing, but it just prompted the children to ask me questions I wasn't prepared to answer. When the children asked why I lived with my father, I told the truth. I hadn't yet mastered the principles of lying. I told them how Daddy and Momma got a divorce and that my brothers and I lived with our daddy. I told them how my mother drank, smoked, and played cards for money every weekend. I told them how my mother had a boyfriend with a wife. I was so glad for the attention. Surprisingly, I had not yet learned that all attention was not good attention.

Even as children, the other kids understood enough about me to know that I was different and not in a good way. The children punished me for being different. I heard them whisper about how crazy my family must be. I saw them point and laugh at me when they thought I wasn't looking. No one talked to me or wanted to be my partner for any events that required us to choose partners. One girl actually cried because she thought she would have to be my partner, asking the teacher if she could team up with another partnership rather than be my partner. The teacher thought it was best to allow her to be the third member of a partnership, and the teacher decided she would be my partner since I was a little behind the class and would need extra care while being brought up to speed. I tried to pretend that it did not bother me that no one wanted to be around me or be my friend, but it hurt badly—very badly. And the rest of my first week back at school went very much the same way.

Her Choice

I was relieved a few days later when Daddy came home from work and told us that he was going to bring the rest of the family home. I didn't mind eating Kentucky Fried Chicken every night and not having a bedtime, and I surely didn't miss being whipped for everything, going to church, or having my hair done every day, but I didn't want to be treated differently. I wanted to fit in with the other kids at school. I decided to dress like a girl again. I didn't want Momma to be mean again if she came home, and I hoped that this time would be different. All children are supposed to have a mother. This time, I told myself, things would be normal.

In the car, Daddy asked Jake and me if we would be able to find the house we had lived in with Momma. We told him to take us back to the school that David and I had attended, and we could find our way to the house from there. Jake and I went on to explain how we had learned our way home from school. We told him about the events that led up to us walking home that day when I had been beaten up so badly. The more we talked, the more Daddy began to fidget in his seat. Whenever he asked us a question to gain a better understanding, his voice sounded strained. Daddy listened and grew angrier with every word.

When we got to St. Louis, Daddy found a gas station attendant who knew where our school was. Once we arrived at the school, he woke us up and told us if we wanted him to bring Momma home, it was up to us to find the house. Jake and I sat up and pointed the directions as he drove. We had to take him through alleys because that's how we got home from school. Finally, we arrived at the back of our mother's house.

"Are you sure this is the right house?"

"Yes, this is the right house."

We leaned in toward Daddy and began to tell him where everyone was located in the house.

"That window at the top of the house on the right is Angel's room. The window on the left is the upstairs bathroom."

"Where is David's room?"

"His room is in the front of the house upstairs. You can either take the front steps or the back steps to get upstairs."

"Are you saying there's two ways to get upstairs in this house?"

"Yes."

"Where's your momma's room at?"

"Her bedroom is downstairs on the right side of the house."

"How many ways in and out of the house?"

"Just two, the front and back door."

"Okay, I think I got enough to go in on. Dorthea and Jake, I want you two to stay outside with Andre." Then he reached into his jacket pocket and handed Andre a pistol.

We sat back in our seats and caught our breath when we saw the gun, neither of us saying a word. I don't know what was going through Jake's or Andre's mind, but my mind felt as if it were running a marathon. What was Daddy doing with a gun? Why had he decided to go into the house without us? Why had he given Andre a gun? What was really going on inside Daddy's mind?

Neither Jake nor Andre said a word. They sat in silence, watching our father gather his belongings as he prepared to enter the place that had been our shelter for a short time. I could not call it home, because to me home was supposed to be where you felt safe and loved, and I had never felt either of those feelings in that house. As I came out of the fog of my mind, I heard Daddy speaking. Andre sat stiffly in his seat, listening intently to Daddy.

"Listen to me carefully, son. I want you to wait here for ten minutes. If I'm not back by then, I want you to go, and if you hear gunshots or see the police, then you leave. Go straight to Uncle Andre's house. Uncle Andre will make sure ya'll get to your grandparents' house."

"Come on, Daddy. Let me go in with you. I can help you."

"No, son. Look at these kids. I need you to stay with them, and I need you to get them to your grandparents' house if things don't go well. No arguments. I'm counting on you."

Daddy handed his wallet to Andre, and then he was gone. We could not see which direction he walked in, because everywhere we looked, it was dark. I don't know if my eyes were playing tricks on me, because everywhere I looked, I saw movement in the shadows.

We sat outside in the dark. We were scared, realizing that maybe we had done something wrong by telling Daddy all that stuff about Momma.

"Andre, why did Daddy have a gun? Is Daddy going to shoot Momma?"

Andre turned around and looked at us in the backseat while pointing his finger at us. I could tell he was just as shocked and scared as we were by his trembling, even though he masqueraded the fear with raw anger.

"Sit back and shut up. I don't know what's gonna happen, but whatever happens, it's your fault. You shouldn't have told him all that stuff about Momma having a boyfriend. If Daddy doesn't come out of that house, then it's your fault—both of you."

Jake and I sat back and cried. We watched the house, hoping and praying for Daddy and Momma to come out the door. Time went on forever, and no one came out of the house. Andre turned around and told us to be quiet. I was glad that he was no longer screaming at us. However, I could still hear the fear in his voice as he spoke. I also noticed the perspiration on his forehead. The perspiration shouldn't be there; it was October and pretty cold outside. All of a sudden, Andre turned around in his seat and informed us he was going to need to leave us in the car alone while he went to check on Daddy.

"Don't open the doors, and get down low in the seats so no one will see you," he said.

"Wait, Andre. Daddy said for you to stay in the car, too. Daddy said you're supposed to take care of us."

"Yeah," Jake added. "Don't leave us in here alone."

"I've got to go see if Daddy's all right. Don't you want to know if he's okay?"

"Yes," we wailed.

Just as Andre began to open his car door, Daddy bolted from the house with Momma and David. At the car, Daddy opened the door, pushed David in the backseat, threw Momma in the back next to David, and got in the front seat. Daddy pointed a pistol at Momma's head. David was crying and clinging to Momma for life.

"Get off your momma!"

"Please, Daddy, don't hurt my momma," David cried out, still not releasing his grip on her body.

Momma was wearing her nightie, and David wasn't wearing a jacket or shoes.

"Hurry up and start the car! Back this car up, and don't turn on the lights!"

"I can't see where I'm going without the lights!"

"Yes, you can. Let's go! We've got to be out of here before anybody notices she's gone!"

Daddy had to move quickly because Momma's boyfriend was due to arrive to pick her up. Andre started driving, without Angel. Angel had been out with her boyfriend when we got there, which angered Daddy more. Daddy and Momma screamed at each other while Andre drove.

"Where is Angel? Where she at? She should be at home at this time of night."

Andre turned toward Daddy and asked, "Should I drive to Uncle Andre's house or just drive straight to the highway and head toward home?"

Momma screamed, "Yes, Andre! Take us to your Uncle Andre's house!"

Daddy screamed louder than Momma. "No! Don't stop this car until you see the sign that says Kewanee exit!"

Then Daddy turned back around in the seat, pointed the gun in Momma's face, and began to scream at her again.

"If you don't want your children or me, then you shouldn't even want to live. I ought to just kill you now. You let that man touch you. You don't give a damn about your own kids. What the hell is wrong with you?"

Momma began to sob loudly. "Ace, please don't kill me in front of my children."

"I'll never let you live with another man. You should know that by now," he growled at her.

Scared what Daddy might do to Momma, Andre knew he needed help to calm Daddy's anger, so he began to ask him questions. "Daddy, can we stop at Uncle Jimmy's house?"

Momma, sensing the danger she was in, screamed at Daddy, "Ace, let him stop so I can get a change of clothes and use the bathroom."

"No! Andre, keep driving this car and do what I told you to do."

Turning back around in his seat and looking at Momma, he told her, "My brother can't help you. The only person can help you now is God! So if you want to live, you better start praying!

"You ain't got to go to the bathroom anyway. I know what you want to do. You just want to rat me out and try to stop me from taking you home—home where you belong. If you gotta pee, then just pee on yourself because we ain't stopping this damn car until we get to Kewanee."

"You can't do this. You can't just force me to go home with you," she wailed.

They screamed at each other the whole way home. Apparently, Daddy had tried to shoot her with his shotgun, but it had jammed, so Momma reached for the nightstand to get her pistol. Daddy was too fast and dove on her. Daddy and Momma wrestled for the gun. Daddy was too strong. He hit Momma in the head and took the pistol from her. David awoke when he heard the fighting and ran downstairs, but when he heard Daddy's voice, he ran back upstairs and hid.

* * * * *

Daddy's wife came into the room where I sat reminiscing about the past and offered me a drink. I snapped out of the past and focused on my present situation.

"Dorthea, we are so glad you came to visit your daddy. Can I get you something? Do you want something to drink? Do you want something to eat?"

"No, I'm fine," I answered. When she retreated to the kitchen, I looked over at Daddy again and began to think to myself. Was this really happening? Was I really sitting here next to my daddy? Lost in thought, I quickly went back to my memories, the very memories that seemed to hold me captive and would not let me go. As I drifted back into my memories, I could hear the constant chatter of my sisters in the kitchen, speaking with their mother. I could hear the television program that Daddy was watching. And I saw my past continue to unfold once more.

* * * * *

In the midst of the fighting, Daddy asked Andre for the pistol he had given him to hold. When Andre told him it was in the glove compartment, Daddy retrieved the gun and gave Momma the pistol. He told her to shoot him so he could shoot her. Then they would be free from each other, he said. All of us children screamed. We begged Daddy not to kill Momma. We begged Momma not to kill Daddy. In a panic, Andre swerved the car, and both Daddy and Momma lost their pistols. Each of them scrambled to get a pistol before the other. Momma got her pistol first and pointed it at Daddy. He laughed and grabbed her. Then he grabbed her pistol and hit her in her head.

For a while, we rode in silence, listening to Momma cry. After about an hour, Momma asked, "Ace, can we stop to get some food and use the restroom? I went to bed early without dinner, and I really have to go pee."

Daddy mumbled under his breath but turned to Andre and spoke, "Pull over at the next exit so we can get gas and food." When we stopped, Momma and Daddy got out of the car and went into the gas station while Andre pumped the gas. Daddy came out with drinks and snacks, but Momma was not with him.

"Where's your momma?"

"We don't know. We thought she was with you," Andre answered nervously.

Daddy began to look around nervously. He gave the food and drinks to us in the backseat and went back into the gas station. We sat there quietly, none of saying anything, wondering where Momma had disappeared to. Minutes later, both Daddy and Momma appeared walking to the car. Daddy was practically dragging Momma to the car. He had a firm grip on Momma's arm. Daddy had found Momma at the pay phone trying to place a call.

After Daddy opened the back door and threw Momma inside, landing on top of us, they immediately began to yell at each other. "Ruthie Ann, who were you trying to call?'

"I was calling Angel to let her know where David and I had gone to. You do remember Angel, our daughter. I thought she must be worried sick, and I wanted her to know we were all right."

Daddy immediately calmed down and asked, "Did you tell her where you were and who you were with?"

"No, she did not answer the phone."

Andre started the car and pulled out of the gas station, heading toward the highway, the highway that would take us back home. Momma looked into the bags and began to hand out drinks and chips to each of us. We were glad to have the food. I don't know if I was really hungry or if I just welcomed the distraction, but I relished the food all the same. The food must have been the magic trick that calmed the storm brewing within the confines of the car because we rode the rest of the way home in silence.

When we reached the house, my parents were speaking to one another calmly. Daddy went to sleep while Momma cooked us supper and fixed our plates. As we ate, she asked us questions. She began with Andre. "How have you been?"

"Pretty good, Momma. Been busy trying to take care of Daddy."

Then she turned her attention to Jake and me. "Which one of you told Daddy where I lived?"

Jake and I didn't answer her question—we felt guilty. Using a sweet voice, she continued to probe us. "You can tell me. I'm not angry with either of you. I just want to know who can keep a secret."

Fearing her wrath, Jake told her that I had blabbed. I tried to protest. I told her that we both had told, but looking in Jake's eyes, she said, "I believe you, sweetie."

After we finished eating, Momma spoke again. "Ya'll need to go to bed so you can get up bright and early for school in the morning."

"Momma, are you going to do anything special tomorrow for my birthday?" I asked.

Flashing a smile, she replied," I don't know. You'll have to wait and see."

The next morning, we awoke to the smell of breakfast in the kitchen and my mother's laughter. I sat on the side of my bed in wonder. I wasn't used to hearing her laugh. Her laughter was like the Pied Piper, because as I began the walk downstairs to get close to the sound of my mother's laughter, I looked around and there stood all three of my brothers. We all tripped over one another trying to descend the stairs and get into Momma's presence. We raced down the stairway.

"Dorthea, hurry up and eat your breakfast so you can get in the tub. You look and smell as if you have not had a proper bath since you left my house."

Feeling ashamed, I quietly replied, "Okay, Momma." I hurriedly sat down and ate my breakfast. My brothers and mother were talking and laughing, and I decided it was going to be a great day. After all, it was my birthday. I was six years old.

I hurried through my bath, taking extra care to wash everything properly. I was glad to have Momma home, since she was being nice. I didn't want to do anything to make her angry. After I finished my bath, I went into her room. She asked me where my clothes were, and I showed her what Daddy had bought me. She let out a gasp.

"Lord, have mercy. This is crazy. These are boy clothes, and you don't need to be dressing like a boy!" she screeched.

"Can I get some new clothes for my birthday, Momma?" I asked.

Momma smiled at me and said, "I'll see what I can do. Now, get dressed and come into the living room so I can do your hair. I know you don't have many girl clothes, but put on a dress. You sho' don't need to go to school looking like a boy."

When I reached the living room, Momma and my brothers were talking. They were asking her what she was going to do for my birthday. As I sat between Momma's legs, I turned to her and asked if she would bring birthday treats for my class. She told me she had so much to do to get ready for my birthday dinner that night, but if she had time, she'd bring treats to my class in the afternoon. For the next few minutes, my brothers tried to convince Momma to make me a chocolate cake for my birthday. I contested, saying that I hated chocolate cake—I loved vanilla cake with white icing.

"Momma, please make me a vanilla cake. You know I hate chocolate cakes. Please, Momma, can I have a vanilla cake? Huh, please, can I? Momma, please no chocolate cake! It is my birthday. I should get to choose the cake. Please, please, please say you will make me a vanilla cake!" Momma gave me a look that said to stop it, and I immediately stopped and grew silent. Now that it was quiet, she changed the subject and resumed last night's conversation.

"Are you all happy living with Daddy?"

"Yes, Momma, but we want you to be here too," we all replied in unison.

"How did Daddy find out where I lived? Did one of you tell him, or did he know on his own?"

Neither of us was quick to answer her questions. Why did both Momma and Daddy ask us so many questions? After what had happened last night, I didn't want to answer any more questions.

Reluctantly I began to answer her. "Momma, both Jake and I told him where you lived."

"How did ya'll know how to get back to the house?"

"Momma, remember the day Dorthea got beat up at school and David and I had to walk her home through the alleys? It was easy. We told Daddy where we went to school, and he took us to the school. Once we were at the school, we showed him how to get to the house from there."

"I'm surprised ya'll remembered how to get home since you only walked home once. How did Daddy know how to find the school?"

"That was easy. I told him where Dorthea and David went to school, and he stopped at a place to get gas, and the lady he gave money to showed him on a map how to find their school."

Smiling at us, Momma replied, "Both my babies are very smart to figure out how to get home." After she sat and looked upon us for what seemed forever, she spoke again. "You boys need to finish getting ready so ya'll don't miss the bus."

"Oh, Momma, will you please take us to school?"

"Oh, I wish I could, but I have a lot to do to get ready for Dorthea's birthday party if I'm going to make treats for her class."

"Momma, can you stop by all of our classes today if you come to school?" Andre asked quietly.

Jake had struggled at school trying to explain to his classmates about Momma, and he wanted everyone to see her. David wanted her to stop by for different reasons. He wanted to make sure she was still there and hadn't left him behind. As we walked out of the house that morning, we believed life was going to be better for our family.

I went to school and immediately told my teacher that it was my birthday, and that if Momma had time, she would be bringing treats to school in the afternoon. The teacher announced that the day was special because it was my birthday, and she told the class that we would be making birthday cards for me. I felt so special.

At lunch, I wanted the children to talk to me, so I told them about my mother bringing cake and ice cream in the afternoon. Word spread throughout our class. The children seemed to warm up to me, and for a moment, I felt normal.

Before afternoon recess, Mrs. Hanson called me up to her desk to ask me what time my mother would be bringing the treats. I didn't know, but I told the teacher to call Momma to ask. I didn't know my phone number, so Mrs. Hanson gave me a note to go to the office to call and see what time she would be bringing the treats. Mrs. Goody, the secretary, was very nice to me. She always smiled at me. Mrs. Goody looked up my phone number, dialed, and handed me the phone. The phone rang until the recording came on that told me that the party was not answering and instructed me to try again. Mrs. Goody must have seen the look on my face.

"What's wrong, Dorthea?"

"It's my birthday, and Momma said if she had time, she would bring treats for my class."

Mrs. Goody had a way of making a person feel better and smiled at me. Trying to give me reassurance, she took both my hands in hers and spoke softly to me. "Dorthea, sweetie, calm down. Your mother is probably at the store picking up the treats as we speak. I am sure everything will be fine. Now hurry back to class before your Mrs. Hanson sends out a search party looking for you."

When I returned to my class, I informed my teacher of the situation.

"I called my momma, but she didn't answer the phone. I told Mrs. Goody, and she told me to come back later and try again."

Mrs. Hanson looked down at me and replied nervously, "Oh yes, that will be all right for you to try again. Dorthea, if you would like to try again, you can always try to call your mother again at recess."

During lunch, my classmates made comments about eating cake and ice cream, and when we returned, I expected to walk into the room and find the treats waiting, but they weren't there. Mrs. Hanson said she wasn't able to get in touch with my mother. She sent two of my classmates to pick up the recess milk and had me go to the principal's office. Mrs. Goody bought some vanilla wafers and gave them to me to share with my class.

When I returned to the classroom, I helped Mrs. Hanson pass out the vanilla wafers. One of my classmates asked if Dorthea's mother was coming with cake and ice cream, and Mrs. Hanson nicely explained that my mother was not coming. While I walked around the classroom nervously passing out cookies, the children asked me questions about my mother's whereabouts. How could I answer their questions? I did not know where she was either.

They started turning to one another and speaking in whispered tones that I was lying and had made it all up. I even heard someone remind another classmate that I had to be lying, because I did not have a mother. Every aisle I walked down passing out cookies, at least two of my classmates accused me of lying about my mother bringing cake and ice cream. I nervously looked around, not knowing what to say to defend myself. In an effort to stop their questions and make my situation seem not too bad, I thought of a lie that would make all their questions and accusations go away.

As I continued to pass out cookies, I began to tell them all before they could ask, "My mother was busy setting up for my party." I told them they were all invited to come. When they asked me how their parents would know they were invited, I told them that Momma was probably getting in touch with all of their parents and that was why she didn't have time to come. Truthfully, I didn't know where Momma was, but I knew that she wasn't getting in touch with any of their parents. Whenever my mother did anything that involved inviting people to our home, she invited only family and church members. Most of the children called me a liar, but a few said they couldn't wait to get home so they could come over and have fun at my party.

David, Jake, and I rode the bus home. My brothers sat with their friends, laughing and talking about school that day. I sat alone, wondering why Momma hadn't shown up at school. When the bus stopped at our address, we all got off and walked home. The station wagon was gone, and we didn't have any keys to get into the house. I had to go to the bathroom. I had been holding it since after we had finished our cookies and milk at school. I didn't put my hand up and ask to go because I didn't want to draw any more attention to myself.

I silently cried as we sat outside on the steps with nowhere to go. After sitting outside for about an hour, my bladder gave up, and I cried even harder. At first, we thought up reasons Momma might be late: Maybe she had a flat tire. Maybe she was visiting friends, letting them know she was back home. Maybe she was still shopping for the party. Maybe she was getting me girl clothes, or maybe she was out of gas somewhere. Any excuse was better than the last one that David suggested.

He said the words, half crying, "Maybe she just left again and didn't take us with her this time."

After a while, when it turned dark, we realized she wasn't coming back—she had left us again. She had broken her promise. Eventually Daddy came home and found us sitting outside on the steps.

Daddy walked over and looked at us, shaking and with tear streaks on our faces. My pants were wet by this time from a second accident.

"Where is your momma?" Daddy yelled. "How long have you been out here? Did Dorthea pee on herself? Why didn't ya'll take your sister to the bathroom?"

My brothers started to answer all Daddy's questions at once, but I just ran over to him, wrapped my arms around his waist, and cried.

Daddy unlocked the door, and we all went into the house. The first thing he did was call into work. "Hello, I won't be able to return to work today. Yeah, today Ruthie Ann done left the kids locked outside the house. Yeah, the way they shaking, I guess they been sitting here since they got off the school bus. Yeah, when I got here, they were sitting on the steps outside waiting for me to come home." Daddy was quiet for a few minutes, listening to his boss before he spoke again. "I don't know why they looking for me. I haven't seen Ruthie Ann since this morning. But I am almost positive that it has something to do with my wife."

Daddy hung up and called the police. Maybe there was a good excuse for Momma not being at the house when we came home from school.

The police informed him that my mother had called them to ask them if they would let him know where she had left the station wagon. They also informed him that the keys were in the ashtray. Daddy sat at the kitchen table and cried. After a while, he turned to us and said, "Your momma is gone. I didn't really think she would leave ya'll."

At that moment, Andre arrived home. Daddy was scared to leave any of us alone, for fear that Momma would try to take us with her. "Dorthea, get a bath and change your clothes. We gotta go pick up your momma's car. She left it at a gas station in Annawan."

While I was taking a bath, Andre asked Daddy and my brothers what had happened. I listened while I hurried to get cleaned up and dressed. I did not want to make Daddy wait any longer than he had to.

We drove the Buick Electra to pick up Momma's station wagon. All the way there, Daddy murmured under his breath, "I can't believe Ruthie Ann did it. I can't believe she left her kids. She always said she would jump in the fire for her kids."

The rest of us sat in silence listening to him. When we arrived in Annawan, we half expected her to be in the car waiting for us. Momma couldn't just leave us. We were her children. On the way home, I sat in the backseat between Jake and David.

While Andre followed us in the Buick Electra, Daddy drove the car slowly with one hand. I leaned forward in the seat to see what he was doing with his other hand and realized that he was drinking from a bottle wrapped in a brown paper bag. He had not had that before, so I assumed he bought it at the gas station when we picked up the car. As we rode back to Kewanee wondering what life would be like without our mother, my brothers snuggled under the blankets from Momma's bed when Daddy had taken her. They still held her scent from the night before. My mother had made her choice—she no longer wanted to be Daddy's wife. She no longer wanted to be our mother.

Neither of my brothers would share his blanket with me, each pushing me away from them. Even though I sat between them on the seat, I felt so alone with no one to comfort me. After all, did anyone remember she was my mother too? When David finally offered to share his blanket, I was so relieved. I felt comforted lying under the blanket that smelled like Momma. It was not long before I drifted to sleep.

I must have been asleep for about ten minutes when I felt David's hand between my legs, touching my privates. I immediately woke up, but I didn't say anything. I tried to shift my body so he would not be able to reach my private parts, but he just waited a few moments and shifted his body closer to mine so he could continue to touch me. Hoping to stop him, I shifted my body again, making the blanket fall from my body. After he waited to make sure I was still asleep, he quickly placed the blanket on top of my body. I sat there holding my breath, my mind reeling. *What is he doing? Why is he doing this? No one is supposed to touch me there. I am his sister. He knows I am his sister. How could he do this to me?* Although I wanted to scream at him to stop touching me, I sat there quietly, pretending to be asleep. I didn't make a sound because I didn't want to add any more trouble to the situation. If Daddy knew what David was doing, he would whip him, and everyone was so sad right now. I also didn't tell Daddy because I felt so alone, and at least someone was paying attention to me. As long as I pretended to be asleep, at least he wouldn't push me away. Even though I knew what he was doing was wrong, I told myself that if I didn't say anything about it, then it wasn't happening. This was a skill that would come in handy in the years to come.

When we arrived home, David refastened my clothes under the blanket as if he hadn't been fondling me. He got out of the car and left me there. I lay there wondering how long I should pretend to be asleep. I couldn't just get out of the backseat and follow him. He would know I hadn't really been asleep. I continued to lie there until Daddy called my name, and then we went into the house—a house with no Momma. Once in the house, I watched David. I wanted to see if he would change his behavior toward me. Maybe he'd give me a smile to let me know we were all going through losing Momma together. I thought since I had allowed him to touch me and didn't tell on him, maybe he'd be nice to me.

"Move out of his way!" He walked toward me, pointing his finger at me, and yelled, "Peabody!"

Then, without any reason, he proceeded to shove me into the doorway, punch me in my back, and went into the bathroom to take his bath. I stood there shocked. Nothing I did seemed to matter to him. I stood there thinking to myself, *Is he always going to be mean to me?*

In the days to come, we came home each day expecting to find that Momma had changed her mind, and with each new day, we adjusted to the fact that she wasn't going to return. In the weeks to come, David became more and more depressed as we all realized that Momma wasn't coming back. The only time he seemed happy was when he would hit me. He punched me everywhere. It was as if the harder he hit me, the better he felt. Then at night as I lay in my bed, I could hear him come into my room. I would hear the creak of the door as it opened and hear him walk across the floor as the floorboards creaked, allowing me to know he was closer to me. I would lie there and pretend that I was asleep when he climbed into bed with me and fondled me.

We went through the winter shut up in the house, not going anywhere but school and home. Andre did the best he could with my hair. Sometimes, he would bring different girls home with him to do my hair. My brothers tried to keep the house clean, but oftentimes, Daddy would bring the wives of his drinking buddies home to clean for pay. I would sit and listen to their conversations while they did my hair or busied themselves cooking our dinner. These same women said that Daddy needed to find a good woman to settle down with to help him raise us. They all made promises while sipping on their drinks of what they would do if given the opportunity to be our new momma. They made statements about my mother being crazy for leaving such a hardworking man. They commented about the way he was raising me, that he needed to take a firmer hand with me and get me out of those blue jeans and back into dresses. They said he needed to make me go into the kitchen and learn how to cook and clean. They told him that I needed to have my hair done more regularly and that I needed to take better care of my hygiene.

He didn't like it when these women would criticize his children, and neither did we. I didn't like them getting into our business. While Daddy seemed to enjoy their flattery and the way they spoke about Momma, he would always stop the conversation when it pertained to us by telling them they could stop for the day and come back another time and finish. To show I did not like it when they spoke bad about me, I would not turn my head and make it easy for them to braid my hair, causing them to become angry at me and raise their voices for me to turn my head. Most of the time, the women ended up drinking with Daddy and going into his bedroom before they left our home. They rarely did any housework. Whether they cleaned the house or went into Daddy's bedroom for a short while, Daddy never let any of them come around more than a few times.

However, when spring came, Daddy knew he needed to find someone to help around the house. He still worked long days and knew that once school let out for the summer, he'd need full-time help.

Daddy tried to get Momma's sister, Aunt Bessie, or some of Aunt Bessie's older girls, my cousins, to help him take care of my hair and the house.

"Bessie, how much you charge to come to my house every day and get my children ready for school, do Dorthea's hair, wash clothes, and prepare meals?"

"Ace, you wouldn't have to pay me to help with my sister's children, but you know Glenn. He ain't gonna allow me to come to your house every day without him."

"Well, what days can you come help? I don't know nothing about raising no girl! I need help!"

Nervously Aunt Bessie replied, "Ace, Glenn isn't gonna let me come over to that house no days. You know he ain't gonna be comfortable with me around you like that."

"Bessie, I won't be there. I'll be at work! That's why I need you!"

"I know that, but it wouldn't look right for me to be there in the house that much. Maybe he will let Dorthea come round to the house and I can help you that way."

"Bessie, I don't need Dorthea to come to your house! I need someone to help at my house. The kids need clean clothes and food cooked every day. What do you mean it won't look right for you to come to my house? Bessie, these are your sister's children. When Ruthie was here, I couldn't keep you away from my house!"

"I wish I could help you, but I can't! Glenn is a deacon in the church, and people will say things if I go to your house without my sister there. I am a married woman. I ain't got no business at no man's house every day but my husband's!"

Angrily Daddy replied, "Bessie, you are as worthless as tits on a bull. These are your sister's children, and I need help!"

Aunt Bessie was my mother's oldest sister, and she and her husband lived right behind us on the next block. Uncle Glenn and Aunt Bessie drove by our house daily on their way home, and we'd run outside and down the yard, waving at them. Uncle Glenn always smiled and returned the wave, but surprisingly, Aunt Bessie and her children turned their heads. It took only one time for Daddy to see this happen before he jumped in his car and followed them home. He threatened to shoot them if they ever drove by us again and treated us like nobodies. After that, they took the side street home, but we could still see them every day on their way home.

Daddy still needed help to raise us, so he turned to the church people he had ridiculed when my mother was home with us. The men didn't want their wives inside a home where Daddy would have access to them. There was one special church family that didn't turn him away, though—the Alexanders.

Mr. Timothy Alexander Sr., whom everyone called Big Daddy, pastored Pentecostal Deliverance Church on the same street that we lived on. He was married to Mrs. Vicki Alexander, whom everyone called Big Momma. I called her Mother Alexander because she was more like a mother to me. Mother Alexander babysat to help subsidize her and Big Daddy's income.

Mother Alexander came to our house every morning, made breakfast, and made sure that we caught the bus. After school, I rode the bus to my house, went in the front door to take my schoolbooks into the house, and went out the back door. Every day, I walked down the alley half a block past my Aunt Bessie and Uncle Glenn's house to Mother Alexander's home. She couldn't come to our house after school because she had a house full of children in her care, but I didn't mind going to Mother Alexander's house after school because there were always babies and children to play with. That's where I stayed on school nights until Daddy or my brothers came to get me.

Mother Alexander and her family were always after me to go to church with them. I loved Mother Alexander, but I didn't want to go to church. When the Alexanders had church on Tuesday and Friday nights, I left their home around 5:30 p.m. Even by the time I walked home, I was still at home by myself. I hated to be at home alone. The house was large and creepy whenever there wasn't anyone home with me. Otherwise, my brothers had to come get me at 7:00 p.m. If my brothers did not have to come get me, they did not have to be home until 8:00 p.m.

My brothers would be down the street playing at the Howards' house. There were two parents and twelve children in that home. Practically all the children in the neighborhood gathered there to hang out and play. Even though it was Mr. Johnnie Howard's family, Daddy didn't want me to play there because of all the boys that hung out there.

Some nights when I came home from Mother Alexander's and there was no one at home, I would sneak down to the Howards' house. The only reason my brothers didn't tell on me was because this gave them more time to play with their friends. I liked it because they played tag, hide-and-go seek, Barbie, Truth or Dare, or red light, green light, dynamite stop. On the nights that I walked to the Howards', my brothers and I made sure we left their home by 7:45 p.m. to beat Daddy to the house before he came home for his break. After Daddy left again for work, we would sneak back down the street to the Howards' home so we could play with all the other children.

The Howard children could be just as nasty and mean as they were nice. They began calling me "baby" when my brothers had to miss out on the fun to go get me at Mother Alexander's house, so I began to leave Mother Alexander's house every night at around 5:30. At first, Mother Alexander wouldn't let me leave without Daddy telling her it was okay, so I told Daddy that all those children at Mother Alexander's house made me have a headache with all their hollering. Daddy was hesitant until I told him I wasn't scared to be at home for a little while until my brothers returned, and then he allowed it.

Mother Alexander and Daddy wanted me to call Mother Alexander every night when I reached the house safely. I would go into the house upon my arrival and call her, hang up, and then walk down the street to the Howards' to play with all the other children. This was pretty much our routine Monday through Friday until summer break came.

When school let out for summer break at the end of May, Andre was fourteen, David was ten, Jake was nine, and I was six. Our mother had been gone for seven months. Surprisingly, we were beginning to adjust, and we were all promoted to the next grade. Daddy was happy, we were happy, and all was right with the world.

Summer started out great because we didn't have to get up early and catch the bus. I got up early every morning, though, to make Daddy his coffee and talk to him while he got ready for work. This time of day was special for me because I got him all to myself. Some mornings, he would tell me to hurry and get dressed, and we would run across town to Mrs. Smith's bakery and grab the best donuts ever made.

Sometimes, after Daddy went to work, I would go back to sleep until my brothers woke me up, or I would lie in bed and watch television until Andre made us all get up. Then I would help clean the house. Some mornings, David would get up before everyone else in the house, creep into my room, and touch me while I pretended to sleep. One morning, Andre knocked on my door, and David hid in my closet while I spoke with him. When Andre moved on and went downstairs to start doing chores, David emerged from my closet, stopping to look at me as he eased out of my bedroom unnoticed. It was then that he knew I was only pretending to sleep while he had been fondling me over the past months.

I thought once David knew I was protecting him, he would be nicer and stop hitting me. However, once he knew that I was on to him, it only made him hate me more. He still hunted me down in between television programs and beat me. The beatings were so ferocious that both Andre and Jake would have to work together to pull him off me. Andre would threaten to tell Daddy if he did not stop, but he never did. Andre felt that David's anger was due to Momma leaving him behind.

When David beat me, he did not leave any part of my body safe. He punched me with such rage that Andre would speculate out loud that he was unbalanced. This caused Andre to instruct both Jake and me to stay away from David as much as possible. Once David figured out that we were purposely distancing ourselves from him, his anger increased even more whenever he did have those anger outbursts. On one occasion, he punched my head so hard that force from the blow resulted in me having a headache and having to go to bed. Luckily, these outbursts were quick, and once they were over, he would ignore me for a while, to all of our relief.

Mother Alexander no longer came to the house daily. Daddy had five mandatory requirements that were to be fulfilled daily: that the house be clean, we be dressed, our hair be combed, our teeth be brushed, and his lunch be fixed when he arrived at the house at noon each day. When Daddy entered the house, Andre would place his lunch on the table while we each walked in for a daily inspection. When we passed the inspection, Daddy granted us permission to leave for the day. Andre would return before midnight, while David and Jake returned before the streetlights came on. After lunch, on Daddy's way back to work, he would drop me off at Mother Alexander's house, where I stayed until he got off work at 3:30.

After work, Daddy and I would visit his friends. He'd stop at the store and get a bottle of a strong-smelling liquid that he held in a brown paper bag. He sometimes took me to the Shell gas station on the north side of town, where the men hung out with one another while the owner fixed customers' cars. We usually returned home around 7:00 p.m.

The summer pretty much went on this way until one day after work, Daddy and I went to Mr. Howard's house. Daddy and Mr. Howard drank from a bottle in a brown paper bag and visited with other men in the garage while I played with the Howard children. Mr. Howard's daughters all came outside and asked Daddy if they could comb my hair for him. Mr. Howard had several daughters, but Angel and Daisy were my favorites. They were nice to me and made me feel special. Every day that week, Daddy and I went to Mr. Howard's house after work, and while they drank and talked, Daisy and Angel did my hair. I looked forward to seeing them every afternoon. I had so much fun with them. They would sing, laugh, and dance for no reason at all, and most importantly, they included me in the fun. I felt normal for once.

One night, we were playing at the Howards' house, and I had to go pee. I was waiting in line, bouncing up and down trying to stop the flow of water that wanted to exit my body. The older children would bully us younger children and make us wait until they were finished. The fear of peeing on myself weighed heavily on me. I knew if I had an accident, the other children would never let me live it down. The fear, coupled with the need to relieve myself, was starting to weigh in on me to the point that I began to perspire. Not only did I perspire, but my head began to throb.

When I thought I could not hold it any longer, I attempted to find my brothers. I walked outside with my back slightly bent and my legs firmly pressed together. Once I found my brothers and they saw me, they began to laugh at my predicament. I slowly walked toward them, taking care to remind myself not to relax or I would have an accident right there in front of everyone. Once I had made my way to them, I asked them to walk me home so I could use the bathroom, but they told me no.

All the men were in the garage, so I knocked on the door, looking for Daddy, but Mr. Howard told me Daddy had left. When I went back into the house, I found out that I had missed my turn for the restroom and again was last in line. Daisy told me to go outside and use the bathroom behind the garage, but I was scared to go in the dark. I tried my best to hold my pee until I could sit safely on a commode. I cried at the thought of going outside in the dark.

I felt the moistness in my panties as my bladder began to relax from the pressure that had built up within my body. I tried to stop it, but I couldn't. Once my bladder decided enough was enough, it would not allow me to take back control. It had a mind of its own, and it wanted relief. I have to admit, the release of pressure was a relief; however, I did feel as if my bladder had betrayed me as it emptied itself.

I ran outside just as the other children noticed that I had stopped whining. They quickly followed me outside, circling me and asking me if I had peed on myself. They were all looking at the area between my legs that would tell them if I had indeed wet myself. Thankfully, it was dark outside, or they would have seen the glistening wetness that the pee had left on my legs. I did not wait around, trying to tell a lie. I knew if I stayed there under their inspection, they would begin to smell the pee. I began to back away from them in preparation of leaving before more attention was drawn to me and more eyes arrived to complete the inspection. As I began to take flight, I could hear their laughter as they called out to me. I did not stop to answer their calls to me as I continued to run toward my house. I just wanted to make it to my house before they caught me and saw the pee on my shorts.

When I got home, I ran inside and went straight to the bathroom. Once I got there, I had to go again. When I finished, I took a bath, then dressed myself and went back down to the Howards' house. It was dark outside, and I was scared as I walked down the street, but I knew once I got there, I would be all right.

When I arrived back at the Howards' house, the children all began to gather around and taunt me. "Pissy pot, pissy pot!" I heard someone yell at me. Before I could respond, they began to yell, "Pissy pot, pissy pot!"

"I did not pee on myself!" I yelled at my tormentors. I was so embarrassed and angry at their taunts that I began to cry.

"If you did not pee on yourself, then why did you change your clothes?"

I tried to be flip with my reply. "Because I felt like it. There's no crime in changing my clothes."

They continued to torment me. "Pissy pot, pissy pot!"

Frustrated at their taunts, I began to cry. When Jake and David saw that I had begun to cry, instead of them protecting me and insisting the children stop tormenting me, they joined in with the other children and began to scream, "Pissy pot, pissy pot!"

Why did my brothers have to be so mean all the time? I didn't have anyone to help me. My brothers had each other. I felt so alone and unwanted. Why hadn't I just stayed home? Frustrated at the children's cruelty, I began to scream. I screamed and screamed and couldn't stop screaming. I was out of control. I began to scream with tears running down my face, "Jake, David, I'm telling Daddy on you!"

I turned and ran from their taunts. I did not stop running until I reached the safety of my house. I was so intent on getting home and away from the taunts of the children that it wasn't until I was halfway home that I noticed how silent it was outside. I was now more afraid than I was angry and wished I hadn't left. Even though I wanted to, I couldn't go back and listen to them teasing me anymore. With each step I took, the chirping of the birds and the "ooh, ooh" of the owls grew louder and louder. The only noise that seemed louder was the thumping of my heart.

As I walked down our driveway, I heard a noise in our garage. I made a sudden stop when I heard something fall to the ground in the garage. I didn't think it was possible, but my heart began to beat even louder. Slowly I began to turn around to run back down the street to the Howards' house, but just as I reached the end of our driveway, I stopped in my tracks. I could not return to the Howards' house, not after the way they had teased me not more than twenty minutes ago. I stood there trying to figure out what to do. Should I go back with the other children and take a chance that they would continue to taunt me, or should I just go into the house and wait for everyone to arrive home? I told myself it was probably a cat or some other stray animal. Accepting that I was not in any danger, I decided it was safer to just stay home.

Still a little hesitant about the situation, I tried to ease past the garage and walk toward the back door of the house—we always left the back door unlocked. Just as I reached out to open it, I noticed someone standing just inside the door. At first, I screamed, until I realized who was standing there. I stopped screaming for a second with relief just as Earl Howard reached out and grabbed me. Earl was one of the neighborhood children, who lived down the street from our house. He was also the son of Johnnie Howard, my daddy's best friend.

I tried to ask him, "What are you doing?" I didn't have time, though, because he held his hand over my mouth and pushed me to the floor just inside the door of our back porch. His hands were all over me—ripping my shirt, touching me all over my chest, pulling my shorts down, sticking his hands inside my panties, and touching me there. I tried to cry out, but he wouldn't stop. He pushed himself against my leg, pressing his private part against my leg, moving up and down ferociously. All of a sudden, just as quickly as he had grabbed me, he got up, ran out the back door toward the alley, and was gone. I lay there in disbelief. I felt something wet on my leg. I lay back in the corner and cried. Why was this happening? First David, and now Earl?

After I finished crying, I got up, went into the bathroom, and took another bath. As I washed, I planned how I was going to tell on Earl for what he had done to me. I made up my mind to tell on both Earl *and* David. As I finished getting dressed, Daddy and my brothers walked into the house. I was trying to find the right words to tell him what had happened to me when Daddy noticed dirty dishes in the sink.

He hollered at us, wanting to know who had left the dirty dishes in the sink. Through a process of elimination, it was determined that David had left the dirty dishes in the sink. Daddy took off his belt and beat David so badly that every time he hit him, Jake and I both yelled out with David. When Daddy finished beating David, Jake and I stood there, looking at David's body lying on the floor trembling. We listened as we heard the truck engine start and back out of the driveway. Neither of us spoke; we just stood there in shock, looking at our brother, both us too scared to say anything. Daddy had never treated us like that—only Momma had beaten us in the past. Daddy had always been the nicer one of our parents. As David began to lift himself off the floor, Jake reached out to help him. I gasped as I saw the swollen bloody lip and the bruises on David's face. He walked bent over, clinging to Jake as if every inch of his body hurt.

I wanted to tell Daddy what David and now Earl were doing, but I didn't want to make matters any worse for David. After the beating I had witnessed Daddy give David, I was not sure when or if I would ever tell on David. But I would have to tell Daddy eventually because I truly wanted both David and Earl to stop what they were doing to me. As I lay in bed that night, I began rehearsing how I would tell on David and Earl, but no matter how much I wanted everyone to leave me alone, I realized that if I told Daddy, he would beat David again, and this time, it would be my fault. No, I could not tell. I didn't want Daddy to beat David because of me, but I still needed to tell him about Earl.

Just as I began to drift off to sleep, I heard Daddy yelling my name downstairs. He must have come back home because he was downstairs and yelling for me to get down there now. I jumped out of bed frightened by the tone of Daddy's voice. I did not know if what had happened earlier to David was about to happen to me. Clumsily I looked for my slippers and tried to get downstairs to the kitchen before Daddy had to call my name again.

"Sir!" I yelled down the stairs to let him know I had heard him and was on my way. When I reached the kitchen, Daddy sat at the table drinking from a bottle covered by a brown paper sack. I could tell by the look in his eyes that he had been drinking, and as I drew closer to him, I could smell it on his breath.

"Dorthea, why did you come home by yourself?"

"I had to go to the bathroom, and I could not wait. I ended up peeing on myself waiting in the line. So I had to come home and get cleaned up." Scared I was in trouble, I nervously and quickly added, "I went back to play, but all the kids were teasing me for peeing on myself, so I walked back home."

I was just about to tell him about Earl when he immediately started firing questions at my brothers. "How come ya'll did not walk with your sister? Where were ya'll when she had to go to the bathroom?" He didn't allow them to answer the questions. He just continued to ask more questions. "Did they tell you that you could not use the bathroom? What did ya'll do while they were teasing your sister? Why didn't ya'll walk her home?" He began to get up from the chair. "Where is the strap? I bet next time you will walk your sister home!"

He ran around the house looking for the strap. David and Jake cried and walked backward to the corner. I didn't want them to get a whipping with the strap, and I especially didn't want David to get another beating tonight. I started to cry out to Daddy, "Please don't whip them, Daddy! It was my fault!"

At that moment, Andre silently walked into the house and saw us standing in the corner watching Daddy. While Daddy went room to room in search of the strap, Andre whispered to us, "What happened? Why is Daddy mad?" David and Jake both answered him, "It's Dorthea's fault! She peed on herself, and now we have to get a whipping because of her." They made it sound like I *wanted* to pee on myself, like I invited all the children to point and laugh at me.

They didn't mention that they had joined in on the teasing. I wanted to yell at them to stop blaming me for everything, but I didn't. David began to plead with our older brother to help both him and Jake. "Andre, please stop Daddy from whipping us! It wasn't our fault. She always gets us in trouble. I hate her!"

I listened to them whine, and I tried to explain to Andre that it wasn't my fault. He turned to face me and very calmly said, "If Daddy gets into any trouble, it'll be your fault. You need to stop being a part of the problem and become part of the solution."

I looked at him questioningly and asked him what that meant. "Well, if bad things happen all the time when you're around, then maybe you need to examine the role that you play to cause these situations," he explained quietly.

I grew silent and thought about what he had said to me. Maybe it *was* my fault. I replayed tonight's events in my mind: I peed on myself. I should have just stayed home after I peed on myself—I knew how the Howard children could be mean to us. Next, Earl attacked me. Maybe I should have stayed at the Howard house until Daddy came back to get me or just waited until my brothers were ready to come home. Maybe I should have just gone to bed. Why did I always feel the need to tell?

I decided in that moment that I would stop telling. I wouldn't tell on Earl for what he had done to me or how he made me feel. After all, telling wouldn't help the situation anyway—it would only make it worse and make everyone mad at me.

Andre talked to Daddy and calmed him down, and then Daddy went to bed. My brothers were happy that they weren't told to stay away from the Howard house. However, I decided I'd stay away from there and return to where I felt safe—Mother Alexander's house.

Over the next couple of weeks, I went back to playing with the children at Mother Alexander's every day. I still felt nervous about walking home in the evenings by myself, so as soon as I arrived home, I called Mother Alexander to let her know that I had made it home safely. I didn't go to the Howards' house to play anymore; instead, I stayed home by myself and watched television.

Since there was no one to cook for me, I experimented. One night when I was trying to cook a hamburger, the fire was too high and I burnt the hamburger patty. I didn't want Daddy to know that I had been cooking, so I put it in a bag, took it out back, and threw it in the alley. As I was walking back to the house, I saw Earl standing in the garage doorway, watching me. As soon as I saw him, I felt my stomach tighten up. I thought I was about to throw up. I felt my heart beat faster in my chest. Panicking, I ran toward the back door, but his legs were longer than mine. He used his body weight and forced his way into the house. I begged him to leave me alone, but he wouldn't. He grabbed me and dragged me into the front room. It was dark, and he could watch out the window to see if anyone was coming. He pushed me down and climbed on top of me. Again, he fought me to remove my clothes. When I tried to fight him, he twisted my arm around me, pinned me to the floor with one hand, and ripped my panties off one leg with his other hand. I could feel his hands all over my body, touching me everywhere. He pinched my nipple really hard—so hard that the only thing that kept me from screaming aloud was him whispering reminders that if I screamed, he would break my arm. The harder he pinched my nipple, the harder he pressed his privates against my leg.

Every time I let out a whimper, he twisted harder until I stopped. When he finished, he got up and stared down at me. "You better not tell anybody, or I'll beat you up!"

Trying to hold back my tears, I stood up and yelled, "I'm gonna tell my daddy."

Laughing at me, Earl replied, "Ain't nobody scared of your stupid daddy." Shocked, I exclaimed, "You better be scared of my daddy. He'd shoot up everyone in your house if he knew what you just did to me!"

"You're not going to tell on me. You didn't tell on David." My eyes widened in shock, and he continued. "Yeah, I know about that. I've been watching you for a while, and one night, I was looking in your window, and I saw you and David. If you tell on me, then I'll tell on your brother. You and David are nasty. That's your brother, and now your brother's your new boyfriend?"

I fought back the hot tears and screamed, "David is *not* my boyfriend!"

He just looked at me and laughed. Before he walked out of the door, he turned and looked back at me. With a serious look, he paused and said, "Even if you don't care about what happens to your boyfriend, you should care about what happens to your pappy. If your daddy does anything to me, then he'll go to jail. I'm a kid, and your daddy is an adult. You don't even have a mother anymore, and if your pop goes to jail, then you and your brothers will be put into an orphanage. You don't like what I just did to you? It'd be a whole lot worse in that place."

The hot tears released, and as I fastened my clothes, I heard the back door open and close. I must have fallen asleep because when I woke the next morning, Daddy was calling me to make his coffee. When I arrived in the kitchen, he asked me why I had slept in my clothes on the living room floor all night. Avoiding Daddy's eyes, I replied, "I fell asleep waiting for everyone to come home." It must have satisfied his curiosity because he didn't ask any more questions. As I walked around the kitchen getting sugar for Daddy's coffee, I replayed the events from last night in my mind. To make sure I wasn't dreaming, I rubbed my chest. It was sore. I wanted to tell Daddy so bad what Earl had done to me, but I heard his words in my head that Daddy would go to jail if he shot up their house. I reminded myself that Earl said he would tell on David if I told on him. I just had to figure out a way to make it stop by myself.

Over the next few weeks, I stayed clear of the Howard house and pretty much stayed to myself. I didn't come home until Daddy or my brothers came to get me from Mother Alexander's house. My brothers were angry with me because they had to leave their friends' house early to come get me every night. Even though they took turns pushing me and punching me all the way home every night, I didn't care because at least I was safe. No one questioned my reasons for changing my mind and wanting to stay late at Mother Alexander's every evening.

After a while, I grew comfortable and began to feel safe with my new routine, until the day Daddy picked me up after work to go to the Howard house. He played cards with the other men in the garage while the kids played baseball in the field across the street. I felt safe because we were out in the open.

I loved to play baseball. When it came my turn to bat the ball, it went out in the field. I ran to first, then second, and when I was coming into third, Jason tagged me, but Earl, who was Jason's captain, said I was safe. Everyone on Earl's team said I was out, but he said I was safe, so I was safe. He stood right by me the whole time I stood on third base, which made me nervous. I kept wondering if anyone could read my thoughts and see what he had done to me.

Luckily, Andre came up to bat next. He hit me in, so I didn't have to stand there long. When we finished playing, all the kids lined up on the side of the house to take turns getting a drink from the water faucet. Earl held the hose and told me to come get a drink, while his younger siblings protested. He turned the hose on them and laughed as they ran away. I walked over to the hose and took my drink, wondering why he was being so nice to me.

Over the rest of the summer, that's how it went. Every couple of days, Earl would come find me and attack me. Wherever I went, he seemed to find me. I tried to avoid him by staying home, but because I was always home alone, he would lie in wait and get me there. On the occasions that I couldn't come up with a good excuse not to go to the Howards' with Daddy, he would find ways to separate me from everyone so he could have his way with me. Eventually, I was so accustomed to his attacks that whenever he got me alone, I told him to hurry up and not to get anything on my clothes. I would just lie there until he was done, and when I didn't fight, he didn't tear my clothes or hurt me anymore. He would just do what he had to do and leave.

As the summer came to an end, Daddy surprised me by taking me to JC Penney to get a bathing suit. I was so excited—I didn't own a bathing suit. He told me that a woman he worked with had a pool and wanted me to come over and swim at her house with her children. I was so excited. I didn't know anyone who owned a pool. I thought I was going to a mansion. I wondered if there was going to be a maid. I imagined myself sitting by the pool sipping on lemonade like I had seen on the television and that I had the coolest daddy in the world. When we pulled up in the trailer park, I thought we were making a quick stop before we went to the lady's house with the pool, but Daddy turned off the car and told me to get out. I looked around and noticed two little boys playing in a blow-up pool in the yard. I was disappointed. The pool was so small, barely big enough for two kids to sit in comfortably at the same time. They quickly got out of the pool, ran over to Daddy, and smiled as they said hi to him.

How did they know Daddy? Daddy told me he had just met this woman today. He introduced me to the children—George, the oldest, was seven, and Mark was five. When I questioned him, he told me to go play with the children, and he quickly went into the house. I looked around wondering what to do. I didn't know these kids. They were white. I had never been to a white person's house before. I got into the pool, but I quickly got right back out and sat in the chair watching the other children play. I must have sat in that chair for about an hour before their momma came outside. She introduced herself and handed us homemade cookies. She sat outside for a minute and watched her children play in the water before she noticed that I was cold. She asked me if I wanted to come inside.

When I went inside, I looked around for Daddy. "Where's my daddy?"

"He is in my bed asleep. If you need him right now, go on in there and wake him up. My bedroom is straight to the back at the end of the hallway."

What was Daddy doing in her bed? She wasn't my mom. How did her children know my daddy?

I decided not to wake Daddy, so nervously I sat on her couch. I sat quietly watching everything and everyone around me, not speaking to anyone. Christie, the mom, sat in the kitchen talking with Cassie, the babysitter. They were drinking Coke and smoking cigarettes. They probably thought I couldn't hear them because the television was on, but I sat there silently listening to them.

"So when do you get to meet his other children?"

"I don't know! After all, it took Ace months to bring his little girl."

"She seems nice, but on the shy side to me, maybe even a little unfriendly." They giggled at Cassie's statement.

"Shy, yes, but I don't know if I would say she's unfriendly. She's probably that way on account of her momma leaving them kids the way she did. Ace told me all about it. It was horrible. I could never leave my children the way she left them kids."

"I want to meet her brothers. Maybe there is one my age. I hope they are cute. Did Ace tell you how old his sons were?"

"I'll bet they are cute if they look anything like their daddy. I couldn't tell how old the boys are 'cause he don't talk about the boys—just her."

"Let's go see what we can get out of her!"

They both got up and came into the living room, where I pretended to watch television. Christie sat next to me while Cassie sat directly across from me. Christie went first. "Do you want another Coke and more cookies?"

As I ate the cookies and sipped the Coke, they asked me questions.

Cassie began to ask questions. "Do you ever talk to your mom?

"No!" I was a little nervous talking to them. Why were they asking me these questions? I didn't know if Daddy wanted me to be discussing our family business with them and did not want to get into trouble for talking too much.

"Has your daddy taken you to any other women's homes besides Chris's home?

"No!"

While they studied me, I studied them. Christie was a grown woman, but Cassie was a kid, like my brothers and me. I decided to ask them questions, too. "How long has my daddy known you guys?"

"I work with your daddy."

"How do your children know my daddy?"

"Your daddy comes over all the time to visit with my family and me after work."

Almost as if Daddy had been listening, he walked into the living room.

Christie and Cassie immediately stopped questioning me and returned to the kitchen. Then Daddy sat down to put his shoes back on.

"Have you been having fun?"

Just as I was about to answer, a little white girl emerged from the same bedroom where Daddy had been sleeping. She looked to be about two years old. Crying, she walked right up to Daddy with her arms outstretched, saying, "Daddy." She whined for Daddy to pick her up. As I watched in disbelief, my daddy picked up this child. This child who did not look mixed, but all white, had called out to him, "Daddy!" My mouth must have dropped open from shock because Daddy quickly put her down on the couch next to him and started to explain. "This is not my child. This is Mags. Christie is her momma." I must have still looked confused because he added," She likes to call me Daddy."

Christie came into the living room and introduced us. Mags stood in front of me and just looked at me. Then, to my surprise, she climbed up on the couch next to me, reached in my napkin, took my cookie out of my hand, and ate it. She wasn't scared of me because I was black. I liked her. She was cute, but she wasn't my sister. Or was she?

Seeing the confusion still lingering on my face, Daddy looked around the room nervously and began to walk toward the door. "Christie, it's time for me to be heading back across town. Chicken, you ready to go?"

I normally loved when Daddy called me Chicken. But I refused to smile and let him off the hook that easily. I did not like this little girl calling my daddy, Daddy. He wasn't her daddy; he was my and my brothers' daddy. No, I did not like this one bit. As I was exiting Christie's house, she stopped me at the doorway and asked me if I wanted to take some cookies home to my brothers. I accepted them, but I did so grudgingly.

Not accepting Daddy's answers and wanting to dig deeper into that little girl calling him Daddy, I began to question Daddy on the way home.

"Daddy, why that little white girl calling you Daddy if you ain't her daddy?"

He laughed before he replied. "Mags doesn't have a daddy. She calls me Daddy. Do you have a problem with that, Chicken?" Again, he tried to butter me up, but I was not going to let him off the hook that easily.

"Yes, I do have a problem. I don't like it. Let her find her own daddy! You are not her daddy, and if she calls you Daddy again, I promise I will cry and never stop crying!"

"Calm down. If it bothered you that much, I will tell her momma to stop her from calling me Daddy."

Satisfied, I sat back in my seat and didn't say anything for the rest of the ride home. We stopped at the Howards' house to get my brothers, but the men called out to Daddy to come join them while they drank in the garage. Daddy told me to go play with the children. I forgot all about the little white girl who had called Daddy her daddy.

When we reached the house, I jumped out of the car, nearly dropping the plate of cookies that rested on my lap. I wanted to tell my brothers everything. I told them about meeting Christie, Cassie, and Christie's children. Even though I didn't care to go back again, I bragged about how much fun I had with them.

"I had two Cokes, cookies, and swam in a pool."

After Daddy got out of the car and went into the house, my brothers began to ask me all sorts of questions about the lady and her children.

Jake whispered to David more so than to me," I wonder why Daddy didn't ask us if we wanted to go. We could have played with her sons."

I answered them, even though I knew they didn't want an answer from me. "I don't know why Daddy didn't take you guys."

David reached out and grabbed the plate of cookies out of my hand and started to walk away but then decided to turn around, walk back toward me, and kick me in my leg. I stood there, fighting back the tears, wondering what I had done to deserve the hard kick, as my brothers laughed at me as they entered the house.

When Andre came home that evening, he asked me about the cookies and the white lady with kids. He was silent while I told him everything that had happened at her house. He didn't comment until I told him about the babysitter wanting to know how they looked. "How old is she, the babysitter, that is?"

"I don't know for sure, but she did look awful young. But she was smoking a cigarette, if that tells you anything." Andre didn't ask any more questions. He just smiled at me as he took a big bite of a cookie.

Before he took another bite of a cookie, he asked me more questions. "What did Mags look like?"

"I don't know. She didn't look like Daddy, if that's what you want to know. She was all white. She ain't mixed like my friend Raven."

My answer must not have reassured him because he still asked questions about Mags. "What color was her skin? Was she white or yellow?"

"Her skin was white like her momma's." This time, when he heard that, he seemed to relax.

"Why do you want to know about her skin color?"

Jokingly, he answered, "I just wanted to make sure she was not an alien."

Changing the subject, he said, "Hey, what was the babysitter asking about us boys?"

Over the last few weeks of the summer, things moved quickly. Whenever Daddy made me go with him to Christie's house, I sat quietly on the couch while Daddy went into Christie's bedroom for a nap. Sometimes I fell asleep on her couch while waiting for him to take me home. Two days before school resumed, Christie took me to lunch and shopping for supplies. She said we needed to get to know each other better. I still didn't feel comfortable around her and her kids. However, I was excited to be going school shopping, though. I hoped she would pick me out some girl clothes for school.

When we arrived at the store, she sent her boys ahead of us to go find their sizes while we went to the girls' section. She took her time picking out things for Mags while I waited patiently for her to walk over to my size. I took little steps toward what appeared to be my size, being careful not to leave her, but able to look at all the pretty clothing in my size. I was sure this is what all the other girls would be wearing at school. When she finished looking for her daughter, she turned to where the boys were playing and walked toward them. I didn't say anything; I just followed her in silence. When she started pulling the sizes off the racks for her sons and instructing them to go into the changing room, I wondered why she hadn't gotten anything for me yet, but I didn't ask.

After about ten minutes of standing there anxiously, I noticed that she had accumulated a pile of clothing on top of the buggy aside from what she had chosen for her sons. I immediately thought these clothes must be for my brothers. When the boys finished trying on all of their clothes, we turned to walk back to the little girls' section. I was so excited. I couldn't help but smile so big that Christie noticed and asked me what was making me so happy. I told her that I was happy to be getting new school clothes. She seemed so happy that I was finally warming up to her that she told me that if I hurried up and tried on my clothing, we'd have time to stop at McDonald's before she had to meet Daddy at her house.

I quickly moved around the girls' section. I was so excited about getting new clothes. I looked around at all the pretty clothes, wondering where to start first. I ran my fingers over all the material, wondering if I should ask Christie for her help or just figure it out for myself. I realized I didn't even know how to select my size. I would have to ask her for help. Just as I built up the nerve to ask for her assistance, she called me over to her and told me to take the pile of clothing that was on top of the buggy and start trying them on. I looked at the pile of clothing, and it all made sense. The pile of clothing she had been forming wasn't for my brothers—it was for me. She must have seen the disappointment on my face.

"Your daddy gave me instructions on what to pick, and I have to do what he asks."

I got angry with her and told her, "I don't want any new clothes then."

Anxiously she asked, "What am I supposed to tell your daddy if we go back with no clothes?"

"I don't care what you tell him. I don't want any clothes, and I want to go home."

We arrived at her trailer just as Daddy pulled into her driveway. She got out of her car, moving quickly toward Daddy. She wanted to get to him and explain what had happened before I could say anything to him. She was worried that my coming home with no school clothes would reflect poorly on her. I could hear her explaining to him what had happened at the department store, nearly in tears. As I listened to her gasping for air, I began to feel panicked myself. Maybe I had overreacted. I began to wonder if Daddy would be angry with me.

Daddy called me over to where the two of them stood in the driveway.

Calmly he asked, "Let me see what ya'll got at the store."

Christie wasted no time telling on me. "Everything was fine, Ace, until I told her that I would not go against your wishes when it came to spending your money. I just don't know why she behaved so badly. I was only trying to do as you asked me to do."

From the sound of the conversation, I knew this wasn't going to end well for me. I stood there with my stomach roiling, waiting to see what Daddy was going do to me. He turned to me and said, "Get in the car and wait for me. I'll be back."

He went into the house with Christie and her children. I thought he'd be right back out, but he went in and stayed for a while. Christie's sons came outside to play on their bikes.

"Where's my daddy?"

"In my momma's room," they replied as they rode down the street, leaving me there to wonder what was taking him so long. I don't know how long I waited, but when I woke up, it was dark outside and Daddy still had not come out of her house. I had to use the bathroom and went to the door of Christie's trailer.

As I walked up to her door, I wondered if something had happened to Daddy. Why did he leave me in the car waiting for him? Why were we still at her house? Christie answered the door. She reluctantly let me in to use the bathroom.

"Where's my daddy?"

Snidely she replied, "He's asleep. He told me not to wake him up until nine o'clock."

I went over to the couch and sat. I sat there for a few minutes before Christie nonchalantly leaned around. "Your daddy told me that if you came in the house, I was to send you back out to the car to wait for him." I did not understand why Daddy had deliberately left me outside in the car all evening. Tears welled up in my eyes, but I quickly left before anyone saw them fall.

I went back outside to the car and waited for Daddy. I was so scared being outside alone—every noise I heard sent an electrical current to my heart. Luckily, it was only about an hour before he emerged. I was so glad to see him.

Daddy and I rode to the Howards' house to pick up my brothers in silence. He didn't get out to drink with the other men this time; he just pulled up, honked, and called out to my brothers. My brothers came quickly and got in the car. Neither of them said anything either. Somehow, we all sensed the tension in the air and rode the block and a half home in silence.

When we got home, Daddy went into the house. I stayed outside, taking my time going into the house because I was sad that I had upset Daddy. I felt so bad inside that I had made him unhappy. My brothers were inside the house for only a second before they called out the back door in unison, "Dorthea, Dorthea, Daddy said to come inside the house!" When I entered the house, my brothers' eyes were bigger than usual when they looked at me. "Daddy said for you to come to his bedroom."

Hesitating with every step, I walked into the bedroom, wondering what was about to happen. I felt myself trembling as I forced each leg to move in front of the other. When I got into the bedroom, I saw Daddy on the side of the bed, looking at the floor. When I entered, he looked up and hollered for my brothers to get the strap. When I realized what was about to happen, I cried out. "What did I do, Daddy? What did I do? I'll wear the clothes. Please just don't whip me. I'll be good—I promise!"

He just looked at me with anger in his eyes, "Dorthea, get over here and lie down on the floor in front of me." I wanted to lie down and be obedient, but I couldn't make myself. I knew what he was going to do with that strap. I kept trying to reason with him, but Jake entered the bedroom with the strap, handed it to Daddy, and retreated out of the room quickly.

Momma and Daddy had designed the strap years ago. It was an old broom handle that had a hole drilled through the top and electrical wires running through the hole. Every time one of us was struck with the strap, the wires wrapped around our body. Daddy again told me to lie down, but this time he was yelling.

I cried out to him again, "Please, Daddy, don't whip me! I'm sorry! I won't do it again." He lunged at me and swung the strap at me. When the strap hit me, it wrapped around my entire body. I cried out. The pain was so bad that I peed instantly. As the urine ran down my legs, he continued to swing the strap at me while screaming that he had found a woman who was willing to help him by taking me shopping. "You not only disrespected me, but you disrespected her as well. That woman didn't have to do a damn thing for you or me. She's not your momma. Your momma ran off and left you," he yelled while slinging the strap continuously. "If I would have known you would disrespect me like this, I would have run off and left too," he bellowed.

He enunciated each word he spoke with a blow of the strap. The strap hit me everywhere. I tried to escape, but he slammed the door closed and latched it. Running from corner to corner of the room did nothing to help me escape because the strap found my skin every time it reached out for me. His words were more frantic when he hollered, "You don't love me, and you don't appreciate me trying to give you a home after your momma left. I'm gonna hafta leave, too. I deserve more respect than this for trying to keep clothes on your back and a roof over your head."

Hearing his words, I ran to him and hugged him. I begged him to stop beating me with the strap, but he continued.

"I love you, and I'm sorry for disrespecting you, Daddy. Please don't leave me," I wailed. I was howling so loudly that neither of us heard my brothers screaming through the door that someone was on the phone.

Eventually Daddy heard my brothers banging on the door, and he paused. He stopped whipping me, opened the door, and took the phone.

It was my grandma. She had heard him whipping me while she waited for him to come to the phone. She wanted to know why Daddy was beating me like that. As he caught his breath, he explained, "Momma, I found a woman to help me with the children. She took Dorthea shopping for school. You know I don't know how to shop for no girl." He was silent for a few moments. "Momma, she wouldn't try on the clothes Christie picked out for her."

Daddy stopped talking to Grandma to inform me what she had just said to him. "Your grandma said that you were disrespectful and needed a whipping. She told him me if I need to continue to whip you, I could call her back. She told me to send you to her so she could straighten you out." He laughed, and they continued to talk.

I got up off the floor and walked out of the bedroom that he had once shared with my mother. I wondered what had just happened to Daddy. Daddy had never whipped me like that before. He didn't even allow Momma to beat me like that. As I stumbled to get up, I felt as if my body were on fire. It hurt so bad to walk. I heard a strange pounding in my head. Slowly I managed to make my way past him as I attempted to climb the stairs to my room. As I climbed the stairs, I could hear him talking with his mother as if nothing had happened. He didn't sound like a man who had just beaten his daughter severely. He sounded like a dutiful, loving son. "Yes, Momma, I will have Christie put a check in the mail tomorrow."

As I lay on my bed, I continued hearing Daddy's laughter while he talked with his mother. I lay in bed crying as I heard him say, "Momma, I am not gonna take my children to the bad children's home and come back home to live with you and Daddy. I'll do what I can to help you and Daddy, but I am not gonna leave my children. Besides, it hasn't been that long, and their momma may come back home." I stopped crying to listen better. "I'm going to give Ruthie Ann a little while longer to change her mind and come back to her kids. If she doesn't, I may put then into a home and come back and help you and Daddy."

It must have been more than my mind could bear because when I awoke, I heard David, Jake, and Andre outside my room. I awoke to David and Jake outside my room in their room. "Daddy was so mad at Dorthea, he said that he was waiting for Momma to come back home so he could leave us with her and return home to his momma."

"Jake, are you sure that's what he said?"

David smiled a big grin and informed Andre, "Yes, that is what Daddy said. I heard him say it too."

While David was happy, neither Jake nor Andre was happy with this piece of news. Andre, who was usually very sympathetic toward me, turned on me this time. "Why couldn't Dorthea just take the clothes? Daddy said we would be with him forever, and now, because of her, he probably thinks he cannot take care of us properly."

I lay there listening to them blaming tonight's events on me. I lay there and listened to them. No one seemed to understand that I wanted to dress like a girl, and that was not wrong. I was a girl and should be allowed to dress like one and not be beaten for it. Never mind that I had just been beaten with that horrible strap. Never mind that I hadn't meant for Daddy to get mad like that. It was the last thing I wanted to happen. I heard them laughing as they mocked me, imitating how I had begged and pleaded with Daddy not to beat me. I lay there in bed crying, wondering why it was so easy for the people who loved me to hurt me. Everyone always blamed me for everything. Again, I realized that no one cared for my feelings or happiness.

The next morning, I awoke to Daddy calling my name to come make his coffee. I jumped out of bed glad that Daddy had called me, but as my feet landed on the floor, pain shot through my body, and the memory of the horrible beating I had received the night before came rushing back to me. I was so glad that Daddy wasn't mad at me anymore that I ignored the pain. I hurried and made his coffee so he wouldn't be late. I kissed Daddy on the cheek as I usually did each morning when he walked out the door.

After he left, I went to the bathroom. As I sat on the toilet, I looked down at my legs and saw the lines that covered my legs. I jumped up, walked to the mirror, and examined my body. I had long, dark-purple welts all over my body. They were on my legs, arms, back, chest, neck, and on the tops of my feet. They felt hot to the touch. I ran out of the bathroom screaming, "Andre, Andre! Andre, come quick. Help me, Andre!"

Andre came running out of his room and practically jumped down the stairs, taking two at a time. In between pants, he asked me, "Why are you screaming?"

Carefully I raised my shirt so he could see what I had just seen. He took one look at the welts on my body and his eyes filled with tears.

"How am I supposed to start school tomorrow? How am I going to explain this to everyone? All the children already think I am strange."

Andre didn't say a word to me. He turned away and sat down at the kitchen table where he was joined by my other two brothers, whom I had wakened with my screams. David and Jake sat at the table with Andre, quietly trying to come up with a good solution to our problem. We all knew how Daddy had gotten custody of us from Momma—it was because Momma had beaten me. As soon as I reported to school tomorrow, there would surely be trouble. What if the authorities found out that Daddy had beaten me? What would become of us? Would they take us all away? Where would we go?

After discussing it with David and Jake, Andre hollered at me. "Why can't you just get along like everybody else? You always have to start trouble. Now, because of your actions, we all might have to go into foster care," he yelled.

I felt terrible both physically and emotionally. I didn't want us to get taken away from Daddy. All I wanted to do was live with Daddy. "The school don't have to find out. I can just stay home," I replied.

"That won't work. They've got special police that'll come to the house. They'll come here to ask Daddy why you're not going to school."

"Well, I can just tell everyone that some kids beat me up."

"That's stupid," David said.

All throughout the day, none of my brothers spoke to me. They formed an alliance, speaking to each other in hushed tones and ending conversations when I entered the room. I tried to go to Mother Alexander's house after I took a bath and got dressed, but Andre wouldn't let me.

Daddy didn't come home for lunch—he had been doing that lately. When Daddy came home after work, Andre hesitantly approached him and asked him what they were going to do about my bruises. He explained to him that we all reported to school on the next day, and there was no way to hide my bruises. Andre reminded Daddy how he had been awarded custody based on the beating that Momma had given me.

I sat on the stairs listening quietly as Andre and Daddy talked. I didn't want to draw any more attention to myself. Daddy made a *harrumph* sound while Andre spoke.

"Andre, what do you think I should do?"

"Daddy, she is going to have to wear jeans and long sleeves to school—that way, her welts will not show."

Then Daddy started to speak softly. "I didn't mean to hurt her, Andre. It's hard for a single man to raise four children. Half the time, I don't know what I'm doing. That's why I need people like Christie to help me. You don't know how many times I've gone to people to ask them for help with you children, and people tell me that I should just take ya'll back to your momma—that a man has no business trying to raise all those children. Heck, even your aunt and uncle live around that corner, and they won't help at all."

There was a pause and a moment of silence before Daddy spoke again. "I swear I didn't mean to hurt her. No one on this earth means more to me than my kids. I just wanted her to understand that she needs to be respectful to anyone who tries to help us. It don't come easy, and if she's disrespectful, I ain't gonna get any help." His voice broke a little. "Andre, just do what you see fit to keep us together."

"Yes, sir," Andre replied.

Listening to Daddy almost cry made me feel that much worse. I had put all of our futures in danger just because I wanted to wear clothes that made me look like the other girls. What did it matter that I looked like the other girls if it cost us living with Daddy? I had to learn to stop being so selfish and think about how my actions affected our family. I was determined to not let him down again. I would do better by both Daddy and my brothers.

The next morning, I awoke and made Daddy's coffee. When Daddy left for work, I got dressed for school before waking my brothers. When I walked to the bus stop, no one questioned why I had on blue jean pants and long sleeves instead of shorts like everyone else. We stood around talking until the bus arrived. The last stop on our route was at the corner of the Howard family's house. As they got on the bus, some of the younger children around my age wanted to know why I was wearing "those hot clothes." I tried to ignore them, but they made jokes about my clothes, making me more embarrassed about the situation.

Neither Jake nor David said anything in my defense—they laughed at each joke as if it were someone else's sister. With each joke, I sank further into my seat, wishing I could be anywhere but on that bus. Maybe if my brothers had just spoken up for me just once, then maybe they would have stopped teasing me.

When I walked into the class, the teacher stared at me for a moment but didn't say anything. I looked around the room until I found my name on my desk and quickly went to my seat. I put my things in my desk and sat quietly, waiting for instructions from my new teacher, Mrs. Kennedy. When the bell rang, she introduced herself to the class and asked each of us to stand up and share something interesting that we did over the summer.

I listened to students describing wonderful vacations, learning how to swim, and playing in the baseball leagues. I wondered what to say when it came to my turn. I thought of everything that had happened to me over the summer. I thought about how Earl attacked me every chance he got. I thought about how I had just been beaten with a strap two nights before, and I thought about how Daddy took me over to his white friend's house to swim. Nothing sounded cool enough for me to share with my classmates. I don't know why I decided to do it or if it was just compulsive, but when it came to my turn, I told a story about visiting my grandparents' ranch in Mississippi. I listened as the words spewed out of my mouth. Surprisingly, my classmates put up their hands and asked me questions, and I made up answers just as quickly as they asked them.

At lunch, I was having so much fun playing with the other children that while playing on the jungle bars, I decided to hang upside down—to impress the other kids. When I did, my shirt fell down and exposed my back. One of my classmates saw the welts on my back and gasped, causing everyone to look. A small group of children gathered around me and asked how I had gotten the marks. I tried to think of something clever to say, but the only excuse I could come up with was another tale. I told them that while I was at my grandparents' home in Mississippi, I had been thrown from a horse and that the horse had trampled me. My classmates were in awe. I was important, and everyone wanted to hear my story. Even though it was all a lie, it made me feel good.

I managed to save the day without feeling entirely embarrassed until I heard Robby Howard telling his sister that the marks on my back looked like welts from a belt to him. Allie agreed, and they both laughed together. The classmates who had believed me asked Robby and Allie why they would say that about me. Robby said that he overheard my brothers telling his older brother on the bus that I had gotten a whipping the night before.

I felt betrayed for so many reasons. I hated Robby and Allie in that moment. Who were they to tell everyone I was lying? They didn't know what happened in my house. What business of it was theirs to tell everyone that I had gotten a whipping? Why were David and Jake telling the Howards our family business?

I screamed at them to stop lying about my family. I told everyone that Robby was lying—my brothers wouldn't tell that lie about our family. Allie and Robby just laughed at me and kept telling everyone that I had cried out and begged Daddy to stop whipping me. Even though I knew they were telling the truth about how I had behaved while Daddy whipped me, I still persisted in telling the children that they were lying. I told them they were just jealous of me because they were poor and didn't have any grandparents who had a horse ranch. When I called them poor, Allie stuck her hand in my face and told me that I better shut up because at least she had a mother who wanted her.

I saw red, and I slapped her. We fell to the ground fighting. On top of her, I beat her in her face and punched her in the chest. She called out to Robby, and he quickly kicked my back. I tried to fight him off while still keeping her down, but I wasn't prepared to fight both of them.

I thought about St. Louis under the Eagle's Nest, and I panicked. Robby pulled me off Allie by the hair, and they both hit me. I fought them as best as I could, not letting either one of them get me to the ground. My brothers, who had been playing elsewhere on the playground, ran up and yelled at Robby to get out of the fight because he was a boy. Jake grabbed Robby and held his arms to protect me from him. Then the older Howard children came over to see what was going on, and they yelled at Jake to let Robby go.

By this time, someone had alerted the playground monitor, who sent the crowd of onlooker children away to their individual teachers while everyone involved had to remain together until it was determined who had started the fight. It didn't take long. I stood beside my brothers as Allie told everyone about the welts on my back. She told how I got angry when she and her brother told everyone I was lying and that Daddy had beat me. Neither my brothers nor I said anything—we were too scared of someone asking to see my body. The playground monitors decided that everyone needed to apologize to one another and report to their classrooms. Robby went to the school nurse to receive a breathing treatment, while the rest of us were sent to our individual classrooms.

When I returned to the classroom, everyone pointed and whispered. They had all pretty much concluded that I was a liar. We all opened our books, and the day continued as usual.

Word got around to Andre, who was in high school, about the fight between me and the Howard children, and when we arrived home from school, he wanted to know what had happened. He instructed me not to tell Daddy what had happened at school. He told me that "sticks and stones will break my bones, but words will never hurt me," and then he yelled at me for getting into a fight with the Howards.

"If you had been sent to the school nurse, she would have seen your bruises. She could have called the police on Daddy," he yelled.

I couldn't believe my ears. How could I be blamed for this mess? I did everything I could to keep my beating a secret. Finally, Andre attempted to find out who had told the Howards about my beating. David admitted that he had told and said that he didn't care because he didn't like me and he thought it was funny. Andre told me there was no need to tell Daddy about the situation because he would take care of it. I wondered why no one felt the need to protect me. No one protected me from anything or anyone.

Mother Alexander came faithfully every morning and made breakfast for us, but I didn't go to Mother Alexander's house after school because I had to do homework in second grade. No matter how much I tried, I just wasn't a good student, but I wasn't the only student who had trouble in second grade. This year, Robby and I seemed to be getting along. We had somehow formed an unspoken truce since the first day of school, and it was easy for us to become friends since we were both labeled troublemakers.

Robby and I were known for alternating between fighting each other and fighting other children, talking back to teachers, and just plain being ornery. He was my friend too. He was tall and awkward, but was all right by me. He really wasn't known for fighting or talking back to the teachers. His biggest crime was lying all the time and being guilty by association with the rest of the troublemakers in my group of friends. My other friend, Raven, was what we kids called a half-breed—her mother was white and her daddy was black. She lived up the street from me with her grandmother because her mother had left her with her daddy. We shared that in common, although it didn't make us any closer. We, too, were known for fighting each other and everyone else. Felicia was another known troublemaker, but I didn't like her at all. She wanted to fight with me all the time.

We stayed in trouble, and most days, we spent our recesses standing on the wall or inside at our desks. Out of our group, no one missed recess more than Robby and me. Even when Robby managed to stay out of trouble, he missed out on recess due to his asthma. At first, I only pretended to hate school like the rest of the group, but over the years, it eventually turned into the truth.

I turned seven in October, and it marked the anniversary of my momma leaving us. A few of the students remembered my embarrassment from last year when Momma didn't show with the treats that I had promised. For the most part, my birthday went unnoticed by everyone—including my daddy, my brothers, and my friends. I pretended that it didn't bother me, but it really hurt that no one wanted to celebrate that I was still here. I tried to bring it up to Daddy, but all he wanted to talk about was the fact that it was the day Momma left him to run off and be with another man. Daddy ended up getting drunk and going to his girlfriend's house, leaving me at home with my brothers. I tried to bring it up to them that it was my birthday, but they only growled that no one cared about me being born, and more importantly, no one wanted to celebrate the day our mother left us.

I hated everything about the holidays, too. I hated going to school and listening to the excitement of everyone anticipating their huge family dinners or their many wonderful presents under their beautifully decorated Christmas trees. This was the first year it really affected us that we didn't have a mother or an extended family with whom to celebrate the holidays. No one was shopping for the children in our home. We weren't smelling the delicious aromas of turkey and dressing on Thanksgiving or tasting the delicious icing on sugar cookies shaped like Rudolph. Nowhere did we see Christmas lights on our house. I hated listening to the other students telling one another about the hoped-for presents under their tree.

With Thanksgiving gone and not one spoon of dressing having crossed our lips, I decided to take a leap of faith. One evening while Daddy watched television with us, I made the mistake of asking him what he was going to do for us for Christmas.

"I don't know—hadn't really thought about it. What ya'll want me to do?"

"I want what all my friends at school have." I described what I had heard them telling one another.

Jake and David informed him," We want what all our friends are getting for Christmas!"

David made an additional request: "I want delicious food for Christmas dinner." At first, Daddy grew silent, staring at the television. We thought his silence meant he was listening intently to us and making plans to make all of our dreams come true, but he abruptly rose from his chair and walked outside. He got into the car and left. At first, we all sat there looking at one another, wondering what had happened.

"I wonder where he went and what he is getting us."

"I hope he brings us back a racetrack."

"I bet he went to get us a Christmas tree to put all our presents under."

We watched television, anxiously waiting for Daddy to return to us with our surprises.

A little over an hour later, we heard Daddy pull into the driveway. We ran to the window and looked out, expecting to see Daddy bringing in a tree for us. Instead, he walked toward the back door of our house, carrying a case of beer under his arm and a bottle of liquor in his hand. We sat back down, disappointed. Still wanting to believe, I whispered," Maybe Daddy is going to surprise us."

They just looked at me with disappointment on their faces and said, "Dorthea, it is highly unlikely that Daddy has anything for us."

Adamantly I replied, "Yes, he does! I don't believe you. You will see, Daddy has presents for us."

As Daddy came through the back door, stomping his feet, I ran up to him and asked him if he had any presents for us in the car. Daddy sat at the table, turned around, and looked at me for a long time without saying anything. He opened a beer and began drinking. Daddy looked strange: his eyes were dark red, and he didn't smile when he looked at me. I don't know why, but I thought he wanted to be alone, so I walked out of the kitchen and back to the living room where my brothers were watching television. As I was leaving the kitchen, Daddy lifted the bottle of liquor and took a long drink.

My brothers and I watched television for about twenty minutes before Daddy called us into the kitchen. He told us to sit at the table because he wanted to talk to us. We all sat down. We didn't know what he wanted to tell us, but we knew it was serious. He took out his pistol and put it on the table. He had finished the bottle of liquor and set it down with a few empty cans of beer that were on the table in front of him.

"I'm doing the best I can to take care of you kids by myself. Your momma don't pay me no child support. I don't know a thing about taking care of no children—let alone a girl. Your grandmomma wants me to put ya'll in foster care. She wants me to come live with her."

He put his face in his hands and began to sob. We sat there silently, unsure of what to say. With tears still running down his cheeks, he continued. "Ya'll don't appreciate what I'm doing for ya'll. You don't care about me. I should just leave ya'll. Nobody cares about me except my momma."

The tears stopped, and his voice turned nasty. "My momma wanted me. She still wants me—not like ya'll's sorry momma." He picked up the gun. "I should just blow my brains out right here. I could just leave all ya'll just like your momma did."

Though we were all scared, we remained silent. After a long pause, he spoke calmly. "I'm gonna call somebody in your momma's family to try get in touch with her. I'm going to tell her to come get you kids. I'm a man. I don't deserve to be tied down to no stupid kids. Hell, I don't even know if you *are* my kids."

By this time, we had all started crying, but our tears didn't mean anything to him. He even told us so. "I cried and begged your momma not to leave me, and she just laughed at my tears. I don't care about your tears. Nobody cared about mine," he said.

Next, he went around the kitchen table and asked each of us the same question: "Who wants me to try and find your momma and convince her to come home?" He paused for a moment before he went on to explain. "You know your momma won't stay in the house with me, so you will have to choose between us."

"Andre, what do you want me to do?"

Andre told him, "I can't choose between my parents because I love you both."

"David, what do you want me to do?"

"I want my momma to return and to live with us. I want to visit you if Momma says it is okay."

"Jake, what do you want me to do?"

"I don't want you to leave us. Besides, I already made my choice when I decided to return home to live with you."

"Dorthea, what do you think I should do?"

I jumped up from where I was sitting and ran around the table and hugged him. "Daddy, I made my choice. I don't want her to come back. I want to stay with you for the rest of my life."

This didn't satisfy Daddy. "David, why would you still want your momma even after she left you to be with another man?"

"Because I love my momma!"

Daddy sat there silently for a minute. In a flash, he picked up the gun, pointed it at David, and started screaming, "If you ever choose her over me again, I'll blow your brains out right here in this kitchen," he yelled. Then, still holding the gun, Daddy went back around the table and asked, "Who wants your momma to come home and live here? Remember, if your momma comes back to live here, then I won't be able to stay."

He looked at Andre. Andre told Daddy that he wanted her to stay wherever she was with that man. Daddy looked at David again. David stared at the floor. Daddy asked him who he wanted to live with. Still staring at the floor, David said that he wanted to live with Momma.

Daddy jumped up and reached David in two steps, and before we could do anything, he had slapped David in the face with the pistol. David fell to the floor, and Daddy began kicking him. Every time Daddy kicked David, we could hear the sound of Daddy's boot as it made contact with the bones in David's body. It made a horrible sound. We thought surely he would kill him if he did not stop soon. Daddy kicked David's head, stomach, back, and face. Whatever body parts Daddy didn't kick on David, he stomped. David was bleeding everywhere. We all begged Daddy to stop. We kept waiting for David to stop crying out, figuring each blow would be the one that killed our brother. When Daddy finished beating David, he screamed, "Do you still want your momma, boy?"

In a gurgling voice, David yelled back, "Yes!"

Daddy picked up the gun and shoved it into David's mouth.

"You tell me right now that you don't want her, or I'll blow your brains out."

We yelled at David, saying, "Just say it!" and "Please, David!"

With the gun still in David's mouth, Daddy said, "Jake, do you still want your momma?" Daddy just looked at him and smiled.

Jake looked at David and said, "No, Daddy. I hate her. I wish she would die."

Then Daddy addressed me. "Chicken . . . "

Before he could ask me the question, I blurted out, "I hate the bitch, and I hope she never comes back." I didn't even know what *bitch* meant, but I knew it was a bad word. I had heard the girls on the playground use the word in anger. The way I said it must have shocked Daddy because he looked at me for a long moment before he began to laugh. He finally pulled the pistol out of David's mouth.

I didn't hate Momma, but it didn't take a rocket scientist to figure out what Daddy wanted to hear. I didn't want to end up like David, and to be honest, she had left us. She didn't want to be our mother anymore. I was happy to see Daddy laughing again.

Daddy sent David into the bathroom to clean up. He sat back down at the table and spoke to all of us once again. "The holidays make me sad," he said. "All I can think about is your momma with another man and us being all by ourselves. We ain't gonna celebrate the holidays this year. I don't feel like it. 'Sides, I don't need a holiday to tell me to do for my children. I do for my children all year round. Christmas is just for mommas and daddies who don't do for their children. I'll take care of ya'll all year long, and I'll leave Christmas to your momma. Now, I'm going to bed."

With that, he got up and left the table. Andre and Jake went into the bathroom to help David. When they emerged and realized Daddy was out of earshot, they began to yell at me for starting a mess. "If you had not been bothering Daddy about presents for Christmas, then he wouldn't have left and gotten drunk."

As bad as I felt for David, I resented their accusations and told them so. "It isn't all my fault. You guys told Daddy what you wanted for Christmas just like I did. Besides, David should have done what Daddy asked. All he had to say was that he didn't want Momma to come home." I knew it was a lie, but what else were we supposed to do? As a matter of fact, at this point I think we all realized it was much safer in this house if Momma did come home.

After Christmas break, we returned to school. As a treat, the teacher went around the classroom asking the children to tell their favorite Christmas gifts. My classmates told stories of their exciting presents, and I stared at the teacher, hoping she would be able to see into me and know that I didn't have a story to share about wonderful presents. When she came to my row, I put my hand up and asked to be excused. I stayed gone until I felt the teacher had passed my row. Somehow, she must have gotten the message because when I came back to the room, she didn't ask what I had received for Christmas. When the children pointed out that I hadn't talked about my gifts, she told them that we had run out of time. I was so relieved.

Winter slowly changed to spring, and life went on at our home. Daddy frequently got drunk and woke us up in the middle of the night to ask the same question. We passed the test, but no matter how many times Daddy beat him, David would always say that he wanted Momma. This led to Daddy picking on him during the wee hours of the morning, with a pistol on the table. We wanted to impress Daddy, so we picked on David too.

I'm ashamed to admit that none of my siblings picked on David as much as I did. I wanted to please Daddy, and during these times, picking on David made him happy. Why couldn't he just say what Daddy wanted him to say? I didn't like it when Daddy beat him or threatened to kill him. Usually, I would distract him by talking about Momma. He liked to hear me talk bad about Momma. If he was beating David, I would scream out to David to just accept that she was a bitch and to hate her as much as we did. It would calm Daddy down. I would tell Daddy that if she came to our house trying to get us back, I would laugh in her face and slam the door. This would make him calm down and stop beating David. No one thanked me. My brothers hated me for joining Daddy. I didn't understand why they hated me. At least I did something to stop him from beating David.

The more Daddy beat David, the more David attacked me. He snuck into my room almost every night and attacked me. When he was through, he would punch me in the back or stomach before he left my room. I couldn't fight back or tell on him, so he held the power, but when we had our nightly sessions with Daddy and Daddy's pistol, I held the power to make his whipping worse. I could jump in right away and begin to call Momma names, or I could wait a while before I said anything, causing David's whippings to last longer. Some nights, I took longer than others. It was the only way I had to fight back for what he did to me when there was no one to protect me from him.

* * * * *

After being cooped up in the house all winter with nowhere to go, it was nice to see the break in the weather. I loved springtime. In spring, everything was fresh and new. The flowers began to bud, and leaves filled the trees. For me, spring always felt like a renewal of life. After the long winter we spent locked inside with Daddy's late night tantrums, I was ready for something new to happen in our life.

One Sunday morning in May, Daddy came home from Christie's house and told us to get dressed because we were going to Chicago to see his sister. Her name was Monique. Aunt Monique, Uncle Dennis, and their son, Myron, all lived in the Windy City. I had never been to their home before, so I was excited to meet them.

My aunt's home was beautiful. We stayed in the car, and Daddy went in first. Then, everyone filed out of the house to meet us. They were all so happy to see us. They hadn't seen us in years. We went inside, and Daddy introduced us to his family. Besides Aunt Monique's family, two of Daddy's cousins were there, too. Uncle Tom was really Daddy's cousin, but everyone called him Uncle Tom. He was there as well as Daddy's cousin John, who brought Princhetta, his girlfriend. All of the adults took turns hugging us and commenting on how good we looked. No one went on about us longer than Uncle Tom. He paid particular attention to me. He held me at arm's length and gushed about how much I looked like Momma.

Then, he turned to the adults. "Lord, he done did a lot and she always stayed with him, so what could he have done to make her leave her children?" he asked.

After the words were spoken, everyone got quiet. Daddy threatened to leave if Uncle Tom didn't shut his mouth.

"Sit down. Calm down. You ain't going nowhere. You just got here, and I been cooking all day," Aunt Monique said.

The food did smell delicious. It had been a long time since we had anything like the spread of food in the kitchen. Daddy looked around at all the food and told her to make us some food to take home with us. Uncle Dennis apologized for Uncle Tom, making the excuse that he had a little too much to drink. Uncle Tom looked over at Daddy and told him he was sorry and didn't mean any harm. Uncle Tom blamed his actions on the liquor. Uncle Tom turned to us and explained that he and our Daddy had grown up more like brothers than cousins and that he loved Daddy best of all.

After things calmed down a bit, Aunt Monique called her son, Myron, into the house and introduced us. He was her only child and the same age as me. Myron took us across the street to an open field where all his friends were playing baseball. Myron quickly introduced us to his friends, and they invited us to play. A little while after we started playing ball, Daddy came outside, got into his car, and left. As he drove away, he yelled out the window at us that he would be back for us. "Be good while I'm gone," he said.

I played until Uncle Tom came outside and called me back across the street. He wanted to talk with me. All the adults had come outside and were sitting together on the patio, talking and drinking with one another. They all joined in the conversation. The questions were coming so fast I didn't know who they were coming from. "Do you miss your momma?" "Do you like living in a house with all men?"

Uncle Tom stood out from all the rest. He informed me, "It's a shame Ace got you looking like a li'l boy. No, I take that back. You look like a little black Annie Oakley."

Uncle Dennis saw the question on my face and asked me if I knew who Annie Oakley was. When I answered no, they all laughed. Still laughing, Aunt Monique spoke up. "Let that child go back and play with the children."

Uncle Tom reached into his back pocket, took out his wallet, grabbed a fifty-dollar bill, and gave it to me. I was so shocked, I just stood there. Uncle Dennis spoke first. "Dorthea, put that money in your pocket."

"I don't have any pockets."

Uncle Tom spoke next. "Put it in your bra."

When I still didn't move, he asked, "Child, do you wear bras yet?"

Embarrassed, I replied, "No!"

Uncle Tom spoke again. "Put it in your shoe."

Thinking that was a good idea, I bent down to do it, but Aunt Monique said, "Don't you do such a thing. Give it to me, and I'll give it to your daddy when he comes back."

Uncle Tom teased me, saying, "You better not let your daddy spend that money on no cheap women." Everyone laughed, but Aunt Monique told me to go play before Daddy returned.

As I ran back across the street, I couldn't help but feel special. For once, everyone seemed to be interested in me. A little while later, Daddy pulled back up and told us to come eat before we hit the road to go home. At the table, I realized that I didn't want to leave. I wanted us to stay there forever. I liked having delicious food to eat. Daddy was a good cook, but most nights, he cooked neck bones and potatoes.

I liked how everyone laughed when they talked. No one threatened to kill us or beat us. Most importantly, I liked how Daddy laughed and talked with everyone. He seemed to relax and enjoy himself. I was sad when it was time to go. Daddy was drunk, but he insisted we had to get on the road, so Andre drove us home to Kewanee. Everyone promised to come and see us soon.

When we arrived home, I couldn't shake the sadness I felt as I walked back into our house. I began to accept that maybe we were missing a part of life by not having a mother. For the first time since Momma left us, I really missed her and all that she brought to our lives. I missed having family at our house and delicious food to eat.

Daddy had such a good time when we went to Chicago that a few weeks later, he decided to return, taking Christie and me with him. I was so glad to be back with my extended family because I didn't have to worry about David or Earl getting me. I could just be a kid. Aunt Monique got up early on Saturday morning and made a huge breakfast for everyone. We had ham, bacon, sausage, pancakes, grits, eggs, and homemade biscuits. It was all so delicious. I tried to eat a little of everything. Daddy, Christie, and I kept telling Aunt Monique how good her cooking was. She laughed and told us that she enjoyed cooking for us.

After breakfast, Myron and I went outside to play with his friends. We played baseball in the field across the street from his house. We had such a good time that when we got back to the house, I walked up to Aunt Monique and gave her a hug. Over the next few years, we returned to Aunt Monique's home often. She was the only family member of Daddy's that he visited regularly.

School let out for the summer, and with summer break came Earl. He was everywhere I went. Between him and David, I felt trapped. If I managed to make it through the day without Earl finding me, David would just come to me in my room at night. I didn't get as much sleep as I should have because I started having nightmares. I began dreaming that either David or Earl was chasing me. One Saturday afternoon while watching Westerns with Daddy, I drifted off to sleep. The dream quickly turned into the recurring nightmare, and I screamed Earl's name. Daddy woke me up and asked why I had screamed out his name. I didn't know what to say to him, so I told him that Earl was picking on me at the Howards' house.

He made me get in the car, and we went to the Howards' house. He told Earl's daddy that I had just had a nightmare about Earl picking on me and that Earl had better leave me alone or else. Earl's daddy called him outside and made Earl apologize to me. I stood there about to faint for fear that someone would figure out that I was lying about the reason for the dream.

While Daddy talked to Earl's daddy, Earl stared balefully at me. I was so scared that if we didn't leave soon, I would open my mouth and blurt the truth about what Earl was really doing to me. I wanted to tell on him. I wanted him to stop using me. I wanted Daddy to beat him up, but all I kept thinking was, *If I tell on Earl, he'll tell on David.* I didn't want David to get into trouble.

The more time Daddy stood there hollering at Earl and Mr. Smith, the angrier Daddy got. I was so scared, I grew nauseous and began to retch. Daddy said Earl picked on me so bad that my nerves were bad, and he started yelling all over again. When I couldn't take it any longer, I threw up right there all over the ground and myself. He blamed that on Earl too, but we finally left.

Something good came out of Daddy going to the Howards' house. When he went to Christie's house, he started taking me with him. He decided that I didn't need all the freedom I had been given. I didn't particularly want to go to Christie's house with her children, but I was glad to be away from David and Earl for a while. I slept on her couch at night and left every morning with Daddy. Because I had to get up so early every morning for Daddy to bring me home, I would go back to sleep in my own bed when I got home. Some mornings, David took advantage of this opportunity to sneak into my room and attack me. However, because I left with Daddy every night, this blocked Earl from getting to me as much. There was still some window of opportunity for him to get me while I waited for Daddy to take me to Christie's, but not nearly as much as he had previously. Daddy and I would arrive at Christie's around seven every night, in time for us to eat, watch television, and go to bed. I rather liked this schedule.

It didn't take long for me to relax at Christie's with her family. I had the most fun with Cassie, Christie's babysitter. Some nights, she would call home and ask her mother if she could stay and spend the night. Cassie and I got along so well that Daddy started allowing me to stay at Christie's house while he and Christie worked. I especially liked this because it stopped David and Earl from getting to me during the days. I actually started to enjoy my life for a change. For the first time since my mother left me, I felt like a kid.

Cassie, George, Mark, Mags, and I had fun every day. Every day, we did something different. Some days, we baked desserts like brownies or cakes. Some days, we experimented, mixing different flavors of Kool-Aid together. There were even days that Christie's friend, the Avon lady, took us to Liberty Pool so we could swim. Things were working out so well that the only time I went home was to get more clothes. On the rare occasions that my brothers asked me questions about my time at Christie's with her sons, I told them that they were cool. My brothers had warned me that white and blacks don't see each other as equals and that one day soon, they would let me know I was not so "cool" to them.

True to form, all good things must end. George and Mark had two friends who were brothers and who played with us in the afternoons. They were both red-headed and blue-eyed with freckles everywhere. We rode our bikes all over the neighborhood together. We sat on the curb at the gas station and ate our chips while sipping on Cokes. We watched the traffic and challenged each other to spitting contests.

The two brothers, Bobby and Robby, began to whisper and giggle amongst themselves. Bobby, the older of the brothers, smiled and turned to me and asked, "Can I see your boobs?"

George, shocked at Bobby's question, replied for me. "Knock it off, Bobby!"

Robby, took a jab at George and said, "Why you getting upset? Is she your girlfriend or something?"

I sat there quietly embarrassed by the brothers' questions. I was glad George had spoken up for me. Lost in my own thought, I did not notice who hit who first, but when I looked up toward where all four of the boys were gathered, George was in the process of punching Robby. Bobby, not wanting George to beat up his younger brother, jumped on his back. When I saw George struggling with both Bobby and Robby, I jumped into the fight, and George and I beat up Bobby and Robby. The gas station attendant, hearing all the commotion, came outside and ran all of us off the property.

When we crossed the street back into Christie's yard, Bobby was so angry at George for defending me that he called him a "nigger lover" for fighting his own kind. I ran at Bobby and knocked him down. Robby jumped on my back and tried to pull my hair. I began to beat Bobby's head into the ground, alternating between punching his face and pulling his hair. George pulled Robby off me and beat him up. Cassie and her friends came running outside after hearing the commotion. Once she and her friends had separated us, Cassie asked what had happened.

I had thought of George and Mark as my best friends, so I was shocked when George started to cry and told Cassie that Bobby and Robby had called him a nigger lover and said that I was his girlfriend. As he cried, he said that he didn't even like niggers, and that he was only being nice to me because his mother made him. I was shocked and hurt, which quickly turned to anger, and I punched him right in the face. Cassie separated us and made the brothers go home. She made George go to his room, and she told me to come into the house. All afternoon, Cassie and her friends assured me that Christie didn't feel that way and that when she came home, George would be in trouble for making such a statement.

No one was more surprised than I was at what happened later that afternoon. When Christie arrived home from work, Cassie told her what had happened earlier that day. We anticipated George getting a stern talking to for what he had implied because of the color of my skin. Instead, Christie called George downstairs from his room and told him to go play. She told me to call Daddy and tell him to come get me. I immediately knew I was in trouble. I remembered what happened to me last time I had upset Christie, and I cried. Cassie saw that I was upset and asked me to go outside and sit on the porch while she and Christie talked.

I heard them talking in the house. While I sat outside on the step, the tears continued to fall. Why did this always happen? Why couldn't I just be happy? Why did I always have to mess things up? I thought about what was there waiting for me back in my neighborhood—David and Earl. I began to get angry about the situation. I knocked on the door and asked to use the bathroom. Christie reluctantly let me in. When I finished in the bathroom, I began to walk back outside and wait for Daddy on the steps when she told me to come into the house and sit down on the couch.

"I'd rather wait outside," I said and kept walking. She yelled at me to come sit my "ass" down on the couch as she had instructed. Her voice scared me, and I jumped and spun around to see her coming at me. She yanked my arm and shoved me to the couch to take a seat.

"You had no right to put your hands on my son. You are a guest in our home and should behave like one!"

"He didn't have the right to call me what he called me either."

Just as she was coming back toward me, Daddy pulled up in the driveway. He came into the house, wanting to know what was going on and why had I called and left a message for him to come get me. Christie immediately told him what I had done to her son. As she was talking, I saw that Daddy got upset. "You was at work with me when all this happened, so you don't know how it went down," he yelled at Christie.

Daddy turned to Cassie and asked her what had happened. She reluctantly told him everything she knew about what had taken place. After Cassie's story, Daddy told me to get my stuff. "We're not coming back here," he said.

Following Daddy out the door, Christie began to question him. "Ace, where are you going? Are you coming back? Are you leaving me for good? Please stop and talk to me! The Andrew brothers don't have to come back to my house."

Chasing behind him, Christie grabbed the door handle and held onto Daddy's car. Daddy started to back out of the driveway with Christie still hanging onto the door. She was crying and continuing to beg him to stop the car. Just as Daddy backed into the street, she reached into the car window, grabbed his hand on the steering wheel, and caused him to turn toward her. Just as he was about to yell at her, she yelled at him, "Dammit, I love you! I don't want to lose you over this."

Daddy stopped the car, looking at her for a moment before he put the car in drive, and began to pull back into her driveway. Daddy put the car in park and turned to look at me before getting out of the car and following Christie into her house. As Daddy walked into the house, he turned back to me again and informed me, "I'll be out in a minute."

I sat in the car for what seemed like forever. After a while, I went back into the house. Daddy and Christie were in the bedroom, still arguing. "Have a seat," Cassie said. "They should be done in a minute." Daddy had told Cassie that he would give her a ride home. Eventually, Cassie gathered her things and the two of us waited for Daddy outside on the steps. While we waited, we heard Mark, George, and Mags eating dinner at the table. As I listened to them laugh and eat together, I couldn't help but wish I could undo the events of the day. If none of it had happened, I would be in there with them, eating dinner and laughing too.

A little over an hour later, Daddy called me back into the house to explain what was about to happen. I was going to go back home and would not be allowed to be there anymore unless he or Christie was there to watch me. I was told that I had to keep my hands off Christie's children, and if they ever did anything to me again, I was supposed to tell Daddy or Christie. I had to apologize to Christie and George. So I told Christie that I was sorry for disrespecting her home and fighting her son. I told George that I was sorry for punching him. Christie explained to me that all children needed to feel safe at home and that I had taken that away from George. He didn't feel safe with me at their home.

I felt like no one cared about my feelings. After all, I wanted to feel safe, too. If I felt safe at home, I would never have wanted to come to their home. When Daddy noticed that I wasn't happy, he asked me if there was something else he needed to know. I wanted to tell him how Christie had snatched my arm. I wanted to ask him why he wasn't more upset about George calling me a nigger, but I didn't.

"I'm fine, Daddy," I said, and I turned around and walked out to the car. I had learned that telling the whole story just caused more problems for me in the end.

We dropped Cassie off at her home, and then Daddy dropped me off at home before he went back to Christie's house. My brothers wanted to know what had happened. They wanted to know why I was back at home with them. Glad for the attention, I told them everything that had happened that day. Andre was angry and couldn't understand why Daddy wasn't angrier about what George and his two friends had said to me. David and Jake reminded me that they had warned me that something like this could happen.

That night as I lay in my own bed, it didn't take long before David entered my room. This time, when he finished, he was even angrier with me. He repeatedly punched me, but before he left my room, he whispered in my ear, "You can run, but you can't hide."

I heard his laughter as he snuck out of my room. Long after he left, I cried myself to sleep. I thought about George's mother telling me that it was important for a child to feel safe at home. Didn't anybody care that I wasn't safe at home?

* * * * *

The rest of the summer went by fast. My summer was split between spending time with my aunt and her family and going to Christie's house and playing with her children. On the trips to Chicago, I enjoyed myself—I was able to be a kid. I loved being with Aunt Monique. She was like a mother to me, and I really wished I could be her daughter.

When Daddy took me to Christie's house, I learned to tolerate their dislike for me in exchange for refuge from home. It wasn't that bad being there unless the Andrews brothers came to play with George. George felt the need to prove to them that he didn't like me and only tolerated me because his mother made him.

When the Andrews brothers came over on the weekends, I didn't remind Christie that she had told Daddy they wouldn't return. I didn't even mention it when George laughed at the racial slurs the Andrews brothers made. I just accepted the fact that if I complained, I would be the one sent home. I learned at an early age that sometimes choices must be made, and I chose the lesser of the two evils. I chose to be called names that hurt my feelings rather than be physically hurt by David or Earl.

Summer ended, and I returned to school as a third-grader. I hoped things would be different. I wanted to be a good girl. Maybe, if I was good, my luck would change. I tried not to let it bother me that all the girls were dressed in pretty clothes while I, again, was dressed like a boy. All the girls wore pretty bows and barrettes in their hair, while I wore cornrows in mine. The girls wore pretty sweaters with matching blouses, while I wore button-down, plaid boys' shirts with blue jean jackets. However, I was determined that it was going to be a new year, and I was going to show everyone that I had a new attitude.

On the first day, I walked into my class, found my name taped to my assigned seat, and sat down. I immediately began to put all my stuff away. After I had put everything away in my desk, I sat with my head down on my desk and quietly waited for Mrs. Ramsey to call the class to order. While I lay with my head on my desk, I secretly hoped that Robby Howard, Raven, and Allie weren't in my room. I didn't have to worry about Felicia. Her family had moved during summer vacation. I heard the children come into the room and find their seats. I heard their laughter as they greeted one another. As I lay with my head on the desk, tears dropped out of my eyes and landed on my desk. I wished someone would hug me. I wished for someone to genuinely care about seeing me again.

I lost myself in a daydream where I was walking down the hallway at school. As students left the classrooms, they approached me and kissed me on one cheek and then the other. I told them all the wonderful things that I had done over the summer, and we promised to get together at recess to talk more. I was so lost in my daydream that I didn't hear Robby calling my name. He slapped me on my back, bringing me back to reality. It shocked me, and I sat up in my seat. Some of the kids laughed at me, but Robby saw the tears and wanted to know why I was crying. I wiped my face.

"I scared you so bad, it made you cry," he yelled. I don't know why I did it, but I hit him, and we began to fight.

Mrs. Ramsey came over and pulled us apart. "I'm not going to put up with your foolishness like your other teachers did," she yelled. With her arms folded, she began to give me instructions. "Gather your things and move your desk to the front of the classroom." She pointed her long, skinny fingers to the corner where I would be banished to sit by myself. As I began to move my desk toward the corner, Mrs. Ramsey watched with disgust. When I had successfully gotten myself settled in the corner, she turned away from me, but not before I saw her rolling her eyes in exasperation.

I tried to hold the tears back, but they flowed anyway. I couldn't stop crying. I moved my stuff to the front of the class and sat with my back to the class. I had such high hopes for a new beginning. The good thing about being in the front of class with my desk pressed against the chalkboard was that no one could see my tears. I tried to focus on my homework, but I couldn't stop shaking and crying. When the teacher announced that it was time for our midmorning break, I put my hand up. "Mrs. Ramsey, can I go to the nurse's office?"

"Yes, but go quickly and come back."

Mrs. Johnson, the school nurse, sat in her office doing paperwork. When I came in, she asked me what the problem was without even looking up at me. I told her that I had a stomachache. She looked up and smiled. I don't know if she could read thoughts or if she saw the pain on my face, but she told me to lie down on the cot in her office. I lay there for a while until she called my name, waking me. She instructed me to go to the lunchroom with my class.

When I woke up, the tears had stopped falling, and I was no longer shaking uncontrollably. As I walked down the long corridors leading me to the lunchroom, I wondered why I hadn't been able to stop crying or shaking. That had never happened to me. I caught up with my classmates and took my assigned seat in the cafeteria. The other students wanted to know where I had disappeared to, and most speculated that I had gone to the office. I ignored their questions. How could I tell them I was being a crybaby and had fallen asleep?

After school, I went to Mother Alexander's house. She wanted to hear all about my first day back at school. I didn't tell her about my crying fit, but I did tell her how Robby had gotten me in trouble. I told her how the teacher made me move my things to the desk in the far right corner of the classroom away from the other children.

"Those teachers don't treat you right," she said.

* * * * *

As fall approached, Daddy decided to enclose the front porch so we could watch television while enjoying a breeze. My brothers never let me watch what I wanted on TV. They always teamed up against me, so Daddy bought me a television of my own to watch in my room. Even though I had a television in my room, I still wanted to be on the porch with everyone else. I hated being by myself. Besides, it was hot in the house, and the porch was cool. We enjoyed watching television on the porch so much that we'd fall asleep on the porch, but Daddy told us to stop falling asleep out there. Time and time again, he told us to go inside if we felt ourselves growing sleepy on the porch. We tried to be obedient, but we were children, after all.

On Saturdays, I always went to Mother Alexander's to get my hair washed and plaited. Once, I drifted off to sleep while my hair was drying, and it had gotten dark by the time Mother Alexander woke me. She tried to contact someone at my house to walk me home, but no one answered the phone. She called Daddy at Christie's house, and he told her that I could walk home alone.

Reluctantly Mother Alexander told me to hurry home before it got completely dark, and she told me to call her when I reached home. Before she allowed me to walk home, she looked up the street one last time, as if someone was there to see who would tell her it was going to be all right to allow me to walk home by myself. When I made it home, I immediately called Mother Alexander, and as I hung up, Daddy entered the house. "Get your stuff together. I'm gonna take you to the Howards' house." Before I could ask why, he proceeded to tell me. "Daisy is gonna watch you while I host a dice game in the garage," he said.

"I don't want to go over there, Daddy. Can I just stay here?"

"No. The adults are gonna be drinking liquor and gambling. With that combination, I don't know what's gonna happen, and you too young to be around all that."

Daddy dropped me off at the Howards' house and left me. From the moment I entered the Howard house, I knew I wouldn't be having fun. Daddy had dropped me off with a six-pack of Orange Crush and a bag of Doritos. I got to go into Daisy and Angel's room while the other children had to stay downstairs. They did my hair and let me listen to them talk about grown-up things. I was having a great time until a car pulled up outside and honked the horn.

Daisy and Angel snuck out of the house, promising me that they would be back in an hour. After they left, I tried to stay in their room by myself, but I grew lonely listening to the other children playing. I ventured outside the room and tried to join the fun, but they wouldn't allow me to join them.

"Can I play with you guys?" I asked.

"No, go eat your chips and drink your pop!"

"If you let me play with you guys, I will share with you."

"Nope, too late. We don't want none of your stuff, and we don't want to play with you!"

I stood there a few minutes, embarrassed and hurt that they would not let me play with them. I did not know what to do but to give up and walk away. I decided to walk home and ask Daddy if I could stay there with him.

I walked home in the dark and knocked on the garage door. A tall, skinny black man answered the door, smelling like liquor. "Can you get my daddy for me?"

I heard the laughter coming from the garage as I waited. The music was loud, and there were loud women in the garage too. Daddy walked toward me, still laughing. "What are you doing home?"

Pretending that I was seconds from throwing up, I said, "Daddy, I don't feel good." Pausing and pretending to gag, I added, "I wanted to come home."

Backing away from me, he replied, "Fine. Go in the house and lie down."

I went to my bedroom and watched television, but it was stuffy in the house, so I decided to take advantage of the empty porch. I took my blanket and pillow and moved to the front porch. It was nice to relax on the porch outside, watching television, drinking my pop, and eating the remainder of my Doritos.

Daddy brought a strange woman into the house to use the bathroom. I could tell by the way he walked her into the house that he was irritated with her. "Now hurry up in there!"

"Ace, I'm going as fast as I can," she yelled from the bathroom to him. I could hear her singing a song to herself while she busied herself in the bathroom.

While Daddy waited for the woman to finish, he checked on me. He looked around the porch before turning to me. "Are you okay out here by yourself?"

"Yeah, Daddy. I love lying on the porch. In between commercials, I like to look up at the stars." The lady came out the bathroom and continued to softly sing her song while walking over to my daddy. I lay there silently as he stood over me watching television.

The lady placed her arms around Daddy's waist. "Ace, are you going to introduce me to your li'l girl? Oh, she so pretty."

Daddy quickly introduced me to her. "This is Dorthea. Dorthea, meet Sue." Sue stepped closer to me and touched my hair.

"Ace, your li'l girl got some pretty hair. Bring her round to my house so my girls can do it for her." I sat up and smiled; the thought of going to Sue's house interested me.

Trying to focus on her in the dark, I noticed how Daddy pulled away from her. I waited for him to respond about me going to her house, but instead, he turned away and began to lead Sue back through the house. Before I heard the back door close, Daddy hollered out to me: "Dorthea, make sure you do not fall asleep on the porch."

Andre came home, found me asleep, and woke me. Then he went into the house to get ready for his date. I started to get up, but decided to watch some more television. I must have drifted back to sleep because I awoke to Earl's weight on top of me, holding me down. I tried to buck my body to force him off, but I was no match for him. I tried to tell him that Andre was home and was going to hear him. He just covered my mouth with his hands. As the speed of his hips slowed, the door to the house opened and Andre stepped out onto the porch. With his mouth gaping open, he just stood there. Earl jumped up and ran past Andre.

Awoken from his daze, Andre ran after him. He didn't catch Earl, but he yelled out into the darkness. "I know where you live, and I bet you I come find you." Coming back to me on the porch, he asked, "Are you all right?" I did not reply to Andre; instead, I looked around, wishing I were someplace else. Anywhere else would do, just not there watching Andre look at me with disgust in his eyes.

As I moved to get up, Andre's eyes traveled down my body. I watched him as he watched me. I saw the look of disbelief when his eyes focused on the wet spot Earl had left on the couch between my legs. Immediately he ran out the door and vomited. When he reentered the porch, David and Jake walked into the house behind him. "What's going on? We heard you retching as we were coming down the street."

Andre ignored their questions. "None of your business. Just go out to the garage and get Daddy!"

"Why? What did we do?"

"Nothing—you didn't do nothing! Andre yelled at them. "Just go get him. Now!"

When I knew David and Jake were out of earshot, I turned to Andre. "Please don't tell Daddy."

"Why wouldn't you want me to tell Daddy? Daddy needs to know what he was doing to you."

"Earl said that if I tell, Daddy will go after him, and then Daddy will get into trouble. If Daddy gets into trouble, then we might have to go to foster care." I didn't tell him about Earl's threats to tell Daddy about what David was doing to me.

Andre sat there for a second and thought to himself. "Daddy won't get into trouble if we handle this right. What Earl was doing is wrong. He needs to be punished for what he's done."

Jake and David returned to the porch and informed us, "Daddy can't come. He said for you to handle whatever was going on."

Andre looked at me for what seemed like a long time, but what was truly only a few seconds, before he looked away. He took painful care to look away from me while spoke, busying himself with removing the soiled cushion of the couch and placing it inside the door that led to the basement. I followed him into the house, wondering why he did not look at me while he spoke to me. He again looked away from me and began to do dishes and tidy up an already clean kitchen before he spoke to me again.

"Go take a bath and go to bed." As I walked past him, he must have seen the fear in my eyes because he reached out and hugged me, but still making sure to avoid eye contact with me, he whispered in my ear, "Everything will be all right."

As much as I tried to force it, sleep wouldn't come to me. I kept imagining Daddy getting into trouble for killing Earl. I kept imagining Earl telling Daddy what David was doing. What if Daddy thought it was my fault for allowing both Earl and David to have their way with me? What if Daddy stopped loving me? Even though I was scared about what would happen tomorrow, I was relieved that someone knew. At least Earl would have to stop now. When we talked to Daddy, I might even tell on David so it would all be truly over, and I would finally be safe.

His choice

The next morning I stayed in bed and tried to imagine that I didn't live there with Daddy and my brothers. I tried to imagine that my mother had come in the middle of the night and had taken me away. I lay there pretending that Momma and I were out shopping and eating lunch. I was so deep in my thoughts that I didn't hear Andre enter the room.

When I opened my eyes, Andre stared down at me. "Come in the kitchen so Daddy and I can talk to you," he said somberly.

I got out of bed slowly, taking my time moving my legs. I was trying to figure out a way to avoid going into the kitchen where the truth waited for me. It wanted to be let free, and I wanted to hold it captive. I didn't want to make any more trouble for anyone, least of all myself.

Andre sent David and Jake outside to play while Daddy and I looked at him anxiously. I knew what we were going to talk about, but Daddy didn't.

"Daddy, something happened to Dorthea that you need to handle." When Daddy didn't seem to be alarmed at Andre's revelation, he continued. "Daddy, when I came home last night, I caught Earl on top of Dorthea, humping her. I tried to catch him, but he got up and ran out the door before I could catch him."

As if telling Daddy wasn't enough, he walked to the basement door and retrieved the cushion and shoved it into Daddy's face. Both Andre and Daddy had tears in their eyes when they looked over at me. They began asking me questions: How long had this been going on? Why had I not told anyone? Had he put his private parts inside my private parts? Where had this been happening?

I cried as I told them everything. I told them how Earl had threatened that Daddy would go to jail and how he said we would end up in foster care since Momma didn't want us. Daddy was so angry. He kept mumbling, "Ruthie ought to be shot. I don't know what I'm doing with no girl child."

Daddy told me that he was sorry and that I didn't need to protect him. Andre wanted to know if Daddy would back him if he went down to the Howard house and beat Earl up right now. Surprisingly, Daddy told him no. "It's too late for that," Daddy said. "If you handle the situation like that, you're gonna get in trouble. When it comes down to it, it'll be your word against his."

"Yeah, but I got proof." Pointing at the pillow, he said, "Ain't that enough? Ain't that DNA evidence or something?"

"I want you to burn that pillow. Chicken, go lie down in your room."

No one was more confused than I was. I thought Daddy would be furious, but he was surprisingly calm. Before going upstairs to my room, I listened to Daddy and Andre speaking. Andre asked Daddy why he wasn't mad. Daddy told him to leave it alone. "I'll take care of it," he said.

"Daddy, what are you going to do to Earl? Are you going to tell Mr. and Mrs. Howard what their dang near-grown son did to our sister? Are you going to press charges? What if he does it again? You know he will if you don't do anything about this!"

Daddy assured Andre, "Earl won't touch her again. As of a matter of fact, he won't even speak to her. I can promise you that."

I was pleased that I didn't get in trouble, but I was also shocked that Daddy didn't do anything else. I just wanted Earl to stop. Because Daddy had remained so calm, I thought about telling on David. For some reason, I chickened out, but at least one of my bogeymen was gone. Just as quickly as before in my classroom, I cried and shook uncontrollably. It was so bad that all I could do was cry myself to sleep. Even though I had just woken up, I was exhausted.

I was surprised when I awoke to a silent house. I had slept all day. Everyone was gone except Andre. Daddy was at Christie's for the night, while David and Jake were at the Howards', playing with Jason. I was shocked that David and Jake were allowed to go to the Howards' house. When Andre saw that I was awake, he asked me if I was okay. I told him that I was fine, but I asked him why David and Jake were at the Howards' house. Andre explained that Daddy let them go because he felt everyone should act as usual. He didn't want it to get out what had happened to me. Daddy felt like people would talk about me if they knew. Honestly, before I heard that explanation, I hadn't really believed I had done anything wrong, but now I wasn't so sure. I felt ashamed.

* * * * *

Monday morning, sitting on the school bus, I was anxious about seeing Earl again. I hadn't seen him since Andre caught him on top of me. I half expected all the Howard children to get on the bus and pick at me, calling me names for getting their brother in trouble. However, none of them did, and it was as if none of them knew what had happened. Earl, however, got on the bus and glared at me. He was so intent on letting me know with his eyes how much he hated me that he didn't notice when Andre deliberately stuck a leg out in the aisle as he walked past. As Earl fell to the floor, Andre pushed him back to the floor. Before Earl could retaliate, the bus driver yelled for him to get up and take a seat.

Over the next couple of days, things seemed to calm down. Earl didn't approach me again, and I began to feel better. I felt like my life would get better. Daddy started taking me to Christie's every night again. Daddy had to explain what had happened between Earl and me for her to agree to me staying. Whenever I had spent the night in the past, the boys and I had all stayed in her living room together. We took turns sleeping either on the couch or the bean bags, but this time was entirely different. She didn't allow the boys to stay downstairs with me anymore. They were instructed to sleep in their rooms. There were nights when either of the boys would fall asleep from a full day of fun and play. No matter how hard it was to awaken them or how long it took, Christie made sure that they got up and retired to their bedrooms. On some occasions, Daddy or Cassie would question her as to why they had to go their rooms, and she would scream irately that they had a bedroom and needed to stay in it.

One evening while Daddy was outside mowing her lawn, Christie sat at the kitchen table and explained to Cassie in whispered tones why Daddy brought me to her home every night. I pretended to not hear them talk about me. She told her that she didn't trust me around her sons. I sat there and pretended to watch the stars as I cried. Why did Daddy tell her my secret? Why did Christie feel the need to tell Cassie? Who else had Christie and Daddy told? Now that Cassie knew my secret, how would she treat me, and who would she tell next? As I cried silently, I thought, *If it's Earl's fault, then why am I being punished?* I began wishing that Andre hadn't caught him. I was glad that I didn't have to worry about him touching me anymore, but I didn't want people to treat me differently. How did this turn into being my fault?

As the days turned into weeks, I settled into a routine. I went to school during the day and spent my nights at Christie's house. I really didn't want to go to Christie's house every evening, but then again, this schedule also didn't leave David much of an opportunity to attack me.

* * * * *

My birthday came and went without any excitement. I was eight years old. Since this birthday marked the second anniversary of my mother's departure, I didn't mention that it was my birthday, nor did I mention that I missed my mother.

Every morning, Daddy would stop at Mrs. Smith's bakery on the way home from Christie's. Once we arrived at our house, he would shave, then change his clothes. While he shaved, Daddy would tell me jokes or funny stories about when he was young. Before he shaved, I would start making his coffee so that by the time he finished shaving, I would hand him his coffee, kiss his cheek, tell him to have a good day, and watch as he hurried out the door with his coffee in hand. I would then get ready for school before I woke my brothers.

One morning shortly after my eighth birthday, we started our normal routine. However, as Daddy walked out, he tickled me. I followed him, laughing, when he reached out and grabbed my right breast. I was shocked at first and stopped laughing, but when I saw that Daddy kept laughing, I chalked it up to a coincidence. It must have been a mistake. Sometimes brothers did this and sometimes neighbors from down the street did this, but daddies didn't do things like this. Besides, Daddy would never do anything nasty to me.

As I hesitantly leaned in to kiss Daddy and tell him to have a good day, he did it again. This time he held my breast in his hand for a quick second. I didn't know what to do this time. I knew it wasn't an accident. I froze. I couldn't move. I was stuck in time. I did not give him the kiss I had intended. I just stood there, looking at him as he looked back at me. Then he turned and walked down the steps, got into his truck, and backed out the driveway, all the while staring at me as I stood in shock, afraid to move.

I don't know long I stood there. It may have been only a few seconds, but I felt as if time had stopped. Daddies weren't supposed to touch their little girls like that. As I got ready for school that morning, my mind ran a marathon in my head. What had just happened? I kept replaying what had happened between Daddy and me that morning. I couldn't stop thinking about it. I got ready quickly and woke my brothers so we could go to school. All throughout the day, I couldn't think about anything else. Why would Daddy touch me like that?

After school, I anxiously waited for Daddy to come home from work and take me to Christie's house for the night, but he never came. I didn't know how I was supposed to act when I saw him. Was I supposed to act like it had never happened, or could I dare ask him why he had done that? Could I tell him that I didn't like the way it made me feel and ask him to never do it again? That was a conversation I didn't have that day because I fell asleep waiting for him to come get me. I awoke after midnight, got out of my clothes, and went to bed. While I lay in bed wondering why Daddy had left me behind, I heard my door opening and saw David coming toward me in the dark. That night, I didn't even have the energy to fight with David. He finished quickly and left me to cry myself to sleep. As I drifted off to sleep, I wondered if this was what my life was going to be like, living in this house with nobody to protect me. Would everyone just use me as they pleased?

The next morning, Daddy came home. He hollered for me to come down and make his coffee. As I got out of bed, all the memories of what had happened yesterday morning came flooding back to me. My stomach tightened with every step I took toward my door. I hoped he wouldn't touch me again. I didn't want to feel dirty again like I had yesterday. How was I going to look at him? Would he be able to tell how uncomfortable I was if he looked at me? I opened my mouth to let him know I was on my way downstairs, but the words wouldn't come out. Would he hear in my voice that I was no longer comfortable around him? I must have taken too long to come downstairs because when I entered the kitchen, he was gone. He had left a box of donuts on the table. I was relieved, but as I went to look in the box of donuts, I noticed that he had forgotten his coffee on the table. Without thinking, I ran to the door with the coffee, but he had already backed halfway down the driveway. He stopped when he heard me call out to him. He told me it was all right and that he'd get some from work. As I went back into the house, I wondered why he hadn't woken me up in time to make his coffee. Maybe he was just as uncomfortable as I was about all of this. With that thought, I began to relax and allowed myself to believe that it was a mistake that would never happen again.

Over the next few weeks, everything returned to normal. Daddy picked me up every evening and we went to Christie's home. Christie continued to try to maintain as much distance between her children and me as possible. She told Daddy that he should start rotating between bringing Jake and me. She reasoned that her sons needed to get to know my brothers. I asked, "Why is Christie trying to get rid of me? I wish you hadn't told her what Earl did to me."

He responded to my question by getting up and walking away from me, but not before stating harshly, "She has a right to feel any way she wants to feel when it comes to her children." He acted as if she had a right to treat me as if I had done something wrong. I sat there and wondered, while Christie was protecting her children from me, who was going to protect me from everyone else?

The next few nights, Daddy took Jake to Christie's and left me alone with David. David acted as if he resented being left at home with me, and he became more brutal than he had ever been. David and I would be alone in the house until midnight on some nights, and he took full advantage of the time alone with me. I tried to avoid him as much as possible. Whenever he would see me, he would yell at me to get out of his way, or he would punch me as he walked by.

Each morning, I awoke before Daddy came home. I met him at the door, begging and pleading, but it always fell on deaf ears. "Daddy, can I please go with you tonight to Christie's house?"

"It's Christie's house and she wants Jake there—not you."

This became our routine pretty much every morning. On the mornings I asked, he would not speak to me and hurriedly got ready for work, even leaving earlier than he had to just so he could avoid my begging and pleading. On the mornings I didn't ask him, he would talk to me while we drank coffee together. I knew the mornings were more pleasant when I didn't ask him, but because of David's cruelty toward me, I couldn't let it go. The more I asked him, the angrier he grew with me, until one day he screamed, "Why would you want to go to someone's house that don't want you there?" Startled, I made his coffee and retreated to my room, where I curled into a ball and cried myself to sleep.

After a couple of weeks, Jake grew bored with both getting up early each morning and playing with Christie's boys. He asked Daddy if he could stay at home and play with David. Both David and I were happy that he decided to return home. I thought this meant that I would be returning to Christie's house, but she blocked my return, stating that the children needed a break from company, but I couldn't understand why her children needed a break from company and she didn't need a break from Daddy.

The more I tried to follow Daddy to Christie's, the angrier he got with me. I would watch the clock daily and walk down the street to Daddy's job and get into the car and wait for him to get off work in hopes that he would just drive to Christie's house from work, taking me with him. However, he would just drive to the house and make a few calls and use the restroom, causing me to get out of the car. As soon as he was done making busy work and I had wandered off to watch television, I would hear the car start up and back out of the driveway. On the occasion that I stayed in the car and read a book, when it was time for him to go, he would just bluntly tell me to get out of the car and go into the house. He couldn't understand why I wanted to go somewhere they didn't want me. I didn't know how to make him understand that I didn't care how they felt about me. I just wanted to be away from David.

* * * * *

One Sunday I enjoyed watching Westerns all day with Daddy. That evening as the sun went down, I drifted off to sleep on the living room floor. I awoke to someone raising my shirt. As I tried to figure out who it was, I pretended to be asleep. I knew from the feel of his hands that it wasn't David. He turned me over on my back, then jiggled me from side to side as he first lowered my shorts, then my panties. I kept my eyes closed, afraid to breathe. My mind reeled as I realized who it must be. I heard him unzipping his pants as I lay there on the floor. I opened my eyes slightly to confirm what my mind was telling me was true. I saw him clearly. As he ran one hand over my breasts, he touched himself with his other hand. He got up and disappeared for a few minutes, and when he returned, he covered me with a yellow blanket. I lay there in disbelief. I was scared to move. I didn't want him to know that I was awake and had seen him. Eventually, I fell asleep.

The next morning I awoke when I heard him getting ready for work. He didn't try to wake me, so I didn't get up. I went back to sleep, hoping he'd leave me alone. When I awoke again, I looked around and listened for Daddy, but he was gone. I lifted the covers to go to the bathroom before getting ready for school. Two one-dollar bills sat on the floor next to where I had been lying. I looked at the money and wondered how it had gotten there. Did Daddy leave the money for me? If he did, why? Maybe it fell out of Daddy's pocket on accident. I picked it up. If no one claimed it, then it was mine. All day at school, I tried to push what had happened the night before out of my mind, but I could think of nothing else.

When Daddy came home from work, I waited for him to mention the money. I thought for sure he'd ask us if anyone had found his money, but he didn't. Once again, he began taking me with him everywhere—even to Christie's. The rules were changing, and this time in my favor. He went out of his way to make sure I was happy. Anything I asked Daddy for, he said yes. Each night on the way home from Christie's house, he stopped at the Fireside Liquor Store and bought himself a bottle. Hesitant to ask Daddy for anything that would cause him to stop taking me with him, I softly asked him if I could have something. "Daddy, can I get some chips for me and the boys?" I asked.

Smiling at me, he replied, "Get whatever you want, Chicken!" Smiling back at Daddy, I placed one bag of Doritos and a six-pack of Pepsi on the counter. What happened next both shocked and pleased me. "Chicken, get another bag of chips and a six-pack of Pepsi for yourself. You don't have to share with your brothers. You can have your own."

I was so happy to have my own and not have to share with my greedy brothers, who didn't always divide things fairly, I skipped while gathering the additional items. I was so happy I didn't stop skipping. I skipped all the way to the car. When we reached the house, my brothers were upset when they saw that while they had to share a six-pack of pop between the three of them, I got an entire six-pack to myself. But I didn't care about any of that. At least Daddy was being nice to me again.

None of us had any particular bedtime; we always just went to sleep when we felt tired. However, that night, after Daddy finished drinking his liquor, he told us to go to bed. As we all got up to climb the stairs, we silently looked at one another wonderingly. After I had been sleep for a while, I heard Daddy coming up the stairs. This wasn't uncommon. He inspected our rooms all the time when we least expected it, so I looked around my room to see if it was clean. He walked straight into my room, but he didn't turn on the light to inspect my room. Instead, he walked to the foot of my bed and climbed in behind me.

What's he doing? Why is he here? I heard my heart beating through my ears. When I heard him snoring, I relaxed and drifted off to sleep. A little while later, I awoke to one of his hands sliding under my T-shirt. He moved it all over my chest. I lay there silently, pretending to be still asleep as I watched the covers go up and down. I peeked out of my eyes to see what he was doing that made the covers move. Stunned, I watched as the movement appeared to come from his private area. When he finished, he slid out of my bed and walked slowly back down the stairs.

I jumped up and ran downstairs to the bathroom. When I moved to get out of my bed, I felt something wet on my legs. I wondered what it was, but only for a second, because I had to make sure I wasn't dreaming. I had to make sure Daddy was really home and I had not just imagined what had happened. As I was going down the stairs, I saw Daddy sitting in front of the television. As I walked past him and went through the kitchen to the bathroom, I knew he had been in my room. He seemed to look at me with a knowing sneer on his face, as if he knew why I had followed him. Embarrassed, I turned away from his stare and continued to the restroom. I sat on the toilet for several minutes, wondering, *Why did Daddy just do that to me?* As I climbed upstairs again to my bedroom, Daddy called out, "Good night."

The next morning, Daddy called me to come downstairs to make his coffee and talk to him while he got ready for work. I really didn't want to go downstairs while he was still in the house, but after he called me again, I immediately began the climb downstairs. When I arrived, Daddy was unusually happy. He kept telling me jokes and coming in and out of the kitchen to make sure I was laughing. He even walked up behind me and tickled me. He seemed to ignore the fact that I was jumpy when he came near me. When I reached to give him coffee as he walked out the door, he leaned down to kiss me, and I withdrew so that he couldn't touch me. I thought he'd be insulted or mad at me, but he laughed and shoved two one-dollar bills into my hand. I looked at him questioningly.

"Didn't you get the two dollars I left for you the other night?" he asked.

I hesitated at first, but then I nodded as I looked down at the floor. He had known all along that I was awake. When he looked at me this time, he laughed, turned, and walked out the door, leaving me standing there confused. He had known I was awake all along.

I wanted to know why Daddy was treating me like this, and now that he knew that I realized it was him, what did this mean? I couldn't concentrate at school all day and kept getting into trouble for not paying attention.

When Daddy came home from work that day and picked me up, I decided to ask him.

"Daddy, why did you give me two one-dollar bills?"

"I just wanted to make you happy."

Not satisfied with his answer, I asked, "Why did you come into my room last night?"

"I've been very unhappy since your momma left us, and I figured since I was unhappy, you were unhappy. I came into your room because I love you, and it made me happy to spend time with you."

"Weren't we doing something wrong?" I asked.

"It's not wrong because I'm your daddy, and I love you. Do you love me, Chicken?"

"Yes."

"Do you trust me?"

"Yes."

He was silent for a minute, and I gathered the courage to ask, "Do you do the same thing to my brothers?"

"No. I don't. I don't love them as much as I love you. You're my favorite, and you're the only one that can make me happy. Do you want to make me happy, Chicken?"

I told him yes. More than anything, I loved when Daddy was happy, and lately, he had been very happy. He had been giving me anything I wanted, including pop, chips, money, and his time.

"Aren't you doing the same thing to me that Earl was doing?"

"No. It's not the same thing. We love each other, so it's different."

I didn't question Daddy any further about the event that had taken place last night. When I pictured what had happened, I still felt uneasy about it all, but I loved Daddy and just wanted him to be happy. Besides, if it made him feel better, then I was happy to do it.

* * * * *

Over the next few months, Daddy snuck into my room almost every night and touched me. When he finished, he always left me either money or something that he got from the Avon lady. Christie always complained about him buying me so much, but he just yelled at her to mind her own business. Daddy had always favored me, but now, he went to the extreme to make me feel special.

Being Daddy's special girl had its benefits. All the girls were wearing brown leather boots with a wedge heel. In the past, Daddy had always bought me the brown hiker boots that my brothers wore. This year, when shopping for winter boots, Daddy allowed me to pick out my own boots. I went to school that winter feeling a little normal—but not quite. Try as I might to forget, I couldn't stop thinking about the price I had to pay to get those boots.

With spring came a special present. Daddy came home from work and gave me a new bike. It was a blue Schwinn bike with blue and white streamers coming out of the handlebars. It had a funny-shaped blue-and-white seat with a big *S* painted on the seat. I was so excited that it was all mine. Immediately, I got on the bike and rode in a circle. I asked Daddy why I had gotten a new bike and the boys didn't, and he told me it was because I was his special girl. I knew what that meant, but at the time, I didn't care.

One day over Easter vacation, I went to the Howards' house on my bike and Jamie asked me to give her a ride. She climbed on the seat and held onto my waist as I stood up and peddled the bike. I came out of her driveway and turned left. We rode past the mailman's house and turned left again at his corner. I didn't want to take this route because I wasn't allowed to leave Denton Avenue. Big semitrucks traveled Junior Avenue daily, and it wasn't safe. Jamie called me a baby, though, and dared me to take that route as I got closer to Junior Avenue. I couldn't think of an excuse for not going there, so not wanting to be called a baby, I turned onto Junior Avenue. There was a large dip in the road on Junior Avenue, and we gained speed, so I was able to just stand and coast.

As we coasted along enjoying the breeze, we heard a semitruck approaching from behind. It came toward us fast on our left side. I began to panic, and Jamie yelled at me to calm down and peddle faster as she kicked her legs out further, enjoying the ride. I steered the bike toward the curb as I continued to peddle to maintain our speed. I hit a rock on the shoulder of the road, and my feet slipped off the pedals. I fell onto the bar connecting the handlebars to the seat, and my knees dragged on the ground on both sides. Jamie and I screamed at each other to hit the brakes as we jumped the curb and headed into the field on the side of Bethel Church of God. We zigzagged through the field as we continued to scream. When the bike came to a halt and fell to the side, we checked each other over for broken bones. We were both bleeding, but I had gotten it the worst. Both of my knees were bleeding, and my elbow was banged up pretty badly. Together, we helped each other walk to the road. While pushing my bike, neither of us said anything to the other. When we reached Jamie's house, I felt better and decided that I could ride my bike the rest of the way home.

As I was getting on the bike, we both broke out laughing and wanted to do it again. We rode around the corner and tried to mimic the accident, but it just wasn't the same. We went back to Jamie's and sat on her porch for a while, teasing each other about how scared we had been, retelling the story every time someone asked about our injuries.

* * * * *

On the nights that Daddy took me over to Christie's house, he still came into my bedroom in the mornings. He would laugh at me because I'd hurry up and get in bed so I could pretend to be asleep. This was something I had to do for me. I wanted to make him happy, but I wasn't as comfortable with our relationship as he was, so in order to make him happy, I had to pretend to be asleep. I pretended that I wasn't there, that he was only using my body—not me. Every time Daddy messed with me, I lost a little piece of myself. I tried to pretend it wasn't happening, but it was getting harder and harder to do.

During this time, David still came to me at night as well. There were nights that both of them entered my room. They somehow managed to never see each other. I don't know how because Daddy had to go through David and Jake's bedroom to get to mine. Every time Daddy left my room, I worried that one of my brothers would see him and know what was going on between Daddy and me. I also worried that Daddy would see David leaving my room. I felt like I was carrying the weight of the world on my shoulders.

I began to act out more and more at school. I would beat on the children in my class. I would wait until recess and pick a random child and chase them until I caught them, then pin them to the ground and beat them until they cried. I fought both boys and girls. The teachers didn't like me playing with their students. They didn't understand why I behaved the way I did, and whenever I was sent to the office, I either sat there with my arms folded across my chest, staring at the wall in front of me and not answering their questions, or I allowed tears to roll down my cheeks without uttering a word. How could I tell them how confused I was? How could I tell them that both my daddy and my brother used me in ways that both confused and hurt me?

On the nights that Daddy and I stayed at Christie's, he wouldn't wait until we got home to mess with me. I would hear Christie's bedroom door open and hear him crawl across the floor toward me. I don't know why he crawled; I guess it made him feel safer. On these nights, I prayed that he'd hurry and finish before someone saw what he was doing. One night while Cassie stayed at Christie's overnight with me, I heard the door open and wondered what I'd do if Cassie saw us. To my surprise, he climbed over to Cassie and began messing with her. At first, I waited to see if she would scream, but she turned over and kissed him. I rolled over and faced the inside of the couch. I was both relieved and shocked, but I thought maybe now that he had Cassie, he'd leave me alone.

A few nights later, I decided that I wanted Daddy to stop coming into my room. I asked him to stop. "If I stop, I'll be very unhappy, and if I'm unhappy, I don't know what I'll do," he explained.

"You won't do anything. You can be just like you were before you started coming into my room. Besides, you have Cassie now. Please stop, Daddy. I don't like it."

"How do you know about Cassie?" he asked, ignoring the now-forming tears in my eyes.

"I saw you at Christie's house," I said.

"I didn't do nothing to Cassie. You must've dreamed that," he explained.

What was he thinking? I knew Daddy when I saw him. I didn't know why he was denying it, but I didn't argue. The tears spilled down my face in a steady stream now. Daddy whispered, "Fine. If that's how you feel, I'll stop. I don't want to do anything to you that you don't want me to do."

Over the next few days, Daddy ignored me and acted very cold and distant. Every time I asked him a question, he told me no before I could even finish. He took turns yelling at us and threatening to whip us for every minor occurrence. I listened to my brothers questioning one another, wondering what was wrong with Daddy and why he was being so mean. To prevent one of us from getting a whipping, Andre took extra care to inspect our clothes, housework, and homework. We tried to be on our best behavior in hopes that his happiness would return.

Daddy stopped taking me with him to Christie's or anywhere else for that matter. "Daddy, why can't I go with you anymore?"

Angrily he answered me with a look on his face I had never seen before. "Ask your momma if you can go with her." The look in his eyes told me that he didn't care how he hurt me—he just wanted to make sure I hurt. I wondered if I had done the right thing in telling him that I wanted him to stop touching me.

One Saturday afternoon, the Howard girls wanted to come with me to my house. No one was home but me, so I let them in because I was bored. We all went up to my room and pulled out the boxes of clothes left over from the family store that my parents had owned together. They thought it would be fun to play dress-up. It was fun, but when they left, there were clothes everywhere. I begged them to help me put everything away before they left, but they told me they had to get home since it was getting late.

I ran out the back door, explaining that I would get a whipping if I didn't get everything put away. They just laughed as they ran down the street. I climbed the stairs to my room, dreading the cleanup work in my room. When I reached my room, I looked around at the mess everywhere and decided I would call the Howard girls back over tomorrow so they could help me clean it in the morning. It was only right, since they helped make the mess. I ate dinner and went to bed.

When Andre came home, he walked up the stairs to his bedroom. On the way, he passed my room. He woke me up, hollering for me to get my room clean, but I was so exhausted I couldn't stay awake. After several attempts to wake my brothers and me, he went to bed, making us promise to clean the room in the morning.

A little while later, I woke up to Daddy flipping the light on in my room and screaming for me to get out of bed to clean the room. Stunned by Daddy's outburst, I struggled to focus my eyes that refused to see clearly. The blinding light refused to allow me to focus on anything in the room. His shouting was so loud, he woke up all three of my brothers. "Dorthea, get out of that bed right now and get this mess cleaned up!" Scared for me, Andre, David, and Jake rushed toward my room to help me clean up the mess, but Daddy blocked the doorway. "She don't need no help. She can clean her own mess." Turning to me, he asked me, "What happened in this room? Why does it look like this?"

Scrambling to the floor, I cried, "The Howard girls come over and played dress-up with me. They left and wouldn't help me clean up the mess." My excuse must have fallen on deaf ears because he became more enraged.

"I don't want them back in my house," he screamed. He looked at Andre and yelled again. "I mean it. Not one Howard in my house."

He turned, looked at me, and bent over to pick up a wire hanger, then began slapping me with it. Once I fell to the floor, he started kicking me. He kicked my face, and when I turned my body, he kicked my back several times. Andre yelled at Daddy to get him to stop. I repeatedly screamed for him to stop, but he just kept kicking me and hitting me with the hanger. When the hanger bent from the force on my body, he looked around the room and found a pair of high-heeled boots. He held the leg part in his hand and hit me with the heel. Andre tried to place his body between Daddy and me. Everywhere Daddy chased me, Andre was there, trying to reason with Daddy. Andre cried out, "Daddy, please stop before you hurt her!

"Andre, get out of my way!"

"Please, Daddy, stop! We will help her clean the room. Just please stop beating her!"

Andre and I were simultaneously pleading with Daddy to stop beating me.

"Daddy, please stop beating me. I will do whatever you want if you just please stop beating me."

After I had yelled this to him a few times, he hollered back at me. "You gonna do just what I tell you to do from now on, ain't ya?"

I looked up at him through one eye, partially closed because of the swelling. Tears ran down my face as I said, "Yes, Daddy. I will do whatever you want." I knew what I was agreeing to. Even if no one else in the room knew, I did.

After Daddy finished beating me, he told everyone to go to bed. "Dorthea, you can clean this mess up in the morning."

As I bent over to climb into bed, I felt a sharp pain that shot through my lower back all the way around to my lower stomach. Just when I thought it couldn't get any worse, I began to cough. With each cough, I thought I would die from the excruciating pain I felt as I tried to hold my stomach. When I coughed, I saw blood spurt out of my mouth and run all down my chin and over my hands. My brothers yelled for Daddy to come back upstairs. Andre asked, "Daddy, are you going to take Dorthea to the hospital?

"Naw, she will be all right. She just needs to lie down. David and Jake, get something and clean that mess up off the floor."

Andre came over and helped me climb into bed. "Daddy are you sure she doesn't need to go to the hospital?"

This time Daddy didn't sound as convincing when he told us I would be all right after I got some rest.

I lay on the side of my bed, watching Andre as he silently cried and cleaned up my blood. He told my other two brothers to get me some clean pajamas. Daddy took a bottle out of his pocket and began drinking. As he turned to walk down the stairs, I saw him smile.

I must have cried myself to sleep because when I awoke, I felt Daddy climbing into bed. All I could think was, *Oh my God, after what you just did, how could you expect me to just lie here?* I tried to pretend like I wasn't there, but he just kept whispering in my ears, telling me to touch him.

When I tried to act like I was asleep and didn't hear him, he whispered into my ear again. "Do you want another whipping?" When I cried, he said, "I knew you weren't asleep. Now you gonna do what you said, or do I have to whip you again?" I allowed him to place my hands on his private parts, but I just couldn't shake the feeling that what we were doing was yucky, so I pulled my hand away. Angrily he reached over, snatched my hands, and placed them on his privates. When I tried to pull away again, he placed his hand on top of mine and held it in place. The more I fought to pull my hand away, the louder he began to breathe. Just when I thought I couldn't stand it anymore and thought I would scream, he stopped, and then my hand was wet. I began to gag. I thought I was going to throw up. With each retch of my body, I remembered the severe beating I had received earlier, because my body still hurt.

"If you don't stop that noise, I'm gonna beat you again," he threatened.

I tried to stop, but every time I thought about where my hand had been, I began to gag again. Frustrated and scared my brothers would return to check on me, he whispered in my ear, "Get up and go wash your hands. When you get back, change these sheets!" He slid out of my bed and crept back downstairs.

My body hurt so badly that I carefully and slowly moved toward the edge of the bed. I lay on the bed, thinking to myself, *Why did he come get us from our mother?* Sometimes he treated us like he hated us. After lying there for a few moments, I mustered up the courage to push myself up into a sitting position. As I looked around the room, I remembered the day at the courthouse when we were all so happy to be home with Daddy.

Easing to my feet, I realized I would not be able to stand up comfortably. It didn't hurt as much if I hunched over and hugged my sides as I walked. I had to walk around the bed and strip it. The thought of what had just happened to me made me vomit into the sheets. The heaving, along with the burning in my throat and the smell, caused both my head and sides to hurt worse. It hurt so much that I started crying, which woke up Andre.

He opened the door to his room and asked me if I was okay. I wanted to scream, "No, I am not all right!" I wanted to tell him what Daddy had just made me do to him. I wanted to tell him that maybe I had made a mistake coming home to live with Daddy and him. I wanted to tell him I was sick to my stomach over what Daddy was making me do to him. At the least, I wanted him to come into my room and help me strip my bed.

But I didn't ask for his help. I didn't want him to find the mess Daddy had left behind.

When I didn't answer right away, he walked across the hall and came to my door. "Dorthea, are you all right?" I could see the worry on his face from the light of the moon entering through my window. He stood awkwardly looking into my room. "Dorthea, what are you doing? Are you all right? I heard you throwing up. I'll help you make your bed. Daddy doesn't have to know that I helped you."

I wanted to take his help, but I looked over at my bed where the wet spot was and wondered how I would explain it and realized, *No, Dorthea, you cannot accept his help.* I would have to clean this mess all by myself. Frustrated by my lack of response, Andre reached for the light switch in my room. Panicking, I screamed, "No, don't turn on the light. The light hurts my eyes. I am okay. I don't need any help. I am just going to the bathroom."

Not sounding particularly convinced, Andre backed away from the door and said, "Dorthea, Daddy doesn't mean to hurt us. He only gets like this when he's been drinking and missing Momma."

When Andre closed his bedroom door, I carefully climbed down the stairs with the dirty laundry. Daddy was sitting in the living room watching television in the dark. He was still drinking from that bottle. He had heard my vomiting and Andre trying to help me, but never even came to my aid.

"Dorthea, put them sheets in the washer." Startled that he even spoke to me, I almost slipped on the stairs, causing me to grab the banister. As I caught my balance to keep from falling, I looked up, and Daddy was looking right into my eyes. I did not like what I saw, looking into his eyes. They were as cold as if no one was there behind them. Unnerved by his stare, I hurried and did what Daddy told me to because I didn't want to make him mad at me again.

As I was cleaning up in the bathroom, I cried so hard I couldn't catch my breath and began vomiting again. Daddy walked by the bathroom door and heard me. On his way to bed, he hollered, "There better not be any mess in there in the morning!"

What had happened to my daddy? Where did he go? Where was the man who loved me the best in this world?

* * * * *

When the school year ended, I wasn't shocked that I had been promoted to the fourth grade. I always managed to get by in school. I didn't get the best grades, but they definitely weren't the worst, although my grades had begun to suffer in light of recent events. I just wanted to enjoy the summer break and relax.

During the summer, I spent a lot of my time with Mother Alexander, helping her with the babies, and both Daddy and David used my body to satisfy their selfish needs. One night, Daddy came to my room right after David had just left. When he reached out to touch me, I said, "Don't. David just left, and if you do anything, David will hear you and know what you're doing."

"What was David doing in your room?" he asked.

"The same thing you've been doing," I said bluntly. I enjoyed telling him. I thought it might shame him enough to stop. He must have been worried at the thought of David catching him because he didn't touch me that night. He just slept there, and sometime before morning, he left my room.

Over the next few days, Daddy came up with work assignments for the boys to complete by the time he got home from work, giving the bulk of the assignments to David. My brothers didn't understand why Daddy was targeting David more than usual, but I did. There was nothing I could do. I couldn't tell them without letting them know what Daddy was doing to me.

One Friday, while we were out running errands, I asked Daddy if we could stop at the grocery store to get me some more shampoo and hair grease for my hair. He asked me what had happened to all my hair stuff. I told him that David had used them. After getting what I needed to get my hair done, Daddy went straight home and called David down to the basement. I grew scared for David because Daddy had that look in his eye that assured us someone was about to get it.

As David walked past me, he mouthed *What did I do*? I ignored him and looked at the floor as he descended the stairs. I stood at the top of the stairs so I could listen to the conversation between Daddy and David. Daddy accused him of taking my stuff, and before David could deny it or explain himself, Daddy took off his belt and began to hit David in the face. Daddy punched him in the chest and alternated between telling him to stay out of my room and to keep his hands off my things. I did not know if David knew what he was *really* getting a whipping for, but I certainly did. I stood at the top of the steps, crying for David because Daddy wouldn't stop beating him. When Daddy finished, I tried to help David upstairs out of the basement, but he pushed past me and told me that he hated me.

When fourth grade started, I was feeling better about my life. Things had slowed down during the nighttime at our house. David no longer came to visit me at night, and Daddy was spending more time between Christie and Mrs. Sandy, which slowed the frequency of his nightly visits. Mrs. Sandy was his new girlfriend and the wife of one of his friends, which caused stress to Christie. Mrs. Sandy didn't have any children at home, so she had a lot of free time to focus on us. She was really nice to us. She left her husband and moved in with us. She even wanted us to call her Momma. She cooked dinner and dessert for us every night. She read to me before bed, even though I was in the fourth grade and could read by myself. When we came home from school, there were cookies on the kitchen table. She didn't know how to do my hair, but it was fun when she tried. She actually showed an interest in us and our well-being. When I asked her why she was so nice to us, she said that it was her pleasure to love on us kids. She also told me that if you truly love a man and he has children, you love the children too. I hadn't really thought about it like that before. I decided Christie really didn't love Daddy because it was obvious she didn't love his children.

Mrs. Sandy was the closest thing we had to a true mother. She even went to bat for us with Daddy when she felt he treated us too harshly. She especially tried to position herself between Daddy and David. One night, Daddy woke us all up and asked the famous question—who wants to live with your mother? He began to beat David. Mrs. Sandy ran out of the bedroom and pulled Daddy off David, threatening to call the police if he ever hit one of us like that again. We were shocked that she stood up for us. Christie knew about the beatings and never stood up for us, not even once. We were happy, but unfortunately, we knew that because she dared to disagree with Daddy, she wouldn't be around much longer.

It seemed the nicer she was to us, the more Daddy didn't like her. He began sneaking around with Christie again and staying out all night. Then, one day we came home from school and all of Mrs. Sandy's things were gone. She, too, had left us. We cried when she left. I began to believe that Daddy wanted to keep us isolated from anyone who cared about us.

When Mrs. Sandy left, Daddy made major changes one night. "Dorthea, get your stuff. You are moving into your momma's bedroom."

"Why, Daddy? Where will you sleep?"

"I'll sleep on the couch for as much as I'm at home. You are getting older and need a room where no one will use your things."

I didn't want to make this move. I knew why he wanted me downstairs and not upstairs with the boys anymore. He wanted to be able to get to me more freely.

Daddy slept at Christie's only part of the night, and when he returned home, he slept on the couch for only two or three nights before he moved back into his bedroom with me. I told him that I wanted to move back upstairs if he was going to be in the bed with me. I told him that it didn't look right, but he didn't care. Besides, he had already given my room to Jake, and he said it wasn't fair to make Jake give up his new room. No one said anything about the fact that I was in fourth grade and sharing a bed with Daddy every night.

When Daddy moved me into his room, he was able to mess with me every night more freely. One night, David came downstairs to use the restroom, when he heard movement and came to my door. Peering into my room, he asked, "What are you doing?"

Nervously I answered him, "Nothing."

Straining to see better, he asked, "Is that Daddy in your bed?"

"Yes."

Nervously, he quickly walked away from my door, went to the restroom, and returned to his room. I thought that someone would ask me in the morning why Daddy slept with me, but no one dared to ask the question.

* * * * *

The last week of school, I woke up with severe cramps. They hurt so bad that I couldn't stand up without holding my belly as I dragged myself to the bathroom. When I finished, I wiped and saw lots of blood. At the sight of myself bleeding, I almost fainted. I screamed loud and strong. I felt dizzy. I wasn't sure if I could stand to my feet, but somehow I managed to pull up my pants and run out of the bathroom, out the back door, and didn't stop until I got to Mother Alexander's door. By the time I got to her house, I was hysterical. I thought I was dying. Mother Alexander let me in, and when she found out what was wrong, she gave me some rags and told me to clean myself. She was older, so she didn't have the supplies I needed. Mother Alexander explained to me that while I was young for my first menstrual cycle, I was a woman and that I could now have a baby.

I immediately cried. She thought I was crying because of my period, but I was crying because I didn't want to have a baby with Daddy. Mother Alexander told me to lie down while she called Daddy at work and explained what had happened to me. Daddy told her that he would send Christie over at lunchtime with supplies for me so I could go to school. After Daddy's lunch hour, there was a knock on the door. Mother Alexander and I were both shocked when Cassie walked in with my supplies. She explained that she was doing a favor for Daddy.

That year around Christmas, Daddy started bringing Cassie around us. He instructed us not to tell anyone about her. "You can't tell anyone that Cassie comes to the house to see us."

He further went on to explain to us, "Daddy could go to jail for statutory rape if y'all tell anyone, and if I go to jail, y'all will have to go to foster care."

At first, I liked Daddy with Cassie, because when he was at home, she was always there to prevent him from getting to me. She lied to her parents, telling them that she was spending the nights with her friends, but she stayed at our house with Daddy. Those nights, Daddy didn't cook neck bones for dinner. He would order dinner from Pizza Hut for everyone, including

Cassie's friends and their boyfriends. Cassie's friends would stay for most of the night, using our bedrooms to have sex and getting drunk on the liquor that Daddy purchased for them.

If Cassie stayed all night or part of the night, she and Daddy used my room. One night, she was leaving my room, and I was asleep at the kitchen table. I awoke as she was about to walk out the back door.

"Are you finished having sex with Daddy?" I asked.

She turned. "What business is it of yours?" she asked in response.

"I can't go to bed until you finish, and I'm tired of sitting up all night waiting for you to get done," I told her matter-of-fact. She simply left. She had tears in her eyes as she walked out the back door.

She came back the next day, and they used my room again. This time, as she came out of my room, I purposely glared at her. He walked her out, and they left together. She went home, and he went to Christie's house. It smelled like sex in my room. I was so mad. The sheets were messed up, my blankets were on the floor, and my pillows were thrown about the room. I climbed into bed and felt something wet on my sheets. I got up to strip my bed and found her bra and panties tucked down in my sheets. I cried as I stripped my bed and replaced the sheets. I knew no one loved me. How could Daddy expect me to live like this?

The next day after school, I told my brothers about finding Cassie's dirty bra and panties in my bed. They told me to shut up before I got us all in trouble. "When she comes over tonight, I am going to say something to her about it anyway."

"Dorthea, just leave her alone."

"Watch me. I'm gonna tell her I know what she is doing and to stop doing it in my bed."

"You are stupid if you think you saying anything to her will make a difference. All you gonna do is get yourself a whipping."

Why was it so hard for me to listen? When Cassie came over that night, I didn't say anything until she was about to leave again.

"Did you leave any more dirty panties and bras in my bed?" I asked.

Again, she turned red before replying. "You better watch your mouth, or I'm going to tell your daddy how you're talking to me."

"I'm not trying to be smart. I just don't like touching your underwear, and I don't like you leaving wet spots in my bed. I know what you do in my bed, and you wouldn't want anybody doing that in your bed."

She walked out the back door, slamming it closed and waking Daddy. He yelled for her, but she kept walking. He hurriedly dressed and followed her.

When Daddy returned, he immediately started yelling. "I own every room in this damn house, and if I want to use every bed in this house, nobody should say anything to me about it!"

He took off his belt and started thrashing me with it, when Andre walked in the back door. "What's going on here?" Andre asked.

"She done got smart with Cassie again. She told Cassie that she don't like us being together in her bed, and it ain't none of her business," Daddy yelled.

"First of all, that girl you sleeping with don't have any right to get in *your* business with your kids, and second of all, your daughter has a right to a clean bed. It ain't right for her to have to sleep in your filth."

After that, Daddy and Andre got into a huge argument, and it ended with Daddy leaving and going to Christie's house, while Andre stayed home with us. When everything had settled down, Andre sat down at the table with me. Putting his head in his hands, he quietly said, "You're going to have to learn to shut your mouth. I don't know how much more of this crap I can take before I have to leave."

Andre didn't leave that night. However, Daddy didn't like Andre standing up to him and deliberately began picking at him. It wasn't too much longer before Andre did leave, and with him gone, there was no one to stick up for us.

* * * * *

Summer went by quickly, and my life didn't change. I accepted the fact that Daddy was the boss and there was nothing I could do about it. I spent most of my days at Mother Alexander's, helping her with the babies.

During the summer, while hanging around the neighborhood, I met a boy named Ty. I complained to my friends that he wouldn't leave me alone, but secretly I thought he was cute, and I liked the attention. After a few days, I agreed to be his girlfriend. We were inseparable. He was my very first boyfriend. Each day, I rushed through my chores so that I could go hang out with him. I knew at the end of the summer he would be leaving to return home to Chicago, which made me sad.

One day Mother Alexander noticed that I looked sad, and she asked me what was wrong. I didn't really know how to respond. I didn't want her to know that I had a boyfriend, so I just told her that I might want to start going to church with her. She was so excited that she called Daddy that night and told him to get me some church clothes. I didn't know that she had called Daddy until I got home that night.

"Dorthea, Mother Alexander called me today and told me you want to start going to church with her." I stood there in disbelief. I couldn't believe she had called Daddy and told him that. Suspicious about Mother Alexander and my conversation, he asked more questions. "What else you been telling Mother Alexander?"

"Nothing, Daddy. You know she is always asking me to go to church with her." Trying to reassure him, I further explained, "Mother Alexander is always trying to get everybody to go to church. I just told her I might go, and now she's calling you and getting stuff started." He looked at me for a few moments before he turned back and began to watch his television program. Apparently, I had eased his suspicions, because Daddy started teasing me about becoming a Holy Roller like my momma.

The next morning after Daddy went to work, I called Mother Alexander and asked her why she had told Daddy I had agreed to go to church when I had not.

"Well, I just want you to come to church, honey," she said.

"I told you that I might want to go. I didn't say that I *would* go."

After a few minutes of me trying to get out of it, I gave in and agreed to go to church with her. That Sunday, I went to church. When I walked in, I could feel them staring at me. Every time I saw them whispering to one another, I felt like they were whispering about me. Even though they had all seen me at some point in the day at Mother Alexander's house, they had not seen me in church since my momma had left us.

It felt weird walking into church without Momma and the rest of the family. But once the service started and the focus was on Big Daddy and the message he brought from the pulpit, I began to relax, and I lost myself in the service. Once I allowed myself to relax, I felt comfortable. It was almost as if I had come home, and in a weird way, I felt close to my absent mother. I decided that I would come back to church. It was only for a few hours on Sunday, and besides, it gave me something to look forward to at the end of the week. I did not know what I was going to do about church clothes, because Daddy had instructed Andre to buy me only one church outfit because he did not want to spend a bunch of money on church clothes if I wasn't going to attend regularly.

Over the next few months, I decided that I loved attending church, and I also decided to join the choir. At church, I was just like the other children. I wasn't the little black girl whose mother had walked out on their family. Everywhere I went, I felt uncomfortable in my own skin, but not at church. For once, I had found a place where I was comfortable in my own skin, where I was comfortable being me. At church, I was just Dorthea Letricia Hughes, a child of God.

During the first few days of fifth grade, Ty and I attended the annual Hog Days carnival in Kewanee. We walked around holding hands and rode all of the rides together. I knew it was risky. What if Daddy found out? He would surely whip me, but I didn't care. Ty was my age, and he made me feel good about myself. I felt normal with Ty. Some of my classmates saw us together and wanted to be introduced to my boyfriend. After introducing him to my friends, we ran from ride to ride, hollering and screaming with joy. It felt good to be normal to my classmates. Ty kissed and hugged me over and over in front of them. I could tell by the way they all gathered close to us and by the looks on the faces that they envied me because I had a boyfriend. For once, everyone was looking at me, and it was not because I was in trouble. It was great.

As the day turned to evening, I ran into my brothers, and they threatened to tell Daddy on me when he and Cassie returned from Chicago. I ran into Christie there too. She was with her children, and she also informed me that she would be telling Daddy when he returned.

I knew what would happen if I allowed people to know that I had a boyfriend, but how could I explain to Ty why Daddy wouldn't want me to like a boy my age? While other parents thought it was cute when their children started showing interest in the opposite sex, Daddy behaved like a jealous boyfriend.

Ty was scheduled to catch a train back home on the Tuesday morning after Labor Day, but for now, for this weekend, I wanted to be normal, so I deliberately ignored every warning. I was willing to take a beating for a few moments of happiness. Eventually, Andre showed up, and David and Jake pointed at Ty and me. I could tell by Andre's clenched jaws that he was angry with me. When he walked over to me, the first thing he said was, "Who is this boy, and why are you holding his hand in public?"

Still holding Ty's hand with a smile on my face, I proudly answered, "He is my boyfriend."

"You do know that if Daddy finds out, he will be furious. Dorthea, why are you always doing stuff to get yourself into trouble?"

I stood there for a moment before I accepted that what Andre said was probably true. Why did Daddy have to mess up everything that brought me happiness? This could not be normal for a parent to want to take away everything that made his children happy. Andre's demeanor softened when he saw the smile leave my face. I reluctantly turned to Ty. "My brother is right. I better go home." When I saw the questions in Ty's eyes, I promised to see him in church tomorrow.

By this time, I loved going to church, and I sang regularly in the choir. Our choir traveled as far as Rockford, Illinois, in one direction and to St. Louis in the other. Churches from everywhere called and requested us to perform at their church functions. They particularly loved to hear "Peace in the Valley." Church was the only place that I didn't have to pretend to be happy. At church, I *was* happy.

After Ty went back home, we kept in touch by phone. I called his house every day, and we would talk for hours. I knew it was long distance, but I didn't care. Before he left that morning, he told me that he loved me. I don't know if I loved him or if I loved how I felt with him, but it was hard for me to let it go just because he lived a few hours away.

I spoke with his brother one day on the phone because Ty wasn't home. "Ain't you worried about what's going to happen when your daddy comes home? Everybody knew that Ty was your boyfriend, and now you running up the phone bill."

I told him I wasn't worried about it. Then he asked me a question that made my stomach flip-flop. "Has your daddy ever messed with you?" After a long pause, he went on to ask, "You know, in an inappropriate way?"

I asked, "Why would you ask me that? That's a weird question, doncha' think?"

"I don't know—just something on my mind." When I hesitated to answer the question, he immediately pressed further. "If you tell me, I won't tell anyone—not even Ty."

I don't know why, but I found myself confiding in him all that had happened to me. Once I opened my mouth, I couldn't close it. Everything poured out at once. It felt good to tell my secrets to someone. He never interrupted me. When I paused, he would just say, "Go on. Get it out. All of it," and I did. After I finished, he said, "You need to tell someone what's happening. You've got to get out of there."

Immediately, I felt bad for telling him. "That's easier said than done," I replied. Though we talked for a little while longer, I didn't feel comfortable talking to him anymore, so I made an excuse to get off the phone.

When the first bill came, Daddy thought it was a little high, but he paid it. He never looked at the bills anyway. When the next month came and I saw how high it was, I threw it away to buy myself more time to figure out what I was going to do. When we let out of school for Christmas vacation, I decided that I had to do something. I called Christie and told her that I had a secret that I needed to tell her. She listened as I told her everything. I told her about David, about Daddy, about the phone bill. She told me that some of the same things had happened to her when she was a little girl. She was very understanding, but she also said that there was nothing that she could do to help me. Before I hung up the phone, she gave me her word to not tell Daddy what I had told her.

Next, I called Cassie at her mother's house and asked her if she would come over so we could talk. She told me that she was busy getting ready for class and could only speak with me over the phone. I made her promise to not tell Daddy what I told her. She agreed, so I told her everything, too. I told her how he came to me every morning. I told her how he slept in my bed and wouldn't leave my room. I told her that every time I asked him to leave me alone and not to mess with me anymore, he would beat me. I told her that he would come home from Christie's in the morning and get in the bed and mess with me.

After I quit speaking, she sounded very concerned. "I'm coming over there tonight after class. Don't let your daddy know that you told me anything. I promise, I won't tell your daddy that I know, and I promise you that I'm going to get you some help. I'm going to get help from the proper authorities. Everything is going to be okay."

I waited all day in my room, scared and not feeling so brave anymore. When Cassie came over, she came straight to my room and asked me if I had told anyone else what I had told her. I lied and said no.

"Okay. Good," she said. "We're going to go down in the basement and confront your daddy about this."

"No. I'm not going with you down there," I said, the fear creeping into my throat.

"If you're telling the truth, then you shouldn't be afraid. I'm going to be right by your side."

As I got up out of the bed and walked through my bedroom door, I glanced at the back door. I thought about just running for the door. Where would I run to? Where would I go? Who would take me in? Who would help me? No one would believe me over him. I was so scared as I walked down the steps to the basement to confront Daddy. He sat in his chair in front of the wood burner, poking at the fire. He often sat and watched the fire whenever he was deep in thought. I leaned forward and whispered into her ear, "Are you sure you don't want to come back later to talk to him?" She turned around, looked at me, and with a firm voice, she instructed me to stay put. Before I could turn and run up the stairs, she blurted it out to him.

"Why are you sleeping in the bed with your daughter? What have you been doing to her?"

He pulled the poker out of the fire and turned to look at me. Ignoring Cassie, he asked, "What are you running your mouth to Cassie for?"

He stood up out of his chair and came toward me with the poker in his hand. I yelled for Cassie to get him, while I tried to make an escape out of the basement. I made it to the third stair when she grabbed my leg. "Hang on. Let's all calm down. Ace, go sit down. Sweetie, just sit right there on the stairs," she said to me.

"I was afraid this was going to happen," I said.

Daddy didn't sit down. Instead, he started yelling. "I ain't listening to any of this bullshit. This is my house, and I can sleep anywhere I want to."

"She don't want you sleeping with her!" Cassie yelled back.

Again, he ignored Cassie, looking directly at me. "If you don't like me sleeping in your bed, then you can get the hell out of my house and go find your momma."

Eventually, he addressed Cassie, but the whole time he yelled at her, he continued to look at me. There was something different about his glance. It was different from any way that he had ever looked at me in the past. I heard the rage in his voice. "Dorthea is lying!"

"Why in the world would this girl make this up, Ace?"

"I don't know. She is probably making it up so she can go live with her mother. I promise you, if I touched her at all, then it must have been in my sleep. It must have been an accident!"

"How am I supposed to believe that? The fact that you're sleeping in the same bed with your daughter is weird enough. That ain't right."

He began to approach me again while screaming, "I just go in there sometimes because it's easier than coming all the way down to the basement. I done told you. I don't know what I do in my sleep. Maybe I was dreaming or something. Maybe I was dreaming about you and touched her by accident, but if I did, I didn't mean nothing by it."

I was shocked when she turned to me. "Are you satisfied with that explanation?" she asked.

I looked over at Daddy. His face told me that if I didn't let it go, I would feel his rage, so I simply said, "Okay."

Cassie turned to Daddy once again. "From now on, you need to sleep in your bed in the basement."

Once he heard the calmness in her voice, he relaxed and sat down in his chair. His voice softened. "Okay. You're right. I'll stay out of her room. It obviously makes her uncomfortable, but she ain't ever told me that I did anything to make her uncomfortable."

When Cassie heard that statement, she turned on me. "You said you asked him to stay out of your bed and he wouldn't."

Making one last effort to make her understand that I was in need of help, I answered, "I did. I asked him to stay out of my bed, and I asked him to stop touching me. He kept on, and he wasn't asleep when he touched me."

They both started yelling at me. "You're a liar, and you better not make me get up from this chair, because if I have to get up, Cassie or nobody else is gonna stop me from beating your ass," Daddy yelled.

"We had it all settled. Why did you have to get it all started again?" Cassie screamed.

I cried. I knew it would be bad when she left.

Cassie asked me why I was crying, and between sobs, I said, "Nobody's ever going to believe me. He's not going to stop, and when you leave, he's going to beat me for telling you."

She turned to Daddy and said, "If you beat her for telling me this, I won't ever come back here. I mean it." She turned to me again and softened her voice. "It's not that I don't believe you. I just think that you got your facts mixed up. If he did something, then he didn't mean to. Now, go on upstairs so I can talk to your daddy."

Between sobs, I climbed the stairs, but I listened in as she talked to Daddy. She told Daddy that he and I needed to take a vacation from each other as soon as possible. She told him to call his sister in Chicago to ask her if I could visit with them for a while. I began to relax. Maybe this was the opportunity I needed to get away. My aunt was a licensed social worker, and if I could get to her, maybe she'd know how to protect me. If she knew the truth, she wouldn't make me come back to live with Daddy.

Daddy yelled for me to get Aunt Monique's number. I hurried downstairs with the number before he could change his mind. I sat on the basement steps listening as Daddy asked his sister if I could come visit over Christmas vacation. He told her he needed a break, and she told him to put me on the bus Friday. I was hoping to leave that night. I didn't know how I was going to stay away from Daddy until then.

Cassie must have seen the fear on my face because she came over and assured me that Daddy wouldn't put his hands on me because he didn't want her to stay away. It was only Wednesday, and I knew there was plenty of time between now and Friday. I don't know how long I was deep in thought, but after a while, I noticed that Daddy wasn't on the phone anymore. He and Cassie made plans for a New Year's Eve party that she could have at the house since I wouldn't be there. Even though I was glad she had gotten him in a better mood, I wondered how she could just dismiss what I had told her and move on so easily.

As they made plans for their party, I turned around, eased my way back up the stairs, and left the basement. Lying in my bed, I wondered why I had decided to speak out. Why did I make those long distance calls on the phone? Why was my life the way it was? Why had my mother left me with Daddy?

I tossed and turned all night, waiting to hear his footsteps, but they didn't come. I should have been relieved, but I wasn't. If he had come in my room and molested me, at least I would have felt like things were back to normal. When he didn't come to my room that night or the next morning, I got even more scared of what he was going to do to me. That morning when I awoke, I cleaned my room while he was at work. I helped my brothers clean the house. I took a bath and greased my hair before Daddy came home for lunch. I tried to do everything that I thought would make him happy. When Daddy came home for lunch, he never even looked at me. He just stared down into his plate of food.

When Daddy came home from work, he went straight to the basement and started a fire. After about an hour, he called for me. My heart started to pound so loudly I thought it would burst through my chest. I started to cry. As I walked out of my bedroom, I looked at the back door and thought of running, but again, I knew I had nowhere to go. As I went down the stairs and into the basement, I began thinking what I could say to beg him not to beat me.

Surprisingly, when I reached the bottom of the stairs, he just told me to put some more wood in the fire. When I finished putting the wood in the fire, I asked him if there was anything else he needed. He turned to me and spoke to me very calmly. "When you go to Chicago, you better not tell anybody what you told Cassie. Those folks are my family, and whatever you think I am, they knew me before you were even born. If you say anything bad about me, they'll turn on you. If you try to start any mess, your aunt will put you out on the street, and I won't be able to help you. You think what I've been doing is bad, well, you don't even want to know what happens to little girls they find on the streets in big cities like Chicago."

When he was done, I went back upstairs and lay down on my bed. When Cassie showed up that night after her class, she came to my room and asked me if everything was all right. I told her yes. I again waited to hear the familiar shuffle of Daddy's feet as he came through the kitchen to my bedroom that night, but it didn't come. The next morning, he woke me to remind me what he had told me about keeping my mouth closed. After he left for work, I got up and took a bath. I wanted to be ready when Cassie arrived to take me to the bus stop. Cassie arrived fifteen minutes before I was supposed to leave on the bus. She had overslept. I had never ridden a Greyhound bus by myself, and I was scared to get on board, but I was also too scared not to go.

It was cold and dirty inside the bus. When I got off at my stop, I thought, What had I done? What if Uncle Dennis didn't come for me? Everyone looked so mean. No one smiled at me like they did in Kewanee. Just when I thought I would scream out in panic, my uncle walked up and hugged me. He grabbed my hand and my luggage, and off we went. He moved in and out of the crowds of people with ease. We rode the L, and he told me to hold on to a strap hanging from the ceiling of the car. I tried to hold on as best I could. Just when I thought for sure that I would lose my hold and the force of the car would send my body hurling in the air across the car, my uncle reached down and grabbed me, giving me a chance to get a firmer grip. If only life were this easy. If only I knew in life that if I were to fall, there would be someone there to save me, but life wasn't that kind. Even at my young age, I knew that most of the time, if you let go and fell, you just fell because no one was there to catch you.

When I arrived at my aunt's home, I expected it to be like all the times I had come before. I expected a huge home-cooked dinner, and since it was only a few days after Christmas, I thought she might have purchased me some gifts. There was no dinner, and there were no presents. Actually, Aunt Monique was in bed on the phone. Myron was in his room playing Atari with one of his friends. No one seemed excited that I was there. I had hoped to get there and tell what had been happening to me, but for some reason, their attitude toward me was different, and I didn't understand why.

Where were my aunt and uncle who loved me so much and constantly begged Daddy to let them have me? When Auntie got off the phone, she informed me that she had been talking to Daddy. She said he had told her that I had been giving him a lot of trouble. She said, "Don't lie to me and we'll get along just fine. Also, you are not allowed to play with Myron's male friends. Understood?"

"Yes, ma'am," I replied.

Daddy had set me up and had already turned my aunt against me. She didn't even ask me about what he said—she just took his side. He had warned me that they would all take his side. Now she treated me like an intrusion instead of the once-loved and wanted niece. I knew I couldn't tell her about Daddy messing with me. I wanted to give it a couple of days and let her see that I hadn't done anything wrong like Daddy tried to make her think.

That night, Myron made a pallet on his floor and gave me his bed. We lay there watching television until we feel asleep, like we had always done whenever I came to visit. I don't know why Aunt Monique was up walking around in the middle of the night, but she came into Myron's room and screamed at me to get up and take my things to the guest room to sleep. I didn't know why I couldn't sleep in Myron's room. I had just been at my aunt's house the past summer, and my cousin and I had shared a room. What was the difference now? What had Daddy told her to make her treat me this way? How was I going to tell her now? Would she believe me? Would she put me out on the streets? Where would I go if she didn't believe me? I had two weeks to figure it out and decided that I would worry about it in the morning.

The next morning when I woke up, both my aunt and uncle had already left to go to work. I suppose the idea of sleeping and not having to worry about Daddy coming into my room or the latest threat of him beating me as retaliation had caught up with me because I didn't realize how long I had slept.

Myron and I spent our days playing Atari. I also spoke on the phone with Ty. During the middle of my second week, my aunt started to relax and treat me like she always had. One night, after dinner, she sat me down and asked me why my underwear was so badly worn. I told her that they were old. She promised to take me shopping before I returned home. Since we were getting along so well, I decided that I would try to get help from her after all. Just when I had worked up my courage to tell her what was happening to me at home, she came home from work very upset.

Daddy had gotten his phone bill. She said she knew about my friend in Chicago. "I better not find out that you've been running up my phone bill by calling that boy," she yelled. She must have noticed the look on my face because she told me that Daddy's phone bill was over six hundred dollars. "After everything your daddy has gone through trying to raise you kids after your momma left, I wouldn't be surprised if he didn't try to find her so she can take you kids back."

I could tell from the tone in her voice that she wasn't happy with me anymore. I answered all her questions and then asked if I could go to my room. Myron came up to the room later and told me that it was time for dinner. I told him that I wasn't hungry. After he left, I thought about what I was going to do. With the phone bill being so high, surely I had given Daddy a reason to whip me when I returned to Kewanee. I decided that I had to seek my aunt's help.

I got up and began to descend the stairs, but before I could finish, I overheard a conversation between my aunt and cousin. "Momma, Dorthea is lazy and sleeps all the time."

Giggling and trying to shush him at the same time, she reassured him, "We only have to put up with her for a couple of more nights. Then she'll be back at home and out of our lives."

"She's isn't like normal kids. She doesn't even like to play. All she wants to do is watch soap operas, sleep, and talk on the phone."

"She must take after her momma. Her momma is as lazy as can be. It's so hard on my brother, taking care of all those children. It's not her fault, really. She's a product of a broken home. You'll never end up being like her because you have two parents who love you and want the best for you."

I went back to my room and climbed back into bed. Daddy was right. She *would* take his side. I couldn't take a chance on making her any angrier with me and risk being put out on the streets of Chicago. I hardly even noticed the first tears as they streamed down my face and fell onto the pillow. I cried so hard that my body shook so much I couldn't stop. I cried myself to sleep.

When I awoke the next morning, I hardly knew where I was. I had almost forgotten what happened until I felt the dampness on my face. Today was my last full day with my aunt and her family. I was torn between wanting to ask for help and knowing that if I did, I ran the risk of making it worse. I opted to enjoy whatever time I had left before I had to return.

That night, my aunt called me into her room and gave me some of her clothing that she didn't want anymore. Even though she was being nice to me again, I realized that telling was no longer an option. I cherished the moments we shared that last night. She laughed with me and tickled me. We played dress-up and snuck down to the kitchen to drink Pepsi while Myron and Uncle Dennis watched television. I felt so close to her that I was almost tempted to reach out to her, to tell her my secret, and to ask for help, but I couldn't take the chance. What if I told her and she stopped loving me?

I went to bed, but didn't sleep as well that night. When I awoke, Aunt Monique was already gone to work. Myron stayed in bed, pretending to be asleep. Uncle Dennis took me to the bus station. I rode the L again before I boarded the Greyhound bus home. The whole trip home, I tried to think of other options on how to get out of that house, but couldn't think of any.

Then right before the bus arrived in Kewanee, I decided that if no one was there, I'd leave. I would run to the police station and tell them everything.

When the bus came to a stop, I got off and looked around, trying to build up the courage to run. My heart pounded as the bus driver took his time lifting the side panels on the bus to retrieve my luggage. He handed me my bag, and I made up in my mind to run as soon as the bus pulled off, but I heard a horn blare. When I looked up, I saw Daddy in a brown Chevy truck pull up to the sidewalk where I stood. I climbed in as he put my suitcase in the back of the truck. We rode to the house in silence. When we arrived, he took my suitcase inside and placed it outside my room, then retreated to the basement.

I went into my room and put away my things. I went to bed that night thinking about what would have happened if Daddy hadn't shown up at the station. Would I have had the nerve to seek help? I like to believe that I would've gone for help. All night long, I listened for the familiar shuffle of Daddy's feet coming to my room, but again, it never came. The next morning, Daddy went to Christie's house before I even woke. I cleaned my room and stayed there all day reading. I loved to read. In a book, I could escape and pretend to be anywhere but 909 Dewey Street.

When Daddy came home, he went straight to the basement to wait for Cassie to arrive. A little while later, she arrived and stopped in my room to ask me how I was doing, before going to the basement. I told her I was good.

"Well, I'm glad you're doing okay, but I want to tell you something. The next time you decide to tell a lie on your daddy, don't involve me."

I immediately jumped out of my bed and told her, "I did not lie to you!"

"You did lie, and you're an ungrateful little brat. Your daddy should've put you in foster care for pulling a stunt like that."

Daddy heard us and called out to her to come downstairs.

* * * * *

Over the next couple of days, no one said anything to me. It was almost as if I didn't exist anymore. I liked the fact that no one bothered me, but I couldn't shake the feeling of dread, as if I subconsciously knew something was about to happen. I went to school every day except Friday, which was good for me. On Friday, I stayed home from school. At lunchtime, Daddy came home as usual. I sat at the kitchen table, reading my book while he ate the lunch I had made for him, when Cassie came in with takeout from La Gondola's Spaghetti House. She had brought only enough for him and her to share together. She got a dish from the cabinet and began to make his plate of food. "Cassie, give that food to Dorthea. I'm already eating."

Both hurt and shocked that he would choose to eat neck bones instead of the meal she had brought for them, Cassie's face began to turn crimson. After a few moments of silence, Cassie walked over to Daddy and stood behind him while rubbing his back slowly. "Ace, I thought we would have a nice lunch together. Dorthea can eat the food she made for you."

Never even looking up from his plate, Daddy said, "Cassie, I'm all right. You and Dorthea eat it."

"I don't want to share with Dorthea. I came to eat lunch with you, not Dorthea!"

Looking up from his plate, Daddy could see that Cassie was upset. However, he continued to eat from his plate. Mumbling under her breath, Cassie complained about sharing lunch she had paid for herself with me and began to pack the food away. Watching as she acted poorly, I marked the page in my book, sat it on the table, and began to laugh.

"What are you laughing at?"

"You don't have any money. All the money you have belongs to my daddy, and I don't want nothing from you anyway," I shrieked.

At this point, Daddy and Cassie began to argue. Raising his voice, he questioned, "Why can't Dorthea eat the food? I can't eat all of it, and I don't want it."

"I'd rather throw it away before giving it to her!"

Even though in my mind I had already envisioned myself finishing the Torpedo sandwich, I said nothing to ease her mind at the idea of giving it to me. Instead, I butted in, "You don't have to throw it away. I don't want your food. It's probably nasty anyway."

"Nothing is nastier than you."

"What do you mean by that?" I asked

"You're an ungrateful daughter who tells nasty lies on your daddy while he works his ass off to take care of a little bitch like you," she screamed.

Looking at her with all the rage I felt at my life, I thought for a moment. I hated being called a liar, but if I defended myself, I ran the risk of inciting Daddy's wrath. I wanted to remain quiet, but how dare she speak to me like that and call me a liar—and most of all, nasty. She who had lain in my bed nightly with my daddy? Who was she to speak to me in that manner?

Before I realized what I was doing, the words rolled across my lips. "Who said I lied? Everything I said to you was the truth!" I was shocked I had allowed those words to leave my mouth, but surprisingly, I was relieved the truth came out of my mouth. For once, I was doing something to defend myself. Even if I feared I would get in trouble later, in that moment it felt wonderful.

"Why would he want you when he has me?"

I screamed right back at her, "Yeah, why is that? Why does he want me when he can have you?"

Finally, Daddy intervened. "Both of you need to shut up. I can't even enjoy my food."

Cassie turned to him and screamed, "You need to whip her so she won't tell any more lies on you."

I shouted back at her, "Daddy needs to whip you for sleeping with a fifty-one-year-old man!"

Daddy pushed his plate away, got up from the table, and walked out the door. Cassie followed him while I cleaned up the mess and returned to my room.

When Daddy came home from work, he didn't have much to say before he went to the basement. After a while, I heard him come up out of the basement and leave. I knew he was going to Christie's house for the night.

I went to bed that night thinking I had been home a whole week and Daddy hadn't once tried to touch me, get in my bed, or beat me for telling on him. I was kind of pleased that he had even defended me when Cassie tried to get him to turn on me. For the first time since I had told on him, I believed I had done the right thing. I slept well that night.

The next morning, Daddy came home after a half shift, and Cassie arrived shortly after. She told him that he needed to do something about me so I wouldn't tell those lies to anyone else. She said that if I went to a schoolteacher or someone else, she wouldn't be able to help him. He told her that he wasn't worried, and that it was all over as far as he was concerned. I went back to sleep only to have my brothers wake me up and tell me that Daddy wanted me to come to the basement. I got dressed and went downstairs to see what he wanted from me. When I got downstairs, I was shocked to see that Cassie had left.

Daddy said, "I want you bring in some firewood."

"I've never done that before," I replied.

"Well, today you're going to learn."

"Jake and David, give Dorthea a pair of gloves and a pair of overalls to wear."

Not believing Dad was serious about me doing the work alone, they continued to put on their work clothes. "What are ya'll doing? Dorthea's gonna do this work by herself today. She don't need nobody's help."

Shocked, they stared at each other, and then they looked at me. They were trying to figure out what was going on. Neither of them said anything to each other, but the fear in their eyes said it all when they looked at me. They understood I had done something to displease Dad, and now he was going to make me pay for it.

My brothers usually completed this task every Saturday morning. One brother worked outside, carrying the wood from the garage and dropping it off at the window, while the other brother worked on the inside of the basement, grabbing the wood through the window and stacking it in the corner. Nervously David spoke. "Daddy, how is Dorthea going to do it by herself?"

"She's so smart, she can figure it out!"

I tried to do both jobs by myself. First, I went outside and dropped the wood into the window, and then I came inside and stacked the wood just as I had seen my brothers do several times before. Dad sat quietly, watching me. I was relieved when David picked up the wood and helped me stack it. It didn't last long, though, because Dad angrily told him to stop helping me.

As I continued to work alone, I realized why Dad was making me do this. I began to work more quickly and tried to anticipate any complaints he might have about my performance. After I had cleared the wood from the window, I went back outside and began dropping the wood again, but Daddy hollered for me to come back inside.

Hearing his voice speak my name, I began to cry. Now I was more scared than ever. I knew he had set me up. This was my payback for running my mouth. I started looking around for a way to escape, but David, who was suddenly beside me, must have seen the look in my eyes because he warned me not to do it.

"If you run, Dad will make us catch you, and then it'll only be worse for you."

As I turned to go back into the house, David looked at me and asked, "What did you do, anyway?"

I couldn't answer him. I was too busy trying to think. As I entered through the back door, I noticed that Dad wasn't in the basement anymore. He had come upstairs and was sitting in my mother's old beautician's chair that sat in front of the living room window across from the stairway. My stomach flip-flopped when I heard his words. "You're not packing the wood quick enough, so I'm gonna have to give you a whipping." He spoke so calmly, I almost did not hear him. "Go get the belt."

"Dad, no," I wailed between tears. "I'll do anything you want. You can come into my room anytime you want. I won't complain anymore."

"Take off your overalls," he replied somberly.

I began removing the straps and cried out again, "Please. I won't tell on you anymore."

He sat silent for a minute, staring at me. I thought he had changed his mind. Then, in a demanding voice, he ordered, "Take off all your clothes."

David arrived with the belt. He handed it to Daddy and turned to walk out the door. "No, David. You stay here," Dad ordered. "Jake," he screamed. "Come down here. I want you to watch this." I stripped down to my panties. Standing up, I tried to look into his eyes while begging him not to beat me.

Ignoring my pleas, he commanded, "Take off your panties, too."

By this time, both of my brothers were standing on the stairs. He made me lie face down on the floor in front of him. Coming closer, he swung and hit me with the belt as hard as he could. He stepped onto my back with his right foot and beat me with his belt over and over.

"You better not tell anything else on me as long as you're alive. Do you hear me?"

As he continued beating me, he screamed again, "Are you going to tell on me again?"

I didn't have the strength to answer him. When he tired of whipping me with his belt, he alternated between kicking and stomping me. With each kick, I saw his steel-toed work boots. Remnants of glue stuck to the boots, and before I passed out, I watched the glue particles turn red before everything turned black.

After a while, I heard Dad say, "Leave her alone, and don't cover her up." I passed out again.

I awoke to Dad kicking my side and telling me to get up and go pack the wood. I struggled to rise, but every time I placed my hands on the floor and tried to push myself up, the pain was more than I could bear. I could not push myself up with my own strength. I tried to reposition myself and just get my body into a sitting position, but both my sides and my back hurt. I lay there wondering how I was going to get myself up from the floor.

As I lay there naked on the floor, feeling more pain than I had ever felt in my life, I wondered why God had been so cruel and not allowed me to die. Surely one of those blows had met my body with enough force to end it all. It would have been the mercy of God to have just allowed me to die. I lay there for a moment and prayed to God to just take me right then and there. I felt the tears fall onto the sides of my face. I felt the salt of my tears as they ran down into first my ears and then the scratches on my neck and head. Just as I thought I could lose myself in my tears, I heard Dad tell me to get up, get dressed, and finish packing the wood into the house.

Realizing, if I made him angry again, he might come back and continue to beat me, I opened my eyes and forced myself to sit upright on the floor. Just when I thought I would not be able to stand on my own, Dad called out to me again, "Dorthea, get outside and start packing that wood like I told you." I don't know where the energy came from, but somehow I pushed the pain to the back of my mind and managed to push myself up onto my knees and then my feet. After I was standing, I moved slowly and put my clothes back on, careful not to move any more than I had to. Somehow, within minutes, I made it outside to finish packing the wood. This time, he instructed both my brothers to help me pack the wood, while he watched us silently from his cot alongside the wall. We worked in silence. This was the worst whipping I had ever received.

That night, Cassie came over and went straight to the basement where Dad was sleeping. After her visit with him, she came upstairs into my room. Feigning concern, she called to me, "Dorthea." Once I turned over and could focus on her eyes, I could see how she carefully checked me out from head to toe. I watched how she studied the bruises on my face. She reached out, carefully raising the blankets off my lower half, and studied my legs. "Is that everything, or is there more?"

Slowly I raised my nightgown and showed first my stomach and ribs, and then slowly I turned on my side and allowed her to examine my back. I thought to myself that surely Dad would get in trouble once she saw how badly he had beaten me, but instead, she cleared her throat and spoke softly. "I'll tell your daddy to keep you home from school for a while until this all heals." Then she was gone, and I didn't know which of them I hated more.

Later that night, I lay there and pretended that my mother was coming to get me in the morning. I pretended that someone had called her and told her all of the horrible things that had happened to me and that she was on her way. If I could just manage to make myself go to sleep, she would be there to get me when I awoke.

Sometime before morning, I awoke to the familiar sound of Dad's footsteps walking around in the kitchen. I held my breath and waited for him to come into my room, but after a while, when the door didn't open, I drifted off to sleep.

I awoke later to go to the bathroom. On my way back to my room, I peeked into the living room. Dad sat on the couch, watching television and drinking out of a brown paper sack. I crept away from the doorway and went back into my room. I tried to go back to sleep, but all I could think about was him drinking from that brown paper sack. I knew nothing good was going to come from that sack.

As I lay there, I began to count sheep. I had seen a commercial that said counting sheep made a person fall asleep more quickly. It didn't work. I was too nervous to sleep, so I got out of bed and turned on the light. I began to read. I don't know how long I read, but reading did the trick, and eventually, I fell asleep.

Jolted from sleep, I felt Dad pulling my panties down my legs. He didn't even care that I let out whimpers as the panties grazed my bruises.

I tried to be still until he finished. After he finished and left my room, I lay there and cried myself back to sleep. I cried because no matter what, there was no rescue for me.

* * * * *

From that night forward, he always made me open my legs and let him fondle me until my body started feeling funny. I tried to will my body not to respond the way he wanted, but I couldn't stop it. One night, when he had finished masturbating, he heard me cry as he was leaving my room. Turning around, with an evil grin on his face, he said, "Whether you want to admit it or not, you like it as much as I do. I know you pretend to be asleep, but I'm not stupid." Then he laughed and walked out, closing the door behind him.

I wondered if I was just as bad as him. My body betrayed me, just as he had said. I was so confused. It seemed because of what he did to me, he went to Christie's house less and less, and even though Cassie came to our house regularly, he came into my room almost every night. The only time he didn't come in was when I was on my monthly, and because he thought I was lying, he always made me pull down my underpants and show him that I was really on my period.

I was so humiliated. I tried in my own ways to make myself understand what was happening in my life. To help me process what was happening in my mind, I stopped calling him Daddy. The man who continued to humiliate me and do nasty things to my body and made me do nasty things to his body wasn't Daddy. From now on, he was just Dad. At first, no one noticed that I had stopped calling him Daddy until one day when Andre came to visit. By this time, he was nineteen years old and I was eleven. They were talking, and I entered the room, saying, "Dad, Mr. Howard is here."

Andre asked me right there in front of Dad why I didn't call him Daddy anymore. I just looked at him for a long time. I looked at Dad, and he didn't say anything to me, so I turned back to Andre. "I'm not a baby anymore, and only babies call their daddies Daddy," I said.

Andre laughed and told me that I was still a baby because I was his baby sister. There must have been concern on my face because when Dad left the room, Andre asked me if everything was okay. I wanted to scream, "No! Everything is not all right!" I wanted to tell him what Dad was doing to me. I wanted to scream what all the dirty boys had already done to me, but instead, I told him that I was fine. I went back to my room, climbed into bed, and read a book.

Sleep didn't come easy for me at night. In the dark, I wondered when Dad would come to me. When I drifted off to sleep, I had horrible nightmares. I dreamed that Momma had come to get me. I was running around trying to get my things before Dad came home, but before we could make our getaway, he arrived and stopped me from leaving. The only time I could sleep was when I knew Dad was at work. I began attending school only sporadically. There were entire months in the sixth grade when I attended only five or six times. It was just increasingly harder and harder to concentrate on my studies, and I spent my time pretending I was anywhere but Kewanee.

Seventh grade was a little better. Dad brought a friend around named Mr. Marvin Henry. I liked when Mr. Henry came around the house. He gave me money and pop. Dad was always with Mr. Henry after work, and as usual, so was I. Mr. Henry used to ask Dad why I wasn't playing with other little girls. Dad told him that he made me ride with him for my protection. It must have made sense to Mr. Henry because he stopped asking.

One day, Mr. Henry came to the house and asked Dad if I could babysit his girlfriend's children. I was excited at the chance to get out of the house. At first, Dad said no, but Mr. Henry kept asking him until he agreed.

Mr. Henry explained to me as he drove back to his house that he knew I wanted to get away from home, and if I did well babysitting his girlfriend's children, I'd be able to babysit again for them. He asked me if I knew how to take care of a baby, and I lied to him because I didn't want him to turn around and take me home. It was okay because when we arrived at his house, he asked his girlfriend, Dana, to show me how to change a diaper and to make sure I knew what I was doing.

His girlfriend was nice to me as she explained how to change a diaper and make a bottle. She laughed a lot and smiled at me all the time. She introduced me to her children, and away she and Mr. Henry went. Ten minutes after they left, I had forgotten everything they told me. Then it hit me. I was alone in a strange house with four children all under the age of seven: Jasmine, six; Dalton, five; Jermaine, four; and Alexis, thirteen months. What was I going to do if something happened? Who would I call? I immediately went and locked all the doors. I was so scared that first night. Every time one of us had to use the restroom, we all went together.

When it was time for their baths, I didn't feel comfortable in the bathroom with them, so I sat on the floor right outside the bathroom, playing with the baby on the floor. When they were done, I quickly gave the baby a bath, and we returned downstairs to the living room to watch television. We watched television together until they fell asleep. One by one, I carried them up to their beds, leaving Alexis downstairs with me. She made me feel special. She immediately took to me, and I felt the need to take care of her.

Later when Mr. Henry arrived home with his girlfriend, they found me asleep with Alexis lying on my chest and every light in the house on. I didn't want to go home. I liked it there. I hoped if they thought I was still asleep, they'd allow me to spend the night, but when Mr. Henry saw headlights in the driveway, he shook my shoulders and told me it was time for me to go home. Dad was waiting for me outside. I heard them discussing the fact that he had come over to pick me up at 3:00 a.m. I was just as surprised as they were.

As I climbed in the car, I wondered to myself why he had come to get me. Why was he always everywhere? Why did he always have to ruin everything for me? As we rode home, neither of us spoke. I sat silently looking out the window at the pretty houses, wishing I was going home to one of them. Any one would do; I just did not want to go home with Daddy.

Riding in silence with Daddy began to make me nervous. I looked over at him, but he just stared straight ahead. When we passed under the streetlights, I could not tell if he was happy or unhappy. Nervously I broke the silence by asking him why he had come to get me. Dad stopped the car in the middle of the street and screamed at me. "You don't know where I'll be. I can be anywhere at any time, so you better not try to run away or sneak around with no boys, because I'll catch you."

I sat back in the seat and rode the rest of the way home in silence while tears rolled down both my checks. He always had a way of taking me to the dark place.

* * * * *

Over the next few months, I began babysitting regularly for the Henry family, and I felt closer and closer to Mr. Henry's girlfriend, and especially to Alexis. I loved the way she cried for me whenever I left to go home and the way she screamed with happiness when I arrived. You might say she was the first person who made me feel loved and needed. I would rush home every Friday after school and pack a bag to go to the Henry household. Dad started to let me stay there during the weekends.

At first, I stayed only one night at a time, but soon, I was staying the entire weekend. I loved it at the Henry house. I was able to sleep at night and be a kid. However, it came at a price. If I tried to struggle when Dad came to me, he would threaten to disallow me to babysit for the Henry family anymore. I had long ago realized that resistance was futile, so I allowed him to do whatever he wanted so I could leave every weekend. It seemed like a small price to pay to get out of his reach.

Whenever I stayed at the Henrys' home, I would get up early, feed the children, get them dressed, and send them outside to play so their mother could sleep in. She would tell me that I didn't have to do this, but I knew that she liked to sleep in, and if I let her sleep in, I got to stay at her home a little longer. I tried to show her and Mr. Henry how helpful I could be if they would allow me to stay the whole weekend.

The first week of December, Alexis came down with chickenpox, and when it came time for Dana to pick me up on Friday, she didn't show up.

I waited until around 9:00 p.m. and then called to ask if she was coming. "Hey, Dorthea, I was about to call you. Alexis has the chickenpox, so we called the kids' aunt over to babysit."

I didn't speak for a few moments. I was torn between worrying about Alexis and worrying about myself. What if the kids preferred their aunt to me? Would I be out of a babysitting job? Realizing there was an awkward silence between Dana and me, I responded to her almost in a whisper. "I understand, and I hope Alexis will be all right." I was shocked when I heard my voice. My voice betrayed me: it told Dana how sad I was; it told her that I was on the verge of tears; it told her that I held a great deal of fear of being replaced.

Hearing the fear in my voice, Dana responded, "Dorthea, no one could ever replace you. Besides, it's just for the weekend."

Dana's words, which were supposed to reassure me, only fueled the panic within my heart. After hearing the word *replace*, I began to panic even more. Before I knew what I was doing, I heard the lie coming from my lips: "I've already had the chickenpox." I wasn't about to let chickenpox make me stay at home with Dad. "I want to come over."

"I wish I had known that. We already picked up LeAnn. I can't afford to pay both of you."

"I don't care. You don't have to pay me. I just want to come over and hang out."

"Are you ready?"

Unable to conceal the excitement in my voice, I said, "Yes, I am ready. Come get me!"

After she and Mr. Henry left the house to go to the bars, LeAnn, the babysitter, began to question me. "Why would you come over if you are not being paid?"

"I didn't have anything to do at home and just like hanging out here."

For the rest of the night, she asked me tons of questions about my life, some of which made me uncomfortable, so as soon as the children went to bed, I did too.

Saturday night, I was left alone with the children while Dana and Mr. Henry went to the bar to meet their friends. Without LeAnn there asking her probing questions, it was as it should be—just the four children and me. Sunday evening, I went home and dreaded the five-day week that bridged the gap before I could find refuge at the Henrys' house again.

When I got home, I didn't feel well, so I went to my room and watched television until I fell asleep. Sometime that night, Dad came home from Christie's and entered my bedroom. I was so knocked out that I didn't even hear him as he climbed into my bed. I awoke when I felt his rough hand touch my breast. I looked around the room, wondering when he had entered my room. As I tried to focus my eyes in the darkness, I felt my head pounding hard. I reached up and grabbed my head, only to have my stomach tighten up while my mouth filled with the contents of my stomach.

I barely made it to the bathroom before my stomach emptied itself. I don't exactly know how long I sat on the toilet before I gathered enough energy to make my legs cooperate and hold me while I stood on them. For some reason, the spinning in my head was not as bad if my eyes were closed. I could barely make it back to my bed because my head was spinning so badly. I staggered back to my room with one hand on my stomach and one protecting my forehead. I took a few steps with my eyes open, and then I would take a few more with them closed. As I climbed back into my bed, Dad looked at me from the other side of my bed and said, "Uh huh, I knew this was going to happen."

I didn't know what he was talking about, but I felt horrible. To keep my head from spinning, I closed my eyes. I kept wondering why Dad was still there. Why wouldn't he just leave me alone? Surely he saw how sick I was. No such luck. As I drifted off to sleep, he slid out of the bed onto his knees. I heard him coming around to my side of the bed, and he pulled the covers off my body. I started crying, thinking, *Will I ever get a break*?

I must have drifted off to sleep because when I awoke again, Dad was standing at the entrance of my room, telling me to stay home from school because I had chickenpox. I wanted to get up and go look in the mirror, but my head hurt too bad.

I awoke later to hear my brothers standing over me, looking at my pox and saying they didn't want it. I cried. The only thing on my mind was the fear that on Friday I wouldn't be able to return to Dana's to watch the children. My brothers thought I was crying because I couldn't go to school. That was the only thing that did *not* bother me. I hated school. The children all teased me because I dressed like a boy or because I was a bully. This morning, I wasn't going to have to call Mrs. Goody in the office and pretend to be sick. I actually *was* sick.

At lunch, Dad came home, woke me up, and told me that Dana was there to pick me up. She was going to take me home with her so she could take care of me at her house with Alexis. Dad didn't want me to give it to my brothers. Besides, Dana said she felt responsible for listening to me and not making sure with Dad that I really had had chickenpox before she brought me around Alexis.

When we arrived at Dana's house, the first thing she did was give me Bayer children's aspirin to make my fever go down. She would wake me every couple of hours, giving me cold compresses and asking how I was feeling. She wanted me to go upstairs and get into her oldest daughter, Angel's, bed where I would be comfortable, but I didn't want to be upstairs alone. I wanted to be around Dana as much as possible. For the next two weeks, I lived on her living room couch. I slept most of the time during the first few days.

While Dana made a quick run to the store to get both Alexis and me some calamine lotion, I decided to take a bath. It felt so good to get into some water. Dana hadn't let me take a bath since I had been there, only allowing me to wash up with cold water. I must have fallen asleep in the tub because when I woke up, Dana had returned, and she was standing in the bathroom and screaming at me to get out of the tub.

I was so scared at hearing her screaming at me that I forgot I was naked. As I jumped out of the tub and began to dry off, I realized that I was standing in front of her naked. She shook her head as she looked at me. Her eyes had turned red and had filled with tears. She left the bathroom and came back, ordering me to finish drying off, but not to put my clothes on. She made me look in the mirror. When I saw my reflection, I cried. I was practically covered head to toe with chickenpox. I had them everywhere. Dana put as much calamine lotion on me as she could before she called Dad at work to see what he wanted to do. I was at Dr. Jacobi's office within an hour.

Both Dr. Jacobi and his nurse said it was the worst case of chickenpox they had ever seen. Apparently, the hot water had made all the chickenpox come to the surface. While they were deciding if they were going to admit me into the hospital, I cried and begged Dana to just let me stay with her. She told me that my chickenpox was too bad, and she didn't want to be responsible for me getting any sicker. I promised her over and over that I wouldn't take any more hot baths if she would just let me stay with her. Something in my eyes must have touched her, because she tried to convince Dr. Jacobi that she was capable of taking care of me, and later that afternoon, I was tucked back in on the couch in her living room before the children came home from school. My chickenpox was so bad that I had to go see Dr. Jacobi every week until they were gone. This bought me an additional three weeks at the Henrys' house away from Dad.

Dad came to see me only one time while I recuperated. While he was there, I kept scratching, and he noticed. He asked Dana if there was anything to give me to stop the itching. She explained that she had given me everything she could. Dad told her that his momma had tied their hands when they were children. He didn't want me to have scars from the pox. No matter how much everyone yelled at me to stop scratching, I felt a sort of relief from the scratching that was much more than alleviating the itchy feeling. I liked to pick my scabs until they bled. I don't know why, but whenever I felt bad about something, I would pick one of my scabs until they bled, and I felt better.

I returned to school after Christmas break, only to have given the children more excuses to pick on me. Now they picked on me because of all the scars I had from scratching my chickenpox. They teased me because I would come to school with oozing sores that I would pick until they bled. I didn't know how to stop myself. Whenever a sore would start to scab over, I would pick it until it bled again. These actions caused me to have brown spots all over my body. One day Dad asked me why I made scabs all over myself that made me look ugly. I wanted to scream at him that the ugliness on the outside just matched how he made me feel on the inside. I wanted to scream at him that if I was so ugly, how come he wouldn't leave me alone? My only joy was going to Dana's house. It wasn't long before I had settled back into my routine of enduring Dad Monday through Friday so I could stay at Dana's on the weekend. For the rest of seventh grade, that was my life.

When school let out for the summer, I figured out ways to make Dana want to keep me around more. When I would go over on the weekends, I would do all her housework—the laundry, the floors, rearranging furniture, and anything else to get her to see that she needed me. I noticed the more work I did for her, the longer I was allowed to stay. It was a win-win situation for both of us. She got to enjoy more of her life, and I got to stay away from Dad. I loved it. I know it appeared as if all Dana and I shared was a working relationship, but there were a lot of times that she came and got me even if she didn't need a babysitter. We became friends. She came and got me to just hang out with her. We watched scary movies and talked about all sorts of things all summer long.

There were times when I wanted to tell her my dirty little secret, thinking she might rescue me, but I was always afraid of what would happen if she didn't believe me. I would lose a good thing. It was better to have a slice of freedom and suffer less than open my mouth and risk getting put out of their home and not have any freedom.

The more we talked, the more she took a personal interest in me. Dana was the first person to speak up about how I dressed like a boy. She made it her mission to change my daddy's mind. At first, she tried to persuade him to let her do my shopping, but when he refused to pay for clothes to make me pretty, she decided to help me save my babysitting money until the end of the summer so she could take me shopping for my school clothes.

When it came time to take me shopping, Dana got a babysitter so it would be a day devoted just to me. I don't know why I was nervous, but I was. I even told her that she didn't have to take me shopping. I told her that she could use the money on her kids. She would have no part of it.

She made me try on everything. It took a long time for me to relax and enjoy the day, but I did. Even though we only went to Kmart, it was the most fun I had had in years. She purchased all my school supplies. She bought me supplies that a girl would use. I felt like a princess. We finished the day at McDonald's, and then she took me home.

I started the school year off with the right clothes and school supplies for once, and I believed the school year would be different. After all, I was in eighth grade. The eighth-graders that had picked on me from last year had gone on to high school. I was at the top of the food chain now. Unfortunately, nothing changed. I still hated school. I still hated to be around the other children. I still found their conversations and petty bickering annoying. I was still known as a bully to most and therefore didn't get invited to parties. Even when I tried to wear my new clothes and fit in with them, they only laughed at me.

Again, I gave up on having any type of life except my weekends at Dana's. Those two days gave me the will to survive the following five days until I could retreat into the sanctuary that I had made for myself at Dana's.

This is pretty much how eighth grade went until the day I got off the bus and Dana was waiting for me. That was unusual. She usually came around 5:00 or 6:00 p.m. She had something she wanted to tell me that she didn't want someone else to tell me. As I packed my stuff for the weekend, I couldn't help but feel nervous about what it could be. I allowed myself to daydream that maybe Dad had moved away and she had gotten him to leave me to her. Maybe there had been a horrible accident and Daddy was in a coma, and I was going to live with her. Maybe Dad had told someone what he was doing to me, and he had gone to jail, giving me to Dana. She would be my new momma, and I would live with her forever.

I didn't know what her news was, but I knew it was big. Somehow, as we got closer to Dana's house, I knew this news wasn't good for me. The tightness in the pit of my stomach told me all I needed to know even before we pulled up at her house and I saw everyone packing. As Dana got out of the car, I looked around at all the people taking things out of her house and putting them on top of the trucks. The feeling in the bottom of my stomach got worse.

When Dana saw that I wasn't getting out of the car, she came around to my side and decided to tell me the "good" news. She told me to follow her to the backyard. With every step, a voice in my head told me that this wasn't going to be good. I wanted to run away. Dana told me that earlier that day, she and Mr. Henry had gotten married. They were moving to Monmouth, Illinois. She told me that even though they were moving, she would still come get me every weekend just like she had been. She reassured me that nothing would change between us.

I heard her talking, but she began to sound like the teacher in the Charlie Brown cartoon. I looked around the yard and saw my daddy's truck being filled with Dana's things. I wondered when his truck had gotten there. Had it been there when we pulled up? As I was trying to take it all in, Dad came over, stood at the corner of the house, and smiled at me. Immediately, I knew what that smile meant. It meant that after she was gone, he would have me all to himself again. I told Dana that I had to go to the bathroom. Just as I made it into the bathroom, I felt the contents of my stomach coming up. When I finished emptying my stomach, I lay on the bathroom floor and cried. I cried and cried until I lost myself watching an ant walk across the floor.

I came back to reality only when I heard Dana calling my name outside the bathroom. All the trucks were loaded, and they needed to get going if they were going to make it back tonight. I was supposed to stay at Dana's house and watch the children while they unloaded the trucks. I told her I was all right.

I realized that there was only one thing I could do. I had to tell her what was happening to me. I couldn't let her leave me with Dad. I remembered the yard of men outside. They would have to protect me. They wouldn't let my father get me. If I told her, maybe he would be so scared of going to jail that he would let me go with her. I would be able to leave and be safe. He wouldn't be able to come into my room again. As I quickly tried to get downstairs, it all seemed clear to me what I had to do. With each step, I heard the pounding of my own heart. I was so scared, but I had to do it now.

As I descended the last stair, I noticed it was quiet. I didn't hear the many voices of everyone shouting orders or laughing at one another. I realized quickly, before I even looked out the front door, that they were all gone. As I closed the door and turned around, the children informed me that the pizza would be there any minute and the money to pay for it was on the kitchen counter. I walked out to the kitchen to get the money and noticed that all the appliances were gone. I quickly went back upstairs and looked in all the bedrooms. They were empty, too. This was real. They were really leaving me. The upstairs was completely empty except for a few hangers in one of the children's closets and a change of clothes for everyone.

I noticed that the only furniture downstairs was the couch, loveseat, recliner, television, kitchen table, and Alexis's playpen. Everything else was gone. *It's not too late*, I thought. *I can still tell her everything the first chance I get.* I wasn't going to let her leave me with him. I needed her to protect me.

I waited for them to return that night, thinking I would still have an opportunity to do it with everyone around to protect me. They arrived back at the house late and quickly loaded up the trucks with the remaining items. I tried to get her alone, but she was so busy telling people to load this and make sure they grabbed that. Only two trucks made the trip back to Monmouth—Mr. Henry's and Dad's.

I managed to get Dana to let me go for the last trip so I could see the house. She asked Dad, and he said it would be okay. I told Dana that I had to talk to her in private, and she said that she would make sure we got a chance to talk before Dad took me home. I must have been acting suspicious because the whole trip down the highway, Dad told me repeatedly how nobody would ever take his children from him.

"I ain't scared of nobody but my momma and God," he said. I sat there silently, but my stomach flip-flopped when he said, "I'm glad that white woman is leaving Kewanee. I slipped up by letting you get too close to her. I ain't worried about it, though. She's white, so she don't really care about you. It won't be long till she finds a new babysitter to replace you. If your own momma didn't care about you, then what makes you think this white woman would? She's got her own kids to worry about—she ain't got time to care about you."

I said nothing, but as we rode down the highway, I stared out the window, looking at the lights of the cars as they passed us while tears fell down my cheeks. I didn't want to believe him, but my own momma *had* left me, so did Dana really care about me?

As everyone unloaded the two trucks and the children ran through the house claiming their new bedrooms, I walked around and silently asked myself if I wanted to take a chance on Dana. What if I told her and she didn't believe me? What if I told her and she told Mr. Henry and that caused Mr. Henry to fight with Dad? Everyone knew that Dad carried a pistol at all times. What if Dad shot Mr. Henry in a heated argument? Surely Dana would hate me then. No, I decided to keep my mouth shut and hope that she didn't forget about me.

When it was time for Dad and me to hit the road, Dana came over and asked me what I wanted to talk to her about. I told her nothing. She gave me a hug and told me she would see me the next weekend.

* * * * *

Dana kept her word to me. The next weekend around 7:00 or 8:00 p.m., she showed up at my house to get me. I was packed and ready from the night before. As soon as she pulled up in the driveway, I grabbed my coat and headed to the door. Dad, who usually went to Christie's, was awaiting Dana's arrival. He said to me, "Who told you that you was going anywhere? You ain't going nowhere. I want you to help me clean the garage tomorrow!"

However, Dana came in to talk to Dad when I didn't immediately come out to the car. After Dana pleaded with Dad, he finally let me go.

I had to go through this almost every weekend. I would be so upset, but Dana would only laugh and say that she had my daddy under control. For the first few months, Dana came every weekend to get me just as she had planned. Then, for no reason, she slacked up, stating that she didn't go out anymore, so she really did not need a babysitter. She also said that she couldn't afford the price of gas to come get me to visit. Dad enjoyed asking me every weekend where Dana was and gloated that she no longer came to get me.

Since I wasn't babysitting for Dana on the weekends, it left more time for me to hang out with my old crew, which consisted of Jamie, Nora, Raven, and Shana. Nora and Jamie were the same age, and two years older than the rest of us. I believe fate and geography made us all friends. I hated being around them at times, while other times I thirsted to be with them.

After a particularly lonely weekend, Jamie sat across from me on the school bus as we drove to school. She asked me to go skating with the crew on the weekend, and I told her I would do everything I could to be able to go. Apparently, Wheels Away was hosting an all-night skating party. The party had a live band coming from Galesburg, Illinois. I knew some of the members of the band—they were related to Mother Alexander.

I raced home and made sure my room was clean before I went out to the garage to clean it. When Dad arrived home, he found me rearranging his tools in his tool room. He came in and looked around at what I was doing. He didn't comment on what a nice job I was doing, but he rarely commented on anything he found any of his kids doing to make him happy. I finished a little after 10:00 p.m. that night. I made sure to lock everything back up before going into the house.

That night, I waited patiently for him to finish using my body, and as he was leaving, I pretended to just wake. "Dad, can I go skating this weekend with the girls?"

"No!" he replied, never even slowing his step.

I jumped out of the bed and followed him to the kitchen. "Why?"

Ignoring my question, he ordered, "Run my bathwater, make some coffee, and wake me when everything is ready so I won't be late for work." He then left the kitchen, so I couldn't ask him any more questions.

When I woke him, I asked him again, "Dad, can I please go skating this weekend?"

"I don't have time to talk about this. I gotta get ready for work."

After he had gone to work, I thought that maybe he would say yes if I could just make him happy.

When Jamie got on the school bus, she came and sat across from me and asked me if I was going to get to go with them on the weekend. I smiled and replied maybe. She, along with everyone else in our crew, was shocked, as they had all expected me to say no. Even though the chances of me going were slim, it was nice to pretend that I was a part of the group for a while. I sat back and listened to them talk about the dance steps they had made up last night.

Raven questioned me as to if I was really going to be able to go with them on the weekend.

"I don't know, but I am really going to try."

"If you want, I can ask Mom to call your daddy and ask if you can spend the night at our house." She had it all planned that we would go from her house.

"I don't know. What if my daddy found out? He would come out to the skating rink and embarrass me."

"Dorthea, you gotta grow up and be more like me. My mom doesn't give me permission to go to half the places I go to. I just tell her that I am spending the night with someone and go where I want to go." Both she and Rose told me they really wanted me to be able to go with them. Rose was my closest friend. She lived a couple of houses down from me. I really wanted to go skating, and now that the girls had actually told me they really wanted me to go with them, I couldn't just give up without asking again.

In the past, I had asked Dad if I could go skating, but he had always said no, so I wasn't hopeful that he would change his mind this time. Usually, I would have let it go, but because I really wanted to go, I continued repeatedly asking him. One morning as he finished messing with me, I asked him again. Because I wouldn't let it go, he grew suspicious and questioned me about having a boyfriend. He told me not to ask him again or he would beat me. I cried silently. Why couldn't I go places like other girls? Why did Dad have to make anything that could bring me pleasure for a moment in my life impossible?

Friday after school, I snuck down to the Howards' house to tell Jamie that Dad wouldn't allow me to go with them. She told me it was all right. No one really believed I was going with them anyway. She then asked me if she could wear the outfit I had gotten for my birthday. I reminded her that I had not worn it yet, and if I let her wear it, it would be returned to me ruined with spots of bleach all over it. Jamie persisted, promising me that she wouldn't let her mother wash it. She promised that she would return it early in the morning while doing her paper route. I didn't want to let her use it, but I didn't want her mad at me either, so I gave in, and we walked to my house so she could get the outfit.

On the way to my house, I saw Dad driving toward us, so I ran through the alley and beat him to the house. I answered the door as if I had been home all along. Dad surprised Jamie and me by telling me that he was going to allow me to go to the skating rink for the party, but that I couldn't spend the night. Jamie and I both screamed with happiness and jumped up and down holding onto each other. I couldn't believe it. I was actually going to get to hang out with the girls.

After Dad left, Jamie screamed some more and joked about his almost catching me coming home from her house. "Girl, ain't you glad he didn't catch you at my house? I'm almost sure he wouldn't have agreed to let you go."

I wiped my brow and pretended I was removing sweat and sighed a sigh of relief. While she was only almost sure, I was positive that if Dad had caught me, it would have played out completely differently.

"Girl, you better start getting ready."

"I know. I want to make sure I'm out of here before he changes his mind. He has been known to do that at the last minute." Then we both agreed that we had better get ready or we'd be late. As I turned to go back into the house, Jamie grabbed the screen door and followed me inside the house. I turned around to see what she wanted. "What's up?"

"I need the outfit you promised me."

"Surely you don't expect me to give you my birthday outfit now that I'm going too. What am I going to wear?"

"Dorthea," she said, as she looked straight into my eyes with a sneer on her face, almost mocking me, "you are not as pretty as me, and the guys expect me to dress a certain way. Besides, I have the boyfriend, not you, and I have to look good when we show up tonight."

Fighting back tears, I reluctantly gave her my outfit. It was moments like this that I truly disliked her, but what could I do? I really wanted to go, and what would be the point in going if she was mad at me? She wouldn't have allowed anyone to talk to me.

When Dad arrived to drive me to the skating rink, he asked, "Why ain't you wearing your new outfit?"

Looking away to avoid his eyes, I lied. "It's too dressy, and besides, kids don't dress like that anymore."

How could I tell him that I had allowed Jamie to wear it? If he knew, it would have been bad for me on so many levels. He would have driven me to the Howards' house and made me get the outfit back. Then Jamie would have been very angry with me. He would have whipped me for letting her borrow it. I had gotten a whipping for letting Jamie borrow clothes in the past. He would have told me I couldn't go to the party.

Before Dad would allow me to go inside and meet my friends, he had to lecture me yet again. The whole time he talked to me while we sat in the truck, within sight of the skating rink, he looked around slowly, watching everyone as they got out of their cars. "Who are their parents?" he asked over and over again. I tried to answer all his questions correctly and as quickly as he wanted. I didn't dare do anything to make him mad. I was too close to getting what I wanted.

After what seemed like forever and traffic on the outside had died down, it seemed as if he was still not going to release me. I allowed the tears to slowly fall down my checks. Why did he always have to ruin things for me? Why did I have to be a girl? He didn't do Jake and David like this every time they wanted to go somewhere with their friends. It seemed like he was going to ask me questions all night. I decided I might have to answer his questions, but I didn't have to pretend like I was enjoying being outside with him more than being able to hang out with my friends, so I began to give him short quick answers.

Just when I thought he was about to end my suffering and take me home with him, he informed me, "Don't leave the skating rink or go anywhere else, and I mean nowhere! If I'm late, just wait until I get here no matter what time it is, or else don't ask me no more." Slowly I began to realize he was going to allow me to stay. I was so happy that I began to get light-headed. I tried to not allow myself to get too happy because he could change his mind for no reason and not allow me to stay.

Just then he started up the truck and drove slowly toward the entrance of the skating rink. I fought hard within myself not to allow myself to show too much happiness at the idea of staying with my friends. In the past, Dad had seemed to take delight in building up our hopes and then killing our dreams. When the truck came to a stop momentarily, I held my breath, causing me to become light-headed yet again. I slowly reached for the door handle but did not dare open it, for fear he had something else to say and would see it as disrespectful for me to leave while he was still talking to me. Surprisingly, all he did was remind me, "Dorthea, don't leave here until I get back." When I didn't move, he asked me, "Have you changed your mind? You don't want to stay?"

"No, I want to stay. I was just waiting for you to finish talking before I got down."

That seemed to make him happy because then he told me, "All right now. If you keep sitting there, I am going to take you with me. I got stuff to do and need to get a move on it."

This time I allowed myself to turn the door handle and slide out of the truck. When both of my feet touched the ground, I wanted to take off running, but I did not. I maintained control and walked nonchalantly toward the entrance. Just as I was about to reach for the door handle and push, I turned back toward my Dad and called, "Thanks, Dad!" That must have calmed his nerves because slowly he began to pull away. I waited until he was gone and I could no longer see his taillights before I entered the building.

I had a wonderful time. I didn't know how to skate, but I managed to stay upright for a good portion of the night. I was so glad when everyone started taking off their skates and met up in the middle of the floor to dance.

Michael and Benji Mason, the two guys from the band who were related to Mother Alexander, were sitting down enjoying some food from the snack bar and noticed me dancing with my friends and came over to speak to me. Everyone came over to say hi to them, and everyone was shocked that I knew them. Jamie, noticing the commotion around Rose, Raven, and me, left the side of her boyfriend and came over to see what the commotion was all about. Once she realized what the fuss was about and overheard everyone's desire to meet Benji because he was so "fine," she instructed me to introduce her to him. "Dorthea, introduce me to your friend!"

Benji was asking me about my family when Jamie rudely interrupted. Not waiting for me to make the introductions, Benji spoke to her quickly. "Hi!" he said, then turned back and continued to talk to me.

"Ahem," she fake coughed. "Benji, do you think I look nice?"

He looked at her, frowned, and said, "Sure," but then he turned back to me and said, "I think you look nice too, Dorthea."

I looked down at what I was wearing and immediately resented Jamie for wearing my new, pretty clothes while trying to upstage me. Jamie must have seen the sadness on my face because she went for the kill.

"Do you think she's prettier than me?" she asked.

I could've just died. I was so embarrassed. My mouth just dropped open. I felt myself getting hot all over. I began to look around for an exit. I tried to think of a reason to leave the conversation before he could answer her. Surely he would pick her. Why did she always have to do things like this when she thought she was not getting enough attention?

Just when I had figured my route of exit, he smiled at me and drawled out, "Something can be ever so pretty on the outside, but rotten to the core on the inside." He excused himself after he gave me a hug.

I tried not to smile, but couldn't help it. Jamie turned to me and said, "Don't get a big head. He's way too old for me anyway. Besides, all the young guys like me the best."

* * * * *

As the night came to a close, Jamie and Nora decided they wanted to walk across the street to get some cigarettes. Everyone who was anyone was getting their stuff together to walk across the street. This was the nightly routine while everyone waited for their respective rides to come for them. I reminded them what Dad had told me, but Jamie had a way of convincing me to do things, and she convinced me that it wouldn't take long. After all, we were just going across the street and would be right back. We arrived at the store together, but everyone was taking too long, so I decided to walk back across the street even if it meant I had to go back by myself. Rose, who wasn't supposed to go anywhere either, noticed how uncomfortable I was and offered to go back and wait with me. I whispered in Jamie's ear that I was going back across the street to wait for my ride.

As I backed away from her, she hollered, "Man, your breath is hot. You know breath that hot got to be funky." While I stood there in shock, everyone laughed at me. I heard them still laughing as I crossed the street.

Then I looked up and saw Dad pulling into the parking lot. He watched me come from across the street. He began to yell at me. "Get into the truck. Dorthea, I told you not to leave. I'm gonna beat your butt when I get you home." I was so embarrassed because all the kids from my school were standing outside waiting for their parents.

As I climbed into the truck, he slapped me in front of everyone as we sped away. All the while he drove home, he yelled at me as I sat in my seat and cried, all the time thinking about what all the kids were saying to one another as we drove away. "I bet you were meeting some boy. Oh, I'm going to enjoy beating you when we get home. Was it worth it?"

"Please don't beat me. I will do anything you want. Just don't beat me." When we arrived at the house, he told me to go into my room and get undressed, that he'd be in the house in a minute. I quickly went into my room and got undressed, thinking he would do what he usually did to me.

Unfortunately, this time he had something else in mind when he entered my room. He came into my room completely naked. I was shocked and turned my head from him. He laughed and told me to come to him. He made me look at him while he stood there naked in front of me. I cried and tried to look away. "Have you ever seen anybody else naked?"

"No!" I told him.

He pointed to his private parts and asked, "You didn't even see Earl's?"

I looked past him, pretending to look at him, and replied, "No!"

"Remember what you told me about doing anything I wanted?" When I didn't reply to his question, he told me what he wanted me to do to him. I hysterically told him, "No!"

He screamed back at me, "Okay, then go get my strap. I told you not to leave the skating rink, and now I get to beat your butt for not listening. When I get done with you, you're going to beg to do whatever I want you to do.

"You better get over here now, or else."

Instead of moving, I began to cry louder.

The next morning Jamie knocked on my window. I slowly got up out of bed and walked to the back door to let her in. She was so busy telling me about how much fun she had after I left and how everyone from school was talking about the scene my daddy had made before I left with him that she didn't notice me until I had lain back in bed and turned my back toward her. She was shocked and let out a gasp accompanied by a low scream. Somehow, hearing her shock brought all the memories and pain back to my mind, and I began to cry softly. She moved closer to me on the bed and began to examine my swollen eye and the red and purple marks from the strap all over my body. She immediately began to ask questions, wanting to know what had happened to me. I told her that I got in trouble for crossing the street, but she didn't buy it.

She knew I had been beaten by Dad for years, but this was the worst she had ever seen—and she didn't believe it was just because I had crossed the street for ten minutes. I asked her if she could keep a secret and if she would keep mine. I cried. I don't know if it was from the pain of moving my body, moving my mouth to talk, or just the pain of moving through life, but I blurted out the truth to her. I had to tell someone, or I was going to explode. I didn't tell her all of it, but I told her enough. She came over and hugged me, and we cried together as she promised to never tell anyone. She told me that her older sisters had gone through the same thing with her daddy, but she never had.

Moments after Jamie left the house to complete her paper route, I panicked. Had I done the right thing by telling her what had happened? What would happen to me if she told someone? I tried to be good the rest of the weekend and forget about telling Jamie my secret. If she was going to tell anyone, I would know first thing Monday on the bus ride to school.

Monday came and went because I didn't go to school—partly because I didn't want to face Jamie, but mainly because of the strap marks across my face and chest. There was no hiding them. Wednesday morning, I awoke to

Jamie again knocking on my window. This time, when I went to the back door and let her in, I was moving better. There were still traces of the strap marks on my body, though. She asked me to get dressed and help her finish her paper route, saying that she missed me. I was grateful for the attention, so I went.

When we got close to my house, she asked me if I was going to school, and I told her not yet, so she asked me to walk to her house and keep her company while she got ready for school. I didn't mind. I figured after the bus had left her house, I would sneak back to the house and spend the rest of my day in solitude. Just as we entered the back door of Jamie's house, I saw her mother at the stove making breakfast. Jamie quickly mumbled to me that her mother wanted to speak with me and left the room. *Oh my God! Did she tell her mother our secret? She couldn't have—she promised me she wouldn't tell anyone.*

Mrs. Howard took me by the hand and led me to the basement where we were alone. Just as I thought, *This is it,* Jamie reappeared in front of me. Mrs. Howard's voice struck my ears as she asked me if I had told Jamie a secret about my daddy. Just as I allowed the first tear to fall, Jamie told me that she was sorry for breaking her promise, but she had to tell someone. I stood there feeling both betrayed by Jamie and stupid for trusting her in the first place.

Mrs. Howard spoke sweetly to me. "I suspected that something like that was taking place at your house. That's why we don't allow our girls to visit you at your house. I don't know if you know this, sugar, but that's the reason your momma left your daddy."

"Wait," I said. "What do you mean? My mom left my daddy because of what?"

She smiled as if letting someone in on a secret for the first time. "Well, you know how small Kewanee is, so you hear all these rumors. I heard that your daddy was messing around with your oldest sister, and your momma found out. From what everybody says, that's why she left him." I stood there with my head reeling so fast that I thought I was going to faint. Mrs. Howard kept talking, though I barely listened. "I never could understand how your momma could've left you there with that man, knowing what he had already done to one of her daughters. I just don't know how a mother could be so selfish."

My tears flowed freely now. Mrs. Howard began to read to me from one of her Jehovah Witnesses' books, then told me to come to Bible study with her and things would get better for me. In my mind, I was no longer in the basement with her. I was thinking of all the times that I had cried out for Momma to come and save me. I thought of all the times that I had lied to myself, thinking that if she only knew what was happening to me, she would come back, beat Dad up, and rescue me and my brothers. I was so stunned at this revelation that I didn't resist when Mrs. Howard asked me if she could see the bruises on my body from the strap.

After that, Mrs. Howard asked me all sorts of personal questions about my relationship with Dad. She wanted to know how far he had gone with me. I was careful not to reveal any more than what I had already told Jamie. When she had seen enough and was satisfied with her questions, she allowed Jamie and me to leave the basement. Jamie rushed to school, while I walked home in silence. I had allowed Mrs. Howard to hug me as I walked out the door. She told me that if I ever needed anything to let her or Jamie know, and she would help me. I walked home confused. *Didn't I just tell you that I needed help? You just saw the marks with your own eyes. Your daughter told you what my daddy was doing to me! If anyone ever needed help, it was me—and not later, but now.*

* * * * *

The next day on the ride to school, I found out how my slip of the tongue was going to affect my life. Jamie wouldn't speak to me on the bus, and as I looked around, none of the other Howard girls spoke to me either. When Jamie got to school away from her sisters, she confided in me that her mother had sat her and her sisters down the previous night and told them all to stay away from me. Jamie told me to give it a while and her mother would change her mind, but for right now, they weren't allowed to even speak to me. Her mother told them that we were all sick in our house and that she didn't want that sickness to spread to her children. I felt betrayed. Mrs. Howard didn't want to help me—she just wanted to know the details. As I walked the halls of school that day, I came to the realization that everyone wanted to know the details, but no one wanted to do anything to help me.

* * * * *

Just when I thought I couldn't take it anymore, Dana called and asked me if I wanted to come and spend Christmas break with her and the kids. She explained that she had to come to Kewanee to pick up her stepchildren, and she could swing by and pick me up too. She told me if I wanted to come, then it was up to me to get things straight with Dad because she was getting tired of dealing with him and playing his games.

I was so excited at the idea of spending the holidays with Dana and the kids that I asked Dad right away. He responded with a maybe. I knew he would be trying to figure out a way that he could get something out of this. I knew I should be scared, but I didn't care because Dana was coming to get me, and I missed them all so much.

A couple of days before school was supposed to let out for Christmas break, Dad came into my bedroom as usual and told me to wake up. I opened my eyes and focused on his silhouette in the dark. I heard what he said to me, but I didn't want to believe it, so I pretended not to understand. He told me that he wanted to "put it in."

I asked him, "Put what in where?"

He pointed to his privates and then pointed to mine. I looked at him and said, "No!"

"If you don't let me do it, then you're never going to Dana's house again." Then he walked out of the room.

My daddy had Christie. Why would he want to go all the way with me, his daughter? How could I let him do that? I had managed to live through everything else by pretending to be asleep when he came to me, but if I allowed him to go all the way with me, I couldn't pretend anymore. I didn't know what I was going to do, but I knew I was *not* going to have sex with him.

Over the next couple of days, he still came to me every night and did whatever else he wanted to my body, but he continued to remind me that if I didn't let him put it in me, he wouldn't let me go to Dana's for the holidays.

The night before Dana was supposed to come to Kewanee and pick me up, she called and asked if I would be allowed to go home with her. I told her Dad said no, but she asked to speak to him anyway. He told her no, too. I went to my room and cried myself to sleep. Surprisingly, Dad didn't come to my room that night.

It wasn't like we did anything for the holidays. Dad didn't even buy us presents. He always spent the day with Christie and her children. They ate an elaborate dinner and exchanged gifts with her children. My brothers and I were left at home to salvage some sort of meal for ourselves that usually consisted of neck bones and potatoes. My brothers had friends who sometimes brought us a plate of cookies, but my brothers hoarded them in their bedrooms and didn't share with me.

If I had been able to go to Dana's house, I wouldn't have minded that I would be the only child not to have anything to open on Christmas morning. I just wanted to be away from Dad. That would have been my Christmas present, and it would have been enough. Besides, I knew that there would be delicious food to eat and movies to watch. That was better than anything that I had at home.

* * * * *

When I arrived home from school on the last day before Christmas break, I changed out of my clothes and settled in for the night with a book. Every now and then, I glanced at the clock, knowing that Dana was probably in town already and picking up the twins. By 9:00 p.m., I knew they were probably on their way back to Monmouth. I cut the light out and closed my eyes. I liked to dream that I was anywhere but home. As I was drifting off to sleep, I heard a truck pull into the driveway and stop outside of my window. I looked outside into the night. It was Dana. She had come for me anyway!

I hurriedly put my clothes on and ran to the back door. The whole family came in, one after another. Dana whispered and asked, "Where's Ace?"

"He's asleep in the living room."

"Go start packing your things, and stay in your room until I call for you."

Even though I was in my room packing, I could still hear their conversation. When I finished packing, I sat on the end of my bed and crossed my fingers, hoping that Dana could talk Dad into letting me go. Dana went into the living room and said to Dad, "Wake up, Ace. When you need Dorthea back home?"

She just took control of the situation and assumed that he would let me go home with her. Dad woke up and turned on his side for a long moment; neither of them said anything to each other. Then a slow smile crept across his face, as if he saw this as a challenge, before he replied to her. "I don't need her to come home because she is not going with you, Dana." On and on, they argued back and forth. After about thirty minutes, I began to put my bag inside my closet on the floor, my hope deflated. Just when I began to drift off to sleep, Dana came and knocked on my door and told me to grab my things.

I grabbed my bags and said good-bye to Dad, who stood by watching me closely. I ran outside into the night, jumped into the truck, and away we went. During this break, we did everything. We cooked and cleaned, we baked all sorts of goodies, we held dance contests to see who could imitate Michael Jackson's dance routine in the new *Thriller* video, we watched scary movies, and each night after the kids were in bed, we played spades. Even though on Christmas morning I didn't have any presents to open, it was the best Christmas break of my childhood.

* * * * *

After the holiday was over and the New Year had come and gone, I knew nothing would be the same. That was the last visit to Dana's that didn't bring about drama. Dad grew increasingly paranoid of my relationship with Dana and Mr. Henry, even accusing me of having a sexual relationship with them. He increasingly told me that I wasn't allowed to talk to Dana anymore and threatened to beat me for just saying her name.

Dana began to grow weary of Dad's tactics to prove his control. It was like a game to him. The more he made me cry, or the madder Dana got with him, the more he enjoyed himself. Each episode of this cat-and-mouse game grew crueler than the last. He began to make rude sexual advances to Dana just to see how far he could push her.

One time, while grabbing his crotch, he taunted her by asking, "If you want a little Dorthea so bad, why don't you let me give you one of your own so you can leave this one at home?" Just when Dana would complain and tell him that she was leaving with or without me, he would give in and let us leave.

In between visits to Dana's, my attendance at school became more like visits. I stayed home more than I attended school. It was so hard for me to function as a normal teenager and attend school.

The week before I was expected to graduate from eighth grade, Dana called and asked me if I would like to come and spend the summer with her and the kids. I excitedly told her yes, but I worried how she was going to get Dad to agree. Against my better judgment, Dana decided to let Mr. Henry ask Dad, stating that the kids would be out for the summer and Dana needed help. It backfired. Dad stubbornly replied, "No!" and quickly got off the phone, slamming down the receiver. When he looked up and saw me standing in the doorway, he charged at me and slapped me across my face so hard that my head hit the wall. I stood there shocked and wondering what I had done to deserve that as he walked out the back door. Hours later, when he returned home, I could smell the liquor on his breath as he beat me and tried to force me to admit that Mr. Henry and I were lovers.

* * * * *

For the next couple of days, no one understood why he kept beating me, not my brothers or my friends who continually saw me covered in bruises. He would come in from work after he had bought a bottle of some type of liquor, then call me out to the garage where he asked me repeatedly if I was sleeping with Mr. Henry or letting him touch me. The more I told him no, the angrier he got, and eventually, he would beat me.

One day he questioned me as he sawed scrap wood and placed it in a pile to make chair legs later. As his anger mounted, he grabbed a two-by-four from the pile on the floor and beat me everywhere with it. As he delivered each blow, he screamed, "You've got something going on with Dana or Chris, and you're going to tell me the truth."

When he finished beating me, I had huge, swollen bruises all over my body that were purple and hot to the touch. I had a black eye from where the board had struck my face. When he was done whipping me, he would make me go into the house where he would have his way with me before my brothers came home. This went on repeatedly until eighth-grade graduation day.

* * * * *

The week of graduation wasn't as exciting for me as it was for all the other little girls. I sat in each class and listened to them brag about their pretty dresses and the parties they would be attending to celebrate their special day. Each time I heard some girl laugh with delight, I screamed inside my head. I didn't even want to attend graduation. I didn't have anything to wear, and no one was coming for my graduation anyway. Dana wasn't coming to town until the next day to attend her stepsons' graduations and to pick them up for the summer. I had told Dad that the required attire for the ceremony was a white dress, but he was so angry at me that when it came time for my graduation ceremony, he told me to get Dana or Mr. Henry to buy it.

After school, Jamie came to my house and asked me if I was going to attend graduation. I told her I wasn't going. She convinced me to borrow her purple dress and go to graduation, promising me that she would be there to holler out my name as I walked across the stage. After Jamie went home, I went into the house where Dad sat watching television. I asked him if I could go to my graduation.

"Yeah, if you let me mess with you," he said nonchalantly.

"I won't fight if you let me go to Dana's house for the summer."

"No. You're just trying to get away from me."

I went to my room, lay across my bed, and cried. Then I heard him enter my room. When I looked up, he was standing there with a board in his hand, blocking the door. As he entered the room, I yelled out, "Dad, I'm sorry for making you mad!"

"Dorthea, which one of Dana or Mr. Henry is messing with you?"

"Nobody, Dad, is messing with me," I told him through my tears, but he struck me anyway. With each whack of the board against my body, I screamed out for him to stop. I even pretended that he had broken my arm, thinking that would scare him into stopping. "Dad, I think you broke my arm!" But it just fell on deaf ears as he swung the board and tried to hit the very arm I held on display to him, crying it was broken. When he had finished beating me and I lay in a heap on the floor, not able to cry or yell any more, he slid down onto the floor where I had curled up to protect myself. He opened his pants. He reached out and took my hand and made me touch him until he was satisfied.

Standing up as if he had not just given me the beating of my life, and for no earthly reason, he said, "Daisy called here. She wants you to go down to her house to get a dress for graduation."

"I don't want to go anymore," I said.

"Yeah. You're going," he remarked and walked out of the room.

* * * * *

I got ready for graduation, but no one heard laughter coming from me as I entered the high school gym. No one saw a smile on my face as I lined up with all the other girls. No one noticed the tears running down my face as I took my seat. I listened as they called my classmates' names and their families cheered. I wondered who besides Jamie would cheer when they called my name. As I took my turn and walked onto the stage, I scanned the crowd for anyone who had come for me, but I didn't see anyone. Just as they called my name, I heard a familiar voice cheer for me.

I looked out in the crowd. It was one of my brother's ex-girlfriends. I didn't care that she came dressed to hang out and not in a suit like all the other parents. I was just glad that she came. The night after graduation, Dana came over and told me to ask Dad if I could go to the twins' graduation. While she waited outside, I went downstairs to the basement and asked Dad.

"Sure, you can go, if you let me do what I asked you," he said.

I told Dana that I couldn't go, and she left to attend the boys' graduation. On her way out of town, she came back by and asked Dad if he would allow me to go home with her for a while. He told her no and drove away while she stood there. Eventually, she told me good-bye and left.

After Dana left, I walked down the street to Jamie's house. She asked why I had gotten a beating. Ever since I had confided in her the reason for one of my beatings, she always felt the need to question me whenever I got another beating. I told her I didn't know. Ironically, it wasn't a lie. My only major crime in life was being born a girl.

Jamie told me that I should run away. She even called her older sister, Leah, outside to talk with us. Once Leah saw all the bruises on my body, she told me that if I gave her the gas money, she would help me run away. She said she'd take me to Monmouth. While the idea of running away excited and scared me, I didn't want Dad to hurt Dana or Mr. Henry. They were the only two people I could turn to. Jamie and her sister told me that I needed to run away, or he would kill me. I finally relented, and we made plans for Leah to sneak me away the next evening.

That night, when Dad came into my room, I didn't fight or argue. I just let him do what he wanted to do with my body. When he was through, I asked him if he thought I would ever be allowed to go to Dana's house again.

"I don't know. I'm not taking you," he said matter-of-factly.

I asked him if I could go if I had a ride. Walking out of my room, he said, "As long as I don't have to take you, you can go for a couple of weeks—but not for the whole summer."

The next day, I went to the Howards' house and let Leah know that I didn't need to sneak out of the house. I told her that she could come pick me up later. She said that she had to run some errands, but that we could go that evening. I was so excited. I called Dana and told her that I would be there later that evening. I waited anxiously all day. When Dad arrived home from work, I made sure the house was clean, his dinner was done, and that no one disturbed him. I didn't want to take any chance of upsetting him and changing his mind.

When Leah pulled up and honked her horn, I grabbed my bag and told Dad that I was leaving to go to Dana's.

Immediately, he yelled, "You're not going anywhere!"

"But you said that I could go if I found a ride," I yelled back at him.

"Who're you getting a ride from?" he asked.

"Leah," I replied.

"She ain't taking you all the way over to Dana's without money. You paying her?"

"Yeah, I'm paying for her gas money with my babysitting money."

Without another word, he jumped up out of his chair, ran over to me, and slapped me. "You ain't going nowhere. Now go tell that bitch to quit honking her damn horn!"

I got up from the floor, leaving my bag in the house, and ran outside to Leah. "Never mind," I told her.

"Why you tripping?" she asked. "I heard him screaming at you all the way out here. Just get into the car with me, and we'll go to the police. Yo' Dad ain't right, and you need some help," she said.

"I can't," I whined. "Please, just leave before I get into more trouble."

Just as I was about to turn around and head back into the house, Dad came out of the darkness. "Get yo' ass off my property. I heard what you said. You trying to get me arrested?"

I yelled, "I wasn't going to the police. I was coming back into the house."

He continued cussing at Leah, and then he started kicking her car. She rolled up her windows to protect herself. In an instant, he turned on me and punched me in the face. I must have been unconscious for a minute because when I raised my head off the ground, I saw that Leah had backed her car out of our driveway. Dad was standing on the street in front of her car, screaming at her. When Dad saw me getting up, he ran over to me and swung his fist at my head, connecting with my eye. I called out to Leah to help me, but she drove away.

Having nowhere to go, I lay in the yard long after Dad had gone back into the house. I stared up at the sky, crying and asking God *why me?* when I heard Dad screaming for me to come into the house. As soon as I walked into the house, and before I could explain to him that I wasn't about to go to the police, he beat me again. He punched me over and over in my stomach, my face, and my chest.

Just when I thought, *This is it. I'm going to die. Surely he'll kill me this time*, the phone rang. He stopped to answer the phone. I don't know who in his family he was speaking with, but the tone of his voice quickly changed, and I heard him laugh out loud. I took this as a sign that I was free to go clean the blood off my face, assess the damage, and go to bed.

* * * * *

The next morning, shortly after Dad left for work, the phone rang. It was Dana! Leah had gone home crying and told her older sister what she had witnessed. Leah's sister called Dana and Mr. Henry with the details. They wanted to know if I was all right. I heard Mr. Henry in the background wondering why my daddy had snapped. Dana wanted me to know that she would be arriving a little before noon to see the damage.

"We'll go from there," she assured me.

I didn't know what was going to happen, but I felt better knowing Dana was on her way to see about me. I got up and did my chores. My brothers woke up, saw my new bruises, and never asked a question about what had happened. Shortly before noon, Dana pulled into our driveway. She took one look at my face and arms and cried. Covering her mouth, she cried out. She instructed me to turn around and lift my shirt as she examined my bruises. She told me that she was going to ask my daddy again to let me go stay the summer with her. "If he won't let you, then I'm going to have to do something else," she said, "because this has to stop."

When Dad pulled up for lunch and saw Dana, he said, "Come in the house. We can talk while I eat my lunch." When they were finished talking, Dana told me to go get my things because I was going home with her for the summer. I didn't know what they talked about, but it worked, because less than an hour later, I was on my way to Monmouth.

When Mr. Henry arrived home from work that evening, Dana called me into the living room. Mr. Henry made small talk while he pretended to read the newspaper. I saw him looking at my bruises, though. I waited for either of them to ask about the bruises and the abuse. I even fantasized about telling them the horrible secrets of my life, if only they would ask me. They didn't. When Mr. Henry finished his small talk, I was sent back outside to hang out with the twins and their friends.

When I had not been allowed to come for the weekend, Mr. Henry found another babysitter. She was the sister of one of the twins' friends. She wanted to meet me and hang out for the summer. From the first moment I met DeLisa, I knew we'd be best friends. She was shy like me and sort of a tomboy. For the next week, we were inseparable. We did everything together. Either I was at her house or she was at Dana's, and for the first time in my life, I began to relax and enjoy things in life like other teenagers.

One day, the twins were being particularly nasty toward Dana and she was having a bad day. Before I had met DeLisa, when the twins were acting rudely, I would have stayed in the house by Dana's side and not spoken to them. DeLisa tried to make me understand that I was a kid and needed to act like a kid. So instead of staying in the house with Dana and boycotting the twins, after I had finished my chores, I went outside to watch the twins and their friends breakdance in the driveway. One of the kids came to the door and told me that Dana wanted me, so I jumped up and went in to see what she wanted, only to have her tell me that I needed to come inside and do my chores. I told her that they were all done and went back outside to hang out with the children.

I wasn't outside more than ten minutes before Dana came to the back door and screamed at me to get my things together because she was taking me home after her husband came home from work. I immediately jumped up from the spot where I was sitting on the side of the driveway and followed her inside the house. I begged her to let me stay.

"I didn't go get you and put up with your daddy for you to come to my house and spend all your time with the twins. I brought you here so you could spend time with me," she yelled before storming out of the room.

At noon, she called my daddy and told him that she would be bringing me home later that day. I immediately realized that in order to stay in Monmouth, I had to make a choice between being a kid and being Dana's companion. I begged her all day to please let me stay. When Mr. Henry came home from work, he gave Dana the gas money to take me home, but not before lecturing me as to why I had come to their home. He reminded me that I came there to help Dana, not hang out with DeLisa or his sons.

"Your first priority, he said "is to make sure Dana doesn't need you to do anything, and then you can hang out with the other children." He told me he was disappointed in me for disrespecting Dana and refusing to do my chores.

I realized that she must have told him that I was talking back to her and refusing to do my chores. I was smart enough to know that I couldn't tell him I had done my chores and that I had not disrespected her, so I apologized and asked Mr. Henry if I could stay and help her for the summer. I promised him that I would stop hanging out with DeLisa and the twins if he would just let me stay and not send me home. He told me that it was up to Dana, not him. He reminded me that it was Dana who drove to Kewanee to get me when they heard how my daddy had beaten me.

As Dana and I drove down the highway, I cried as we got close to Kewanee. I begged her not to make me go home. Only after I had begged her for twenty minutes did she relent and tell me that she would bring me back with her. I begged her not to even go to Kewanee, but she insisted that she at least had to go talk to my daddy. She insisted that she could get him to let her bring me back with her. I begged her to just turn around and call him from her house, but on we drove.

When we arrived at the house, Dad was upstairs in my brother's bed asleep. Dana tried to get him to come downstairs and talk with her, but he told her if she wanted to talk with him, she had to come upstairs. At first, they were just talking and laughing, but when she asked him about taking me back with her, he told her no. She began to cuss him out for being so ornery, and he grabbed her and pulled her down into the bed with him. She fought him off and screamed that she was telling Mr. Henry on him.

From the bottom of the stairs, I continued to listen to them as a part of me died inside. When she left, I knew nothing would ever be the same. I knew that the refuge I had once taken behind Dana's walls was gone. As she ran down the stairs, screaming obscenities back up at my Dad through her tears, I heard him laughing.

I ran behind her, screaming and begging her not to leave me, but as she got into the car, Dad poked his head out the back door and called out to her to come back into the house. She told him no—that he had gone too far. He laughed again and told her that he was sorry. "I'll let you take Dorthea if you come back in the house and talk to me," he yelled.

She kept sitting in her car. I stood there in between the door and the car, not allowing her to close the door and leave me. "Please go back in and talk with him, Dana. He said he was sorry! If you go back in, I know he will change his mind and let me go with you."

Dana turned to me abruptly and said, "There is nothing in the world that will make me go back into the house with that man. I'm sorry that I can't take you back with me." With that, she got into her car and backed out of the driveway.

I don't know how long I stood their crying before I heard Dad calling my name. When I went into the house, he began to question me. "What happened at Dana's house to make her bring you home?" Before I could answer, he jokingly continued to question me. "What happened? Did she catch you and Marvin fooling around?"

Insulted by his continued accusations, I replied, "Dad, if I had been fooling around with her husband, she wouldn't have wanted me to come back."

"Yeah, maybe or maybe not. I don't know how everybody else thinks she might have liked you messing around with Henry." That must have satisfied his questioning of me, because he told me, "If I ever find out that you were messing with Marvin, I'll kill both you and him.

That night I lay in my bed, replaying the events of the day. I came to the conclusion that it was my fault. Last night, I had gone to bed in Monmouth whispering secrets back and forth with DeLisa, and tonight I lay in my bed waiting for the sound of Dad's footsteps to let me know he had arrived in my bedroom. I had not lasted even two weeks at Dana's house. I blamed myself for everything that had happened. If I had just kept my distance from DeLisa and the twins, I would still be there. I didn't need friends. I needed a place to go where I could be safe, and because I had dared to believe that I could be a kid and relax, I landed myself back at home with no chance of ever going back to Dana's. Who would give me a break now?

* * * * *

Over the next couple of weeks, I pretty much stayed in my room. I slept most of the time. I woke only long enough to clean my room, help my brothers clean the house, and go back to sleep. I guess Dad realized that I needed a female companion, because one day he brought a woman from Columbus, Mississippi, home with him. Her name was Ms. Sammie. He had sent for her to come and help with us. She would sit on the porch and talk to me for hours. She wasn't Dana, but it was nice to have someone to talk to.

My friend Rose came over to see what I was doing and asked if I could come outside and talk to her. I hadn't realized how much I missed hanging out with her. Next to Dana, she was my favorite person to talk to. She came over to tell me that a boy we both knew named Garth said he liked me and wanted me to be his girlfriend. She knew this would make me happy; I had liked him for few months. No one understood why I liked him so much, but for some unexplainable reason, I did.

"He told me to ask you if you'll go with him," she said. I told her to tell him yes.

Now that I was going out with Garth, I would walk down the street every day and meet him in the evenings. I liked him, but we fought a lot because I wouldn't have sex with him. He told me that I was just a little girl and not old enough to be his girlfriend. I would wait until Dad left for Christie's house for the night and then sneak out to the alley to meet Garth. During the day, I would promise him that if he came over at night, I'd give in and let him have sex with me, but every time he showed up, we fought because I didn't want to do it. After about two weeks of us fighting every night, Garth broke up with me, but by the next day, we went out again. After about a week of this, I went over to his house to find him getting ready to go across town. I asked him where he was going, and he told me that he was going to the north side of town where "the girls give it up." He was tired of playing games with me. I promised him that if he came to my house that night, I would give in to him. He walked out the door and left me standing there alone. I watched him get on his bike and ride away with his older brother and cousin. I walked home in tears.

* * * * *

I awoke to the sound of the phone ringing. It was Raven calling to tell me that the Dunns were having a barbecue for the Fourth of July. She wanted me to walk to her apartment so I could go with her. I told her that I didn't want to go, but when she told me that Garth would be there, I gave in and told her that I would try to come. I asked Dad, but he insisted on giving me a ride to Raven's house. When we got there, he said that I could hang out with Raven, but he gave explicit orders not to cross the field and go to the Dunns' house. Raven wanted to go to the barbecue, so I told her to go ahead and that I would walk home.

As I left her apartment complex, Garth, his brother, his cousin, and his friend Benny called out to me. They came to the front of the apartment complex where I was standing. Benny offered Garth and me the use of his sister's apartment to have sex if we wanted to.

When I told Garth no, he said, "Fine. I'm done with you for good." He returned to the party, leaving me standing there.

I walked home in silence, realizing that I'd never have fun if I left it up to Dad. I didn't know why I couldn't go to the Dunns' barbecue. They weren't doing anything wrong. As I entered the alley, I looked back toward the party just as they began to play baseball in the field next to the Dunns' house.

When I arrived home, Sammie was waiting for me on the porch. I sat with her, and we talked until we both fell asleep. When we awoke, Sammie decided to walk uptown and get some soda pop. She asked me if I wanted to join her. I called Dad at Christie's house and asked him if I could go. He said that it was all right.

As Sammie and I walked to the gas station, we passed a house where Garth and his friends sat on the porch. They were hollering at girls as they drove or walked by. Since we were walking on the opposite side of the main strip, they hollered at us too. We laughed and told them we would stop to see them on the way home.

While Sammie and I finished walking to the gas station, she asked me questions about Benny Crowe, the grown man with Garth. She thought he was cute. There wasn't much to tell. He was married, his wife was pregnant, and he lived upstairs in the duplex where they were sitting on the porch.

On the way home, we stayed on the opposite side of the street from Garth and his friends, but when they saw us, Benny hollered out to me that Garth said he loved me. I laughed and kept walking. I asked Sammie if we could go back and talk with them, but she said no.

"That man's married, and I don't want to be sitting at no wife's house when she's not home, and I don't want your daddy to catch us over there," she said.

As we passed the house, Benny called out to us and asked us if we were going to stop, and I told him no. He ran across the intersection and walked alongside me. Sammie remained a comfortable pace in front of us. Benny asked me why I wouldn't sleep with Garth. I told him that I was too young.

"Age is nothing but a number," he replied.

"Well, Garth is mean to me anyway, and I don't want to do it with him or talk to him anymore."

Benny laughed at my answer. Then he asked, "Well, what about me?" When I didn't reply, he said, "I just want to know if I have a chance."

"Why do you want to talk to me?" I asked.

"I just want to talk to you as a friend. You're cute, girl, and I want to get to know you better."

Stopping dead in my tracks from shock, I replied, "You're married and have a baby on the way. What would I look like talking to a grown man?"

"Naw, girl. You don't have to worry about that. My wife is leaving me at the end of the summer. I just want a friend, someone to talk to."

Even though it went against everything I knew to be right, I told him that I didn't mind being his friend, and I told him to call me sometime. By this time, Garth and his other friends had also crossed the intersection and were walking ahead with Sammie. Every now and then, Garth looked back and gave me the evil eye for talking and laughing with Benny. The madder Garth got, the more I enjoyed myself. I really wasn't listening to what Benny was saying. Instead, I was watching and enjoying how uncomfortable Garth seemed.

When we were almost home, Benny decided to turn around with Garth and his friends and head back to his house, but before he left, he asked for my phone number and agreed to call me on Monday at one o'clock.

Sammie and I walked a little farther when two women in a passing car hollered at us. Sammie asked who the women were, and I explained that it was Benny's sister-in-law and wife. Sammie became furious with me, saying that she was going to tell Dad how I had walked down a main street in Kewanee carrying on a conversation with a married man. To keep her from telling on me, I lied to her and told her that Benny did not want to talk to me.

"He wanted to talk to you," I lied. "He was only talking to me because he wanted to know more about you. Besides, I was just talking to him because he was telling me how much Garth really liked me. I gave him our number, and on Monday, he said he'd call to talk to you." That seemed to satisfy her.

For the rest of the weekend, I thought of nothing else but Benny telling me I was pretty and asking if we could be friends. By Monday, I was looking forward to his call. Promptly at 1:00 p.m., the phone rang, and it was him. Sammie watched me from outside on the porch to see what I was doing, so I took the phone into my bedroom and talked to him. Before I knew it, the time was 3:40 p.m., and Dad was pulling into the driveway from work.

After Dad changed his shoes and left for the night, Sammie asked me why I hadn't given her phone if Benny wanted to talk to her. I told her that he had changed his mind and wanted to talk to me. She looked over at me as we both sat on the porch. "I'm warning you, honey. You're playing with fire, and if you don't watch it, you going to get burned, talking on the phone to a married man."

I nervously walked off the porch and down the street to Rose's house. How could I get burned when Benny and I were just friends who enjoyed talking to each other? That was all it was. Why did she have to make it something bad? Benny was my friend.

Over the next couple of weeks, Benny called me faithfully every day at 1:00 p.m., and we talked every day until Dad came home from work. If Dad went straight to his girlfriend's house, then we'd stay on the phone until evening time when Benny would hang up and return home to his wife and children, but not before promising to call the next day at the same time. Before long, the only thing I had to look forward to in my life was my daily conversations with Benny.

I loved talking to Benny. He actually listened to me and asked my opinion about all types of subjects. He never made me feel stupid or said rude things to me. He actually treated me like he wanted my opinion.

Before long, the afternoon time slot wasn't enough time to get in everything that we wanted to say, so he began to call me every morning around 8:00 a.m. We would talk on the phone until Dad came home for lunch, and then we'd resume our conversation at 12:30 p.m. as soon as Dad returned to work. This is how I spent my days until one morning while we were talking, Benny asked me if he could come over and talk with me in person. Even though I was nervous and knew it was dangerous, I couldn't help but be excited at the idea of him coming over to see me. I agreed to let him come over and meet me in my daddy's garage.

After I knew no one was following me, I came out and met him. Before long, when I woke up in the mornings, he was waiting for me in the garage, and that was how I spent both my mornings and afternoons with him. I would sit on the back of Dad's motorcycle while Benny would sit on a pile of wood. We would talk for hours. He told me all about his life, and I told him all about mine, with the exception of Dad's nightly visits to my bedroom. He told me that he already knew the stories of how badly my daddy beat his children. He asked me why our daddy treated us like that. I blamed it on Dad's drinking. Benny said he knew someone else's father who used to get drunk and beat them. He told me that he hated that for me and that I didn't deserve it. He told me that he wished he could run away and take me with him so no one would ever hurt me again. I secretly wished he could do just that.

* * * * *

Summer was coming to an end, and Benny and I confided in each other that we had enjoyed each other's company more than we expected. We didn't know what we were going to do when I had to return to school and could no longer spend my days with him. One day, as we were laughing and telling each other how much we would miss each other when school resumed, he asked me if he could kiss me. The next thing I knew, his lips were on mine. First, he just placed his lips on mine for what seemed like a second. Just as quickly as it started, it was over, and he was looking into my eyes. Because I didn't say anything, he asked me if I was all right. Honestly, I did not know if I was all right. I couldn't stop the tingling in my stomach, and I was too ashamed to ask him why it happened when he kissed me. I just smiled at him.

Over the next couple of days, that's how we spent our time together—talking and making out. We tried to get as much time together as possible before I had to return to school.

One morning, I went outside to meet Benny, and he wasn't there. I waited for a while and looked up and down the alley, expecting to see him. After thirty minutes, I went back into the house and waited for him to call me, but the phone never rang. I waited all day, but he never showed up or called. I was sad all day, wondering where he could possibly be.

The next morning, he called and explained that his wife had decided that she wasn't leaving him. His wife concluded that since he disappeared every day and was no longer begging her to stay, he must be seeing someone else. She decided that she wasn't sure she wanted to walk away from her husband anymore. He explained that every time he tried to leave the house, she wanted to come with him or follow him. I asked him if that meant that he wouldn't be my friend anymore.

"No way," he said. "I don't care if she's staying or not. I ain't giving you up for nobody or nothing. You're my girlfriend, and I'll never leave you."

Before I could respond to him calling me his girlfriend, he told me he would try to call me tomorrow or come by for a few minutes, then hung up the phone. Long after I hung up the phone, I stood there looking at it—savoring the memory of him calling me his girlfriend and telling me that he would never leave me. No one had ever made such a strong declaration concerning me.

Before the end of the week, he was back to calling me on our old schedule. He didn't come over, but we still spoke on the phone. He told me that he missed my kisses, and he wanted to touch my breasts the next time he saw me. I was shocked when I heard him say that. How could I tell him that no one had ever touched my breasts but my daddy, and that I didn't like it?

I told him that I didn't feel well and hung up the phone before he could say anything else. He called back later, but I wouldn't answer, and each time my brothers answered the phone, they complained that someone just kept calling and hanging up the phone. I knew it was him, and I knew he wanted to know why I wouldn't talk to him, but I just didn't know what to do. I did not take his calls that afternoon when he called either.

I decided to walk down the street to the apartment complex and see what Raven was doing. As I walked past Benny's sister's apartment, I saw him come running toward the door. He asked me what went wrong, but I just waved at him and kept walking to my friend's house.

After I left Raven's house and began walking home, Benny reappeared at his sister's apartment door and asked me to come talk to him, just for a moment. When he saw that I was going to ignore him, he called out to me to please come talk to him again.

"I need you," he yelled.

No one had ever said those words to me before. When I turned and saw the sadness in his face, I was torn. I wanted to see him so badly. I hadn't seen him in a week and missed him. Before I knew what I was doing, I ran into his sister's apartment. I knew it was risky, but I couldn't help myself. I was drawn to him. Finally, someone cared for me.

Once inside, behind closed doors, Benny asked me why I was avoiding him. How could I tell him that the thought of someone touching my breasts grossed me out? When I didn't answer, he reminded me of the last conversation we had before I stopped speaking to him. He wanted to know if that had anything to do with me avoiding him. He told me that sometimes he forgot that I was only thirteen years old and apologized for rushing me. He reassured me that he would never make me do anything I was uncomfortable doing. He said that he just got carried away because he wanted to make love to me so badly. He told me that even though I was only thirteen and he was twenty-seven, he loved me, and that I understood him more than any woman ever had in his whole life.

When he began to kiss me and push me down on his sister's couch, I let him undo my shirt. I let him lift my bra, and then I let him cup my breasts in his hands. I don't know why I let him, but I felt secure as he whispered how much he loved me and reassured me that I could trust him. He promised that he would never leave me and that I would always be able to count on him, and I believed him.

I let him unbutton my pants. I let him caress my stomach, but when he began to slide my shorts and panties down, I panicked and grabbed his hands. I sat up and began to put my clothes back on. He asked me if he had done something wrong. I looked into his eyes as he tried to get me to lie back down, promising me that he wouldn't hurt me, but I wouldn't let him push me back down onto the couch. I told him I had to go home.

As I tried to button my clothes, he took my hands and said, "Do you love me too?"

Reluctantly I answered his question. I tried to look away when I answered his question, careful to avoid his questioning eyes, mostly because I was ashamed to admit it out loud to him or anyone else. "Yes, I love you."

Pulling me down toward him and placing me on the couch next to him, he began to unbutton my blouse again. "Don't you want to make me feel good and make love to me?"

Again looking away from him and answering him almost in a whisper, I said, "I don't know how."

Rubbing my back softly and slightly pressing my body backward until I was almost lying beneath him, he said, "Baby, I will teach you." Kissing me on the forehead lightly, he reassured me, "There is nothing that we could do wrong to each other's body because we love each other." I still fought the pressure of his weight trying to push me down, so he continued to try to persuade me to relax. "Do I make you happy?" he asked. When I nodded yes, he continued to gently press me backward. I noticed that he was no longer sitting beside me and had somehow maneuvered himself so that he was sitting between my legs. "Don't you want to make me happy?"

I *did* want to make him happy. How could I tell him that I was scared that if I let him touch me down there that somehow my daddy would be able to tell? More scared of what I might do than of what he was doing to me, I pushed him off me abruptly and stood up to go. Startled by my reaction, he quickly reached out to me and took my hand. "Please stay with me," he said. "I don't want you to leave me yet. I promise we won't take our clothes off again. I just need you to be with me a little longer."

Touched by Benny's display of affection, I sat back down on the couch with him, and we just sat there holding each other. "I am sorry for falling in love with you. I know I have no right to be in your life. I know that everything I feel for you is all kinds of wrong. I know the things I want to do to you, the things I want you to do to me. Heck, the things I want us to do to each other are wrong, but I need someone like you to love me and that I can love. I know you are too young for me, but I've waited a long time for someone like you to come into my life."

I felt so intoxicated by his words that I didn't say anything. Never had someone told me they loved me this much. I didn't want to be anywhere else but in his arms, so I just sat there and let him hold me. I felt so good, but at the same time, I felt bad that I couldn't give him what he wanted. So many before him had used my body for their selfish pleasure, but the one person who asked me politely, I wasn't able to give him what he wanted.

I started home just as it began to turn dark outside. I didn't know what to do or where this was going, but I knew that I finally had someone in my life who loved me.

* * * * *

That night, I heard Dad's footsteps coming into my room. I didn't argue or try to fight. I just thought of the conversation between Benny and me. I replayed every kiss, every word, and every promise, and before I knew it, Dad had finished and was leaving my room. I realized that Dad could not hurt me anymore. I did not care what he did to my body. All I had to do was think about Benny, and I went to a different place. I was no longer in that bed in the dark on Denton Avenue—I was with Benny, and he was telling me how much he needed me and loved me.

The next morning after Dad went to work, there was a knock on the back door. It was Benny. He told me that he didn't care if he was caught. He had to see me. He told me that he hadn't even slept the night before because all he could think about was kissing me. He told me how his wife had yelled at him and accused him of having another woman, but he didn't care anymore. He told me that he just sat there the whole time smiling at her because he knew in the morning, he'd be seeing me. I told him I had to take a bath and that I would meet him in the garage.

As soon as I entered the garage, he kissed me and squeezed me tight. He told me that he had heard a new song last night that made him think of me. I asked what it was, and he told me it was called "Some Guys Have All the Luck" by Rod Stewart. When I told him I had never heard the song before, he sang it to me. Just as I thought my life couldn't get any better, a man was actually singing a song about loving me. *Me, Dorthea—Dorthea that no one cared about.*

As he finished singing the song, David strolled into the garage. He stood there looking at us. I stepped back from Benny and kept right on talking to him as if it were no big deal that this twenty-seven-year-old married man was standing in the back of our garage with his arm around my waist, singing to me.

Benny looked at me and whispered in my ear, "What should I do?" I told him to just keep right on talking to me. I told him David wouldn't tell on me because he didn't want me to tell things on him. When David heard what I told Benny, he smiled at Benny and picked up a basketball that lay on the floor. He bounced it on the floor a few times while he locked eyes with Benny, and then he turned and threw the ball into the wall so hard that it burst. It sounded like a gun went off.

Jake came running into the garage to see what had happened and saw David, Benny, and me standing in the garage. Benny and I were looking at David in shock while David just smiled at Benny. Jake didn't hesitate to let me know that he wasn't stupid and he knew what was going on. He said that he wouldn't tell on me, not because he liked what I was doing, but because he figured Dad would kill me if he knew. They both told me they wouldn't tell, but they made me promise that if I got caught, I wouldn't tell anyone that they knew what I was doing. They ignored Benny and spoke directly to me.

After they both walked out of the garage, Benny turned to me and asked, "Is your brother David soft, touched in the head, or just plain crazy?"

I looked at him for a moment, and then we both just laughed.

On a more serious note, Benny's voice grew soft so that no one could hear his question to me. "What is it that David doesn't want you to tell on him?"

I laughed and jokingly replied, "If I tell you, it won't be a secret."

Oh, how I wanted to open my mouth and tell him my secrets. I wanted to tell him about David, Earl, and Dad. I had already told him everything about me except for that, but I did not want him to think I was dirty or unworthy of his love.

Now that both my brothers and Sammie knew my secret, they talked about how Dad was going to kill Benny if he ever found out. Sammie said I should be ashamed of myself if anything happened to that man because he had a pregnant wife and three small children at home. When I told Benny what they were saying, he told me they were just jealous of our love and told me to ignore them. I was scared for him. I didn't want anything to happen to him. I loved him, and his only crime was falling in love with me. I didn't think he should be punished for that. Someone needed to love me.

* * * * *

One morning, Benny asked me if he could come into our house and use the restroom. Since everyone at home knew about our secret relationship, I brought him into the house, but before I took him back outside, I showed him my bedroom. He walked in and sat on the bed, pulling me on top of him. We began to kiss and make out when we heard a noise. It was Sammie.

Clearing her throat, she said, "This is where I have to draw the line. You know your daddy is crazy, even if Benny don't, and if your daddy walked in and found you with this man, he'd kill him and me too for knowing about this mess. Benny, you get out of the house right now. I don't care if you want to lose your life, but as long as I'm in this house, you are not allowed back in. When Ace finds out, and the way you two are carrying on he will, I want to be able to deny knowing anything about this mess."

Once back in the garage, I asked Benny if he was going to leave me alone since he now knew from an adult how crazy my daddy was and what would happen if Dad ever caught him. He told me that he'd never leave me, and Sammie had just proved how much I needed him.

I knew we should stop seeing each other that day, but I couldn't stop myself. I needed him, and he obviously needed me. I needed to hold on to our moments for when my father came to me at night. Benny came to me Monday through Friday. I hated the weekends because we couldn't talk. We never knew exactly when Dad would be home, so Benny never called me on the weekends.

* * * * *

One weekend while I was at home with Sammie, Dad came home and told me to get in the truck because he was taking me to the park to play baseball with the Crowe family—Benny's family. I didn't want to go, but I agreed. Dad stayed in his truck and flirted with Benny's older sister and drank with the men who didn't play. Benny's wife and all the women sat on a bench and waited their turns. I sat quietly on the bench, watching Benny play in the outfield. I had butterflies in my stomach just being that close to him. Benny's older brother, Charlie, began to tease me because I wouldn't play ball with them, so Dad, being competitive, made me get up and play with them. I didn't want to play, so each time the ball was pitched to me, I just let it go by without hitting it. When I had two strikes, Dad couldn't take everyone laughing at me any longer. He ran up to the plate and told me in front of everyone that if I didn't hit the ball, he was going to take me home and beat me. Everyone stopped laughing and talking and waited to see what I was going to do.

When the ball came, I swung and missed. Dad called out to me to come get in the truck, but Charlie told Dad it was a foul ball and not my fault that I had missed. He ran in and switched places with his daughter, Tina, who was pitching. Everyone knew the stories about how bad Dad's temper could be toward his children. They knew he meant business, so this time, when Charlie pitched the ball, he threw it right to me. I swung, and the ball flew to right field, right where Benny was playing. He didn't catch it. While I stood watching to see if he would catch the ball, Dad yelled at me to run.

"You better not get out," he screamed. I started running. Benny had the ball and ran toward me. The other players were hollering for him to throw the ball so someone could tag me out, but he decided to run it in instead.

As I ran from base to base, my mind was reeling. Surely Benny had heard what Dad said and wouldn't tag me out. On the other hand, his wife and kids were right there. How could he not get me out without risking speculation? I was running toward third, and as I looked back, Benny was gaining on me. I panicked and ran faster. Just as he reached out to tag me, he tripped, and everyone yelled for me to continue running home. When I reached home plate, everyone was jumping and laughing—everyone except Dolly, Benny's wife. She just stared at me for a long time.

* * * * *

Summer ended, and school was scheduled to begin on Monday of the following week. Benny and I knew that we wouldn't be able to see each other as much and didn't know what either of us was going to do. "Benny, we have an open campus. I can leave for lunch, so if you wanted to come get me every day for lunch, you could."

"I wish I could, but I don't have the money to come take you to lunch every day."

"You don't have to bring me lunch—just come see me. I don't care what we do as long as we are together."

"I wish I had a job so I could take care of you. If I had a job, I would take you and run away from Kewanee."

I continued to rest in his arms, listening to him while he talked, but all I really heard was that if he had a job, he would run away and take me with him. I liked the idea of running away and never returning—never having Dad come into my bedroom and mess with me again. I stopped daydreaming and turned around and looked into his eyes and asked him point-blank, "Do you really mean it—if you had a job, would you really take me away from here?"

Taking the time to kiss me long and tenderly, he replied, "Yes!"

"My daddy has a good connection at the factory where he works and can get just about anyone hired."

Later that evening, when Dad came home from work, I told him about his friend Charlie's little brother wanting a job at the factory where he worked. I told him how I had told Charlie and Benny that he could get anyone a job that he wanted to. I told him that Benny didn't believe me because his older brother, Charlie, had been trying to get him hired on at the Boiler Shop for four years and wasn't even able to get him an interview. I knew Dad liked to boast about what he could do that no one else could. It worked. That evening, Dad and I rode over to Charlie's house, and Dad told Benny to meet him at his house at noon tomorrow because he was going to get him a job. Dad told Benny that the only thing he wanted from him for getting him a job was a box of cigars.

That night, when Dad came to my room and entered my bed, I tried to argue and stop him. I just wanted one night of peace.

"Why do you have to bother me all the time, Dad?" I asked. When he didn't reply, I asked, "Why can't you just go bother your girlfriend?"

With an eerie smile, he replied, "She's on her monthly, and if you don't let me do what I want, I ain't gonna get Charlie's brother a job."

I lay there in the darkness and began to panic. If Benny didn't get a job, how would he be able to take me away? When I didn't say anything, Dad said, "Well, maybe I shouldn't help him anyway. His own brother couldn't even help him."

I just lay there trying to figure out what to do, but I couldn't think of anything. I didn't want Dad to think I cared if Benny got a job or not. "What does helping Benny have to do with me?" I asked.

"Well, if I don't get him a job, then everyone will think you're a liar and be mad at you."

I thought about what it would mean to me if Benny didn't get the job. Benny wouldn't be able to take me away. Benny would be so disappointed if he didn't get the job. I gave in, but this time Dad wanted more than just fondling me while he masturbated. He wanted to ask me questions, dirty questions. He had never asked me questions before. He had always allowed me to pretend I was sleep. I tried to ignore his questions by blocking out his voice. I needed to pretend I was in the back of the garage and that Benny and I were making plans to run away. When he was finished, he left, and I was able to go to sleep, knowing that it wouldn't be long before Benny and I would leave this place.

* * * * *

The next morning, Benny arrived at my house early. I let him come into the house, and he sat in the living room watching television while I took a bath and got dressed. My brothers and Sammie woke up and saw him and complained about me bringing him in the house again. I explained to them that Dad had told him to come over and to be there for lunch. They all complained because it was only 9:00 a.m., and it was a long time away from lunch. Even though I didn't show it, I was nervous, so I called Dad at work and told him that Benny was already there and asked what to do with him.

"I told that dummy lunchtime," Dad said. "Tell him to just sit there and wait on me till noon," he replied.

Reassured that I wouldn't get in trouble if Dad found out Benny was in the house, Benny and I made Dad's lunch together while laughing and planning for the day when we would leave Kewanee together. The food was so delicious that Dad forgot to be angry with Benny for coming to his home early. Benny explained that before moving to Kewanee three years ago, he had been the head cook at a fancy restaurant in Bowling Green, Kentucky. Dad quickly ate his lunch, gave Benny an application to fill out, gave him instructions on what to say at his interview that afternoon, told me to help Benny, and returned to work.

Benny's interview wasn't until 2:00 p.m., so we sat in the yard at the picnic table and talked. It felt so good to sit in the open with Benny. The time flew by quickly, and Benny left for his interview, promising to come back to tell me the outcome. I kissed him for luck before he left and went into the house to wait for his return. Around 2:45 p.m., Benny returned to tell me that he got the job and was supposed to start on Monday. We were both excited at what this job meant for us.

There was only one glitch. Benny didn't have any steel-toed boots. I told him to ask Dad if he could borrow the money to buy some. He really didn't want to ask Dad for anything else and told me that he was sure he could borrow the money from his brother, but then he realized that if he borrowed the money from my daddy, that gave him an additional excuse to hang around our house. After all, he had to wait for my daddy to get home at 3:30 p.m.

When Dad arrived home, he pulled the truck right into the yard where Benny and I were sitting at the picnic table. He wanted to know how he could "be of service" to Benny. From the look on his face, I could tell that he didn't like seeing Benny still sitting at our house, so I spoke for Benny. I told him that I had been sitting outside in the yard when Benny was walking past our house.

"He stopped by to tell me he had gotten the job," I said, "but he said that he needed steel-toed boots. I told him that you might let him borrow the money if he paid you back."

After hearing my explanation, Dad seemed to relax. "Okay, go into the house and call Kmart. Find out how much them boots cost," he said.

I hurried into the house because I didn't want to leave Benny outside long with my daddy. From the window, I watched them talk to each other while I made the phone call and gathered the information. Dad had me write Benny a check for the exact amount of the boots, telling Benny that he would have to figure out how to pay the tax himself. Benny thanked Dad and quickly left.

The next morning, I awoke to Benny standing outside my window. He wanted me to come outside. I told him that I had to get a bath first. He jokingly asked me if he could come in and get in the bath with me. Then he left, saying he was walking down the street to his sister's apartment. He would be back in twenty minutes, and he wanted me to be in the garage when he came back. I didn't know what he wanted to talk about, but from the tone of his voice, I knew it was serious.

When Benny came back, he asked me if I had told anyone about us because his wife was asking him all sorts of questions about me last night. She told him that if she caught me with him, she was going to beat my butt. Sensing that I was scared, Benny reassured me that he'd never let her hurt me. While we were making out, he unzipped his pants and placed my hands on his privates. Even though it scared me, I didn't pull away. In my mind, I just kept telling myself that he wasn't my daddy and that this was normal.

It had to be normal, or Benny wouldn't be doing it. He loved me more than anyone else in the world.

When I began to relax, he reached down and maneuvered my hand to massage his privates. I continued to tell myself this was different from when Dad made me do this to him. This was real. Benny and I loved each other. What Dad made me do to him wasn't real—it was a nightmare. Benny began to kiss me harder and pull me closer. Then, just as suddenly as he had placed my hand on his privates, he reached down and told me to stop. He asked me when I was going to allow him to make love to me. I told him that I wasn't sure, but I knew that it would be soon. He asked if I wanted him as badly as he wanted me. I didn't know what to say. I didn't know what I was supposed to say. I was still scared that if I let him, Dad would somehow find out and kill us.

I don't know why I did what I did next, but it sounded good at the time. I asked him when his birthday was, and he told me it was in October, on the twelfth. After I nervously told him that my sister's birthday was the same day, I told him that we would do it on that day. Since it was only the third week in August, that gave me plenty of time to figure out something by then. Besides, this way, Benny wouldn't ask me again until closer to his birthday.

After hearing a date from me, Benny relaxed and we kissed a little bit more, but mostly we talked. We talked about how much we'd miss each other when we couldn't see each other while I was in school and he was at work. We talked about how hard it would be because Dad allowed me to go to only a handful of spots, none of which were places where Benny could come to see me. We talked about how much money he would be making and about how long it would take him to save to move me away from here. We were both excited about sharing a future together.

We spent as much time together as possible that week. Benny found excuses to come back at night and hang out with Dad. Dad liked to take wood that people discarded as trash and make lawn furniture or ornaments, so when Benny started work on Monday, he came home with Dad and offered to help him make furniture. Dad wasn't one to turn down free labor and easily accepted his help. By the end of the first week, it was a routine for all of us.

The next week, Benny received his first paycheck. He told me that he wanted to do something nice for me, but I told him no. It had been so long since he was able to do something nice for his children, so I told him to do something for them. He told me that he wanted to do something nice for my daddy too, so I told him to buy him some liquor.

Saturday morning came and went with no sign of Benny. I was worried all afternoon. That evening at 5:00 p.m., Benny pulled into the driveway in his Lincoln, wearing a new outfit and smelling nice. He brought Dad some cigars, the money he had borrowed from him, and a bottle of E & J brandy with Pepsi. Dad was impressed. They drank together, talking about life for a while, until Dad got a phone call from one of his relatives. Dad got up and left the room, but he told Benny to stay, drink, and talk to me until he returned.

As soon as my daddy was out of hearing range, Benny lunged at me, kissing me. "Dorthea, I think I drank too much. I am not used to drinking hard liquor. All I ever drink is a few beers and I get buzzed. I think this liquor is going straight to my head."

Once Dad finished his conversation on the phone, he moved the conversation into the living room, where he could sit and relax while he reminisced about the days of being married to my mother. The more they talked, the more they drank. Eventually, Benny's words began to slur and Dad decided to go to Christie's house. At that point, Benny had passed out on the couch. Surprisingly, Dad told me to let him spend the night. He told me to cover him up with a blanket, and then he left to go to Christie's house. After Dad left, I curled up on the couch next to Benny and watched television.

When my brothers arrived home, they wanted to know what Benny was doing asleep on our couch and where Dad was. I explained that Dad said Benny could spend the night, and they quickly retreated to their rooms, saying that this was going too far and that they didn't want anything to do with it. Sammie arrived home and asked the same question. When I explained what had happened, she angrily shouted, "When your daddy finds out what's been happening in his house—and he *will* find out because nothing done in the dark stays in the dark—then he's going to want to kill everyone who knew because they made a fool outta him. I ain't having no part of it, you hear me?"

She screamed so loudly that she woke Benny. After seeing that he was awake, she yelled at him too. "I'm going to bed, but boy, you better get out of this house. I swear to God, I ain't being a part of this. If you want to get yo' ass killed, then that's fine, but don't you get me involved in it."

Instead of him leaving, we sat up and talked most of the night. I went to my room alone around 4:00 a.m. only to be awakened at 8:00 a.m. by Benny. He stayed around for another couple of hours before he left. I was so happy. I hated to see him go home, but I knew he would be back after work on Monday.

* * * * *

The next week went by quickly. Benny and I stole moments together and talked as often as we could. It wasn't enough. We both missed the hours of talking and making out that we had shared all summer long. On days that Dad didn't want to work on his crafts, he would drop Benny off at his sister's house and go across town to his girlfriend's house. As soon as Benny and I knew that Dad had arrived at Christie's house, Benny would backtrack to the house so we could spend time together. On these occasions, I would call Christie's house every so often to make sure Dad was still there. This is pretty much how things continued until the first week of October.

One evening, after Dad left the house to spend time with Christie, Benny came over. As we sat outside talking in the garage, we heard a car come down the alley behind our garage. Shocked, we looked at each other with an unspoken question on our faces, wondering who could be coming down the alley. We stopped talking and listened to see if the driver was just a passerby. We both nearly jumped out of our skins when we heard the car engine turn off.

Someone got out of the car and knocked on the back door. My heart stopped as we heard a familiar voice call both of our names and continue to knock. It was Mandy, my neighbor. She lived at the end of the block at the entrance of the alley. We tried to ignore her, but she said that she had watched Benny enter the alley and knew he was in the garage with me. I opened the door to hear what she had to say. She nervously began to speak, "My boyfriend, Larry, and I been watching ya'll over the past few weeks. Larry said he is going to tell Mr. Hughes, or better yet, he had a right mind to catch you leaving and beat your tail until you tell Ace yourself. Everybody knows how Mr. Hughes beats you kids something awful, and I don't want to see nobody get hurt."

We thanked her for warning us. Relieved that she understood our dilemma, we ventured outside of the garage and carelessly began to have a relaxed conversation with her while standing outside by her car. While we stood together wrapped in each other's arms, Benny made a confession: "I love Dorthea, and I will deal with the outcome no matter what it is."

We were still talking when we heard a noise behind us. Benny and I turned around to see Dad standing there with a board in his hand. He looked threateningly at all of us, and then just as quickly as we had noticed him, he dropped the board, turned around, and walked into the house.

We all just stood in shock, wondering what to do. Mandy gasped before she spoke. "Should I go call the police? Mr. Hughes is crazy, and I'm scared for both of ya'll!"

Benny stood there quietly looking at me, while I looked at him hoping no one could hear my heart beating. I knew all too well how crazy my daddy could behave. I took a deep breath before I replied, trying not to sound as nervous as I truly was inside.

"No," I said. "If you call the police, then Benny will go to jail for being my boyfriend. I don't want that."

"Well," Benny said, "do you want me to go talk to your daddy?"

"No. You definitely don't need to talk to him right now. Just go home. I'll call your sister and let you know what happened."

I watched as Benny got into the car with Mandy and drove away before I entered the house. I half expected Dad to be heading back outside with his gun, but what I found instead shocked me. Dad was calmly watching television, and when I tried to talk about it, he said, "Not now. I don't want to talk about it until I get back from taking Sammie to work. Just go to your room and wait until I get home, but don't tell anyone about this until we talk."

I went to my room and lay in my bed. I lay staring at the wall, curled up in a ball and glancing at the door every few seconds, wondering why he hadn't entered my room yet. I wondered why I didn't hear him yelling. I wondered why he wasn't beating me. I wondered why he wasn't shouting and getting his gun. The wondering and waiting for what was to come next must have affected me physically because my stomach began to hurt. I ran to the restroom and emptied my bowels. I didn't know why, but I had a severe case of diarrhea. I almost did not make it. After I washed the sweat off my face, I exited the restroom only to run into Sammie. I must have not looked too good because she followed me to my room and watched me curl back into a ball on my bed before she spoke. "Dorthea, come help bring the clothes in off the clothesline before I leave for work." I must have looked worried because she asked me, "What is wrong with you?"

"Dad caught me outside with Benny, and he had his arms wrapped around me."

She didn't have a sympathetic ear at all. She began to give me a tongue-lashing like never before. "What did you think would happen, the way you been carrying on with this married man twice your age? Because of you, a nice man is going to have to leave his kids and go to jail. Then it's gonna be all your fault, and everybody's gonna blame you. And they should, because you ain't got no business being so fast."

Waiting for an opportunity in between her words, I asked, "What if I run away? Will Benny still get in trouble?" Tears threatened to fall from my eyes.

"Why in the world would you run away, child?"

"Because I wouldn't get a whipping, and Benny couldn't get in trouble if I'm not here for the police to question," I replied.

"Naw, girl. That would only make things worse for Benny. You just thinking about yourself. You a spoiled, selfish little brat, and you don't want to face up to the consequences. You gonna get what you deserve, but I hope Benny don't get in no trouble. If I had it my way, he wouldn't get in no trouble just because of yo' fast ass."

At those words, the tears began to flow, and I sobbed loudly. "What you crying for, girl? You knew what you was doing was wrong!" Sammie railed. She abruptly turned and walked away from me.

I looked down the road and thought about running away, but where could I go? I stood there alone by the clothesline, looked up to the sky, and prayed. I didn't care what happened to me, but I didn't want to see Benny punished for caring about me. He didn't deserve to be in prison or dead for being the only one in this world who cared for me.

As Dad was about to leave with Sammie, he called out to me, "Go back into the house while I take Sammie to work. I'll be right back. You better not leave." I walked back into the house and ran to the window to make sure he was gone. When I knew he was gone, I called Benny's sister so she could let him know what had happened so far.

"I'm glad you called, Dorthea. Benny is extremely upset and is refusing to go home until he knows what is going to happen."

He snatched the phone from her before I could respond. "I can't believe that you are calling. I been worried about you. I can't believe he hasn't beaten you or come gunning for me yet." We talked on the phone until I heard Dad's truck pull into the driveway.

As soon as Dad entered the kitchen, he called for me to follow him as he walked to my bedroom. He instructed me to sit on the bed. As I sat down on the bed, he reached in his pocket, pulled out his pistol, and placed it on my dresser top. In an eerily calm voice, he said, "Tell me everything that you have done with Benny. I want all the details. I want to know how long this has been going on, and I want to know if you've been having sex with him."

I answered his questions as best as I could without pointing any blame. He said nothing for a few minutes. Then he sighed and said, "Why Benny?"

"I've tried to have boyfriends, but you always told my brothers to beat up any boy that showed interest in me. You even beat up a boy that liked me, and you threatened to kill that boy who called me on the phone."

"So? That ain't answering my question. Why Benny?"

"Well, all the other boys just wanted to have sex with me, but Benny wanted to talk to me."

"That's bull. All boys want to have sex. I don't believe that ya'll ain't having sex. I'm going to take you to Dr. Jacobi's office. He can look at you and tell me if you're telling the truth."

"You can take me to the doctor. He'll tell you the same thing."

Again, he paused, and I held my breath. "Do you believe that Benny cares about you?" he finally asked.

"Yes," I said, my voice almost a whisper.

"If he cares so much about you, then why did he leave?" he asked.

Tears again streamed down my face. "I love him, Dad. I sent him home so you wouldn't kill him."

Dad looked at me for a long time before he laughed. "You love him, huh? How much do you love him?"

"I love him more than life," I cried.

"Fine. If you love him that much, then prove it."

"How can I prove it?"

"If you love Benny, then you'll let me put it in, and you know what I mean." Seeing the questions on my face, he continued. "I hold all the keys in this situation. If you don't let me put it in, then I'll have to kill Benny. The only way you can really prove to me that you're not lying—that you and Benny haven't really had sex—is to let me put it in."

Stammering, trying to think of a way out of this, I meekly said, "If you kill Benny, you'll go to jail."

"Naw. Mandy was a witness to your relationship, so I can kill him for messing with my child."

"Well, if you kill Benny, then I'm going to tell what you been doing to me, and you'll go to jail for that, "I said defiantly.

He laughed aloud. "Nobody gonna believe you. They'd just think you're saying that to get me in trouble because I killed your boyfriend. You told on me before, didn't you? What did people think then? They thought you were making it up to cover up for running up my phone bill. Everybody'll just think you're bringing up an old lie to cover up something else you've been doing—sleeping with a married man."

"Just give me a whipping, and I'll leave Benny alone. I won't talk to him again."

"Naw, it's too late for that. I need to know if Benny's been sleeping with you."

"I thought you could take me to the doctor. I promise he hasn't touched me," I wailed through tears.

"I ain't taking you to a doctor. You already shaming my name enough by messing with a married man without me taking you to a doctor who can tell everybody in town. It's a shame that Benny is going to lose his life because of you. I'm going to have to kill him."

"But you're friends with Benny. How can you kill a friend?"

"I ain't got no friends. My only friend is my momma," he said with a laugh.

"Please, Dad. Don't kill him. What will everybody think? You said you don't want everybody knowing about it."

"I don't want everyone to know about it, but you ain't leaving me no choice. When I kill Benny, his wife's gonna find out about him, and she's going to beat you up. Then, I'll have to put her in jail, and Dolly's kids will have to go to the bad kids' home. Everybody in town's gonna know how nasty you are, and they're gonna blame you for those children not having any parents. You know you ain't got no business messing with a married man."

"How are you going to kill Benny? He ain't going to get close to you. He knows how you are."

"That's easy. I'll make you call him and tell him to come over here."

"I won't do it."

"Oh yes you will. You'll do what I say, or else."

I wanted to be brave and tell him to just shoot me, but I was scared to die. "Dad, Benny has a family too. If you shoot Benny, then Charlie might shoot you."

Again, he laughed. "You think I'm scared about dying? I don't care if I die. I'm tired of paying bills anyway. Don't forget, yo' momma don't want you, and if I die, then you and your brothers will go into foster care. You know what they do to little boys and girls in there. Do you want that to happen to your brothers? Your brothers are going to get raped in there, and they're going to hate you too for what happened to them."

I didn't know what to do. Frustrated with the entire situation, I began to cry as I remembered the time when Andre and Dad had argued. Dad had grabbed his gun and chased Andre out of the house, shooting at him. I remembered all the times Dad had pulled guns on people and shot at them. I knew that he really would kill Benny. I didn't want to be blamed for Benny dying. I thought of Benny's children. I thought of my brothers. I thought of Benny's family and how they would feel. Surely, they'd hate me and resent me if anything happened to him. I again pleaded with Dad. "Please, just beat me or send me away, but don't make me let you put it in! I don't want to."

"That's your choice. Either you let me put it in, or I kill him."

I knew that was something that would change my life forever. If I let him do that, it would be like I was my daddy's girlfriend. I couldn't let this happen. I looked past Dad at the entrance to my bedroom. Not more than two feet from that entrance was the back door. I could probably make it past him, but could I make it out the door before he shot me? I didn't know what to do. If by chance I did get away, where would I go? No one wanted to deal with my daddy. No one would let me stay with them.

I sat there quietly for a moment and did the only thing I could do. I gave in to his demands. I began telling myself that it wouldn't be so bad. *I've already lived through all the other things he's done. I'll just pretend that it's someone else. I'll pretend that it's Benny. I'll pretend that I'm dreaming.*

"Okay," I finally said.

When I said okay, his whole demeanor changed. He quickly undid his pants. "Get on the bed and lay down," he said.

I had to think fast. "Wait a minute. This is going to be my first time. I don't want the first time to be with you. This is something that I'll never forget. Girls are going to ask me who my first was, and I won't be able to tell them the truth. I need the first time to be with someone else."

"No one else is going to touch you and live," he said.

"Then I'm not doing it," I yelled.

"Okay, okay. You can do it with someone else later, but I'm going to do it first, and we're going to do it right now."

"No," I yelled as he pushed me onto the bed and tried to force my legs apart.

I kept kicking and fighting him until he finally stopped. "You're making this too difficult. I can't even enjoy it. What about Benny?" I tried to remain calm as Dad surprised me and said, "Not only will I let Benny be your first, but I won't hurt him or put him in jail, but then, you've got to stop fighting me. After this, I get to put it in any time I want to without fighting with you."

I didn't know what to do, but it bought me some more time to figure things out, so I agreed.

"Now, if you're going to be with Benny, then you're going to have to use condoms so you won't get pregnant. I'll buy you some condoms, and I'll go over to Christie's house on Friday so you can be with Benny. You can do it then."

I didn't know what I was going to do after that, but at least I had four days to figure it out. "What do I tell Benny?" I asked.

"Leave that to me. I'll take care of it." He buttoned his pants and left my room.

Later, he came back into my room, and I let him touch me. I didn't want to make him mad, so I lay there without fighting him. Luckily, he stuck to our agreement and didn't ask about sex.

The next day, I went to school as usual, but all day I replayed the scene between Dad and me. I tried to figure out how I had ended up agreeing to have sex with him. If only I hadn't stayed outside talking with Mandy and Benny for so long. If I had called Christie's house like I usually did, he wouldn't have caught us and I wouldn't be in this mess right now. At the end of the school day, I went home. Sammie was waiting for me when I got in the house. She wanted to know what happened. I told her that nothing happened.

We sat on the porch, and I tried to avoid her intrusive questions. When Dad got home from work, Sammie and I were both surprised that Benny was with him. Dad went straight to the garage and told Benny to follow him. After a short while, he came into the house and told me to come outside to hold the light for him and Benny while they worked. Sammie began to follow me outside, but Dad rudely told her to stay in the house.

"You ain't never wanted to come outside and watch me work before. Why you want to come now?" he growled. She turned around as if her feelings were hurt, but went back into the house.

Benny and I nervously helped Dad work on his crafts in silence. Dad was silent until after the work was completed for the night. Then, he looked at Benny and said, "I'm going to ask you some questions, son, and you better be honest with me. I'll know if you're lying. First off, I want to know how long you been talking to my daughter. Second, I want to know if you've had sex with her, and I want to know what you plan to do with your wife."

"S-sir," Benny stuttered, "we been talking for a little over three months, but we ain't ever had sex. I love her, sir. I ain't ever loved anyone like I love her. Dolly was supposed to leave me, but she changed her mind, but I ain't got no problem leaving her. I, uh, I love your daughter. I'd like to make *her* my wife."

Dad sat with his head down for a long time before he replied to Benny. In a calm voice, he said, "You were man enough to come to my house tonight, even though you didn't know what I had in store for you, so I believe you. I believe that you love her. I'm gonna let you see her as long as you don't try to take her and run off." He paused a minute before raising his voice. "There will be *no* marriage, though. She's gotta finish school. If you try to run off or marry her, then I'll put you in jail for a long time."

Before Benny could respond, Dad spoke again. "This is my daughter, and I have to protect her. The only way I can do that is if she's here with me. If you run off somewhere with her, I can't protect her from Dolly. I'm going to let you carry on with my daughter, but you are not to leave your wife."

Benny and I both began to protest, but Dad put up his hand. "I have my reasons," he said. "Take it or leave it. Can you live with those arrangements?"

Benny looked over at me and smiled before saying yes.

"Okay then," Dad said. "Don't leave. I'll take you home." Then Dad went into the house.

We thought he was going to the bathroom, but after twenty minutes, I crept into the house to see what he was doing. He was on the phone. I crept back outside to wait with Benny. We talked about what had happened. Neither of us could believe it. Benny kept questioning me about what I had told my daddy the night before. How could I tell him the arrangement I had to make to keep him safe? Even though Dad had agreed to let me have sex with Benny, I didn't know he was going to allow me to have a relationship with him. I was happy that I was able to keep Benny in my life, but I was still scared because I knew Friday was going to come. While I tried to figure out what I was going to do to avoid Friday, Benny began to tell me how the day had played out for him.

Benny said that he had attempted to talk it out with my daddy at work that day, but he wouldn't let him. He told me that when work was over, he exited the building only to have Dad sitting outside the building waiting for him. He told me that all my daddy had told him was to get into the truck.

After hearing his story, I really believed that Benny loved me, and that made me feel even more responsible for him and the mess I had caused by allowing him to spend time with me. I didn't know what would take place on Friday, but I knew that my decision affected so many people.

* * * * *

The week went by quickly. Before I knew it, Friday was here, and I was at school. I walked the halls not knowing what to do. I knew today was the day to either run or stay and accept my fate. I attempted to go see the counselor, but she wasn't in her office. I went to see the nurse, but she had someone in her office each time I tried. The last bell rang, and all the kids exited the building. I rode the bus home in silence. I watched as everyone talked, laughed, and made plans for the weekend. They jumped from seat to seat as the bus emptied. No one noticed that tears streamed down my face. No one noticed that I didn't laugh with them. No one noticed that I was the last to get off at my bus stop, or how slowly I walked home.

When I got to the house, Sammie waited for me on the porch. She didn't notice that I was quiet. I was so deep in thought about who I could turn to, where I could go, and why anybody would stick their neck out for me that I didn't notice that Dad and Benny had pulled into the driveway. Before I could even stand, Benny got out, and Dad drove away. Benny entered the front porch and told Sammie that my daddy said he would be back in a few minutes to take her to work.

Benny and Sammie sat and joked with each other while I wondered about where Dad had gone. About an hour later, Dad pulled back into the driveway. He had liquor, and all three of the adults drank. After a while,

Sammie got up to get ready for work at the restaurant, while we sat and talked for a while longer.

When Benny went to the restroom, Dad slipped me a brown paper bag. "Put this in your bedroom for later." As I began to open the bag to look inside it, he grabbed it and closed it, saying, "I told you to put it up for later." When Dad left to take Sammie to work, Benny and I were alone at the house. We knew he'd be gone for a while because he said he was going to Christie's house.

I was nervous, so I fixed myself a drink and drank with Benny. We sat around talking for a while before we began to make out. I pulled away from him and told him that I was going to change my clothes. When I came back, I had changed into a T-shirt and shorts, and I brought the brown paper bag and set it on the table beside the couch. We picked up right where we left off. As we made out, he told me how much he wanted to make love to me. "It's okay. Look in the sack," I said.

He looked into the sack and said, "What are you doing? What's this for?"

Nervously, I stammered, "Well, your birthday is in a week, and I promised to give you a present."

He immediately began to get undressed, and I slowly followed his lead. When we were both naked, he reached for me and asked, "Are you sure you want to do this?"

"No," I said, "but I know that I want my first time to be with you."

He kissed me, but I couldn't stop thinking about what was going to come next after Dad came home. The whole time we had sex, I wondered why any father would want to have sex with his daughter. When it was over, Benny lay there in the dark singing the words to Rod Stewart's song "Some Guys Have all the Luck." I, on the other hand, lay there crying and wondering why I had such rotten luck.

When one of my tears fell on Benny's head, he jumped. "What's wrong? Did I hurt you?" he asked.

"No, no," I said. "I'm just crying because I'm so happy," I lied.

After we lay there for a while, we showered and went upstairs to watch television until Dad came home. When Dad arrived, he immediately told Benny that it was time for him to go home. "I'm tired, and I need to get some sleep," he said. He walked past Benny and went to the basement. Benny asked me if my daddy was going to give him a ride home, so I went downstairs and asked him.

"Leave me the f*** alone," he said. "Get away from me. Tell Benny to walk home."

When I got upstairs, Benny was putting on his shoes and told me that he had heard my daddy. "Just ignore him. Sometimes he acts strange," I told Benny, but he acted flustered and just kept looking at the floor as he grabbed his stuff to leave.

After Benny left, I poured myself a drink. I needed the drink to do what was going to come next. I knew the time to run was past, and I now had to accept my fate. I didn't know when he was coming for me, but I knew by the way he wanted Benny out of here as soon as possible that it would be soon. I had two drinks before I lay down in my bed, thinking he would come to me that night. Thirty minutes later, Dad called me to the basement and made me climb into the bed with him.

I kept waiting for him to do it and get it over with, but he went to sleep. I kept waking him up and asking him if I could leave, but he would only respond with a "no" and "go back to sleep." Through crying and wondering how I had gotten myself into yet another mess, I drifted in and out of sleep. Sometime in the middle of the night, he woke me up and questioned me about what had happened between Benny and me. He wanted to know if we had done it. He wanted to know what Benny had done to me. I don't know why I thought he would respect my privacy, considering what he was about to do to me, but I did expect it. As he questioned me and wanted a full rundown of whatever Benny and I did together, not only did I begin to grow increasingly irritated, but a wave of nausea was taking over my body the more questions he asked and I was forced to answer.

After he had asked his questions, he told me to open my legs. I started to cry. "Can't you just do the same thing you always do? I'll even masturbate you this time," I cried.

"A deal is a deal," he said. "It's time to pay up."

I tried to pretend like I was asleep, like I had done in the past, but he wanted to talk to me and ask me to do with him what I had done with

Benny. I closed my eyes and tried to ignore him. Then I heard him whisper in my ear. "Move your body," he said. "I know you moved when you were with Benny."

I continued to lie there and pretend that I didn't hear him. I began to quietly hum a church song that we sang in church. It ended quickly after that.

"Get out of my bed, and go take a bath," he said after it was over.

I was glad to go. Just as I went upstairs and began to run my bathwater, Sammie came into the back door. She knocked on the door and told me to come out so she could use the restroom, but I told her I was already in the tub. I was scared that if she saw my face, she would know what had happened. Long after I was done taking a bath, I heard her cussing me for taking so long. She kept threatening to go outside and pee if I didn't hurry up. I felt bad for her, but I couldn't face her. I didn't let the water out until I heard her come back into the house from peeing outside and head upstairs to her room. As the water drained out of the tub, I crept out of the bathroom and entered my bedroom.

I thought about what had happened that night and decided to get up and get something to help myself sleep. I decided another drink wouldn't hurt. As I sipped the drink, both of my brothers walked into the house. They both remarked about the drink, but I didn't care. I drank the glass of E&J brandy mixed with Pepsi and made another. I felt warm and fuzzy inside, and the warmth somehow made it easier for me to fall asleep.

* * * * *

Because Benny and Dad didn't have to work the next morning, Benny came over bright and early. He was so excited to see me. He thought he and Dad would work in the garage, but Dad had already risen and gone to Christie's house. Benny and I hung out all day, watching television and making out. In between making out, we both drank. Later that evening while everyone was gone, we ended up having sex again. When Dad came home that evening, Benny and I were watching television, but he rushed Benny out of the house again.

I wasn't sure what was about to happen, so I again made myself a drink, this time making it a little bit stronger than all of the others. Ten minutes after Benny had left, Dad again called me to the basement. He again made me lie down in the bed next to him.

"Did you and Benny do it again?" he asked.

"Why do you want to know? Isn't that our private business?"

Without a word, he slapped me. I fought back tears. "I asked you a question. Answer me."

Nervously, I said yes.

He then took off his pants. "Then it's time to pay up."

"Please, Daddy, don't make me do this."

"You know the deal. If Benny gets to put it in, then you've got to let me do it too."

"Forget it," I said. "I don't want this deal anymore. I'm not doing this every time. You're not my boyfriend."

"If you don't let me do it, then Benny is going to jail. The two of you have had sex now, and that's against the law."

Again he complained because I just lay there until he was finished. I tried to pretend I was somewhere else. I ignored him when he told me to move my hips. I acted like I was asleep. When he was done, he again told me to go take a bath and go to bed. This time, as I sat in the bathtub, I took a drink into the bathroom with me. I liked how the more I drank, the warmer and fuzzier I felt inside.

Within a couple of days, Dolly found out from one of Benny's nieces what was really going on between him and me. Benny ran all the way to our house to warn me that Dolly knew about us. "Please run away with me," he begged. "We can go to my momma's house. She will protect us."

I wanted to give in to him. I wanted to run upstairs, pack my clothes, and never come back. I wanted to tell him the whole story about the deal I had entered into with Dad, but I was scared. What if he thought I was crazy and left me too?

Benny explained to me that Dolly was coming to tell Dad. Dolly said that if she couldn't have him, no one else would because she was going tell the law what he was doing with me. I reminded Benny what Dad had told him about taking me away, but he told me that he didn't care if he went to jail because his momma would take care of me until he got released. I told him that I couldn't run away with him and begged him not to leave me. He hugged me and reassured me that he wouldn't leave Kewanee without me.

I reassured him that there was nothing to worry about, and that Dad would know how to handle Dolly. Dolly and Benny's sister went to Christie's house and tried to talk to him there, knowing that Benny would run to me, but Dad refused to talk in front of Christie. He told them to meet him at his house.

When everyone arrived, Benny and I were waiting for them. We were very anxious about Dad's decision. We listened as Dolly kept her promise and told Dad about our relationship. It didn't work out the way she had intended, though.

"I appreciate you telling me this, Dolly," he said, "but to be honest, I don't really care what you do to Benny. I will tell you this, though. You better not touch my daughter."

"Well, she's messing with my husband," Dolly shouted.

"I know that. I feel bad for your situation, but several of your family members have told me that you've left Benny before. In fact, I even heard he got down on his knees in the mud and begged you not to leave him. They told me that you just laughed at him before getting in your car and driving off. The way I see it, you gotta expect that he's gonna start looking somewhere else if you treated him like that."

Dolly put her hands on her hips and glared at him, speechless. She looked at all of us. Her eyes scanned all of us—me, then Dad, then from Dad she turned her gaze to Benny, and back to me. Her face changed from anger to disbelief and back to anger.

After a short pause, Dad continued. "Now, I ain't got a problem with you, and as long as you keep your hands off my daughter, then you and I will get along fine. As far as Benny's concerned, like I said, I don't really care what happens to him, but if you go running your mouth, he might go to jail. If he goes to jail, you will have to support them children of yours by yourself. As for Benny, I don't think he will like it in prison. Do you know what they do to perverts in prison?"

Still speechless, Dolly nodded. She began to open her mouth to speak, but Dad interrupted her and began to speak again.

"If he's here on the outside, I'll make sure he keeps his job, and I'll also make sure that he helps you with those babies. If he's in jail, he won't be able to give you money. As far as him and my daughter, they say they got something serious going on, and if I forbid her to see him, then she's only gonna want to see him more. That's how it is with parents and kids." He turned to Benny. "Like I told Dolly, you need to keep your job and give her money to help take care of those babies. As long as you do that, you're welcome at my house anytime."

Even though it was out in the open and everyone knew about our relationship, it didn't get any better. Over the next couple of weeks, Dolly would wait until Benny and I were alone in the house and then knock on the door, pretending she needed to talk to Benny about one of the children. Once he opened the door, she would charge into the house and try to beat me up. She always waited until Dad wasn't home. Fortunately, Benny was always on his toes and headed her off before she got into the house. I would always stand just inside the door while they fought each other. Some nights, this ended with him outsmarting her and getting back into the house. Other nights, he would leave with her.

During the day, she tried to surprise me. One day, while I was walking out of my last class for the day, she was waiting for me. When I saw her, I took off running and made it to the school bus before she caught me. She tried to beat me home and waited for me at my bus stop, but I got off at the bus stop before my stop and took the alleys before she realized what I had done to prevent her laying hands on me.

I didn't tell Dad that Dolly was trying to beat me up, because in a way, I felt like she had a right to try. Besides, Dad's abuse was more frequent, and I didn't want to give him the satisfaction of "protecting" me from Dolly. During that time, my drinking increased. I guess it was a direct result of everything going on in my life. Benny noticed that I was drinking more and suggested that I quit drinking "the hard stuff" and drink wine instead. He introduced me to T.J. Swann's wine. I loved Mellow Days and Easy Nights flavors. He would buy me four or five bottles every couple of days.

Every time Benny and I were about to have sex, I would feel as if I had to pee, but when I went to the restroom, I would no longer have to go. I couldn't understand why it kept happening, and whenever it happened, I used it as an excuse to refill my cup with more wine. I needed the wine to help me relax enough to have sex with Benny, and I definitely needed the wine to numb myself to have sex with my daddy afterwards. Most of all, I needed the wine to dull the pain I was constantly in from having to perform sexual favors for my daddy. I would drink a big glass of wine or a cup of coffee with whiskey in it in the morning before I went to school each day.

Some nights, I drank so much it was hard for me to wake up and go to school the next morning, so I didn't go to school a lot. Benny noticed that I wasn't going to school, and it worried him. He had not been aware of my attendance problems. He did not want my daddy to blame him and make him stay away from me. "Why don't you go to school? What's wrong with you? "If you don't go to school, your daddy is going to make me stay away from you."

"No, he won't. He does not really care if I go to school or not. Besides, I would have gone to school if I hadn't drunk too much last night."

"Great, he will blame me, since I am the one buying it for you. Maybe you shouldn't drink anymore unless it is on the weekends."

How could I tell him that I couldn't stop drinking, that I needed it to dull the constant pain?

Around Thanksgiving, Dolly came over and begged Dad to make Benny take her home to see her parents for the holidays. Benny didn't want to go unless he could take me to meet his mother, but Dad told him no. He told Benny that if he took me with him, there was a chance Dolly might hurt me in Kentucky, so he couldn't allow him to take me. Dad suggested that Benny take Dolly to see her family. Benny didn't want to go, but Dad wouldn't leave him alone until he agreed. Benny called me every day while he was away. By the time he came back home, I was worried almost out of my mind that he wouldn't come back to me.

* * * * *

December brought about new changes in my life. First, Dad came home one day and told me that I had to move to the basement. He said he noticed too much air coming in my bedroom window, and because he didn't have the money to fix it, I had to move to the basement and share his room with him. No one seemed to care that a fourteen-year-old girl was sharing a bedroom with her father.

The other big change came about when Benny and I were making out. I noticed that every time he bumped my breasts, they hurt. I asked him why my breasts were hurting. He grew silent before he replied. He said that since I was having sex, my body was probably just changing. I accepted that as a legitimate answer. A few weeks later, we were making out again, and as we were about to have sex, I felt cramping in my abdomen. I went to the restroom, and when I wiped, I noticed that I had a dark-brown discharge. It scared me at first, but then I thought it must be my monthly.

When I told Benny about it, he grew silent again. This time, he asked me if I had regular periods, and I told him no. I had never gotten regular periods. Dad had made me go to the doctor when I was eleven years of age. At that time, I was diagnosed with endometriosis. Believing my explanation, he told me that since I was having sex, my body was changing.

Two days later, my period stopped, and I again told Benny about it. "How long is your cycle normally?"

"When and if I have a period, it is heavy and lasts all of seven days, nothing at all like this one."

Trying to reassure me that there was no need for concern, he replied, "Your body is just changing because you are a woman now." He explained, "Even though this is not normal for you, you have to take into account that you have never had sex before. It's probably just old blood that is just now coming down because we are having sex."

During this time, that sensation to have to pee during sex kept growing worse, so I also asked Benny why this kept happening to me. "You don't know anything, do you? You got to stop worrying. You are having sex for the first time, and your body is going to go through some changes."

Feeling embarrassed that I didn't know anything, I decided that I would stop asking questions and just accept his answers that the changes occurring in my body were because I was having sex. After all, he was older and much more experienced than I was, so he should know better than me what was taking place with my body.

One day during PE class, I overheard one of my classmates explaining the same sensation of needing to urinate during sex to an upperclassman. Everyone laughed at her. They told her that she was about to have an orgasm, and they advised her to just let it happen.

I couldn't wait to tell Benny what I had learned. When I told him, he laughed and said, "Well, I guess I don't know everything." We decided that the next time I felt the sensation, I wouldn't stop to go to the bathroom. We would, instead, continue with sex and see what happened. Benny had given me orgasms, but not from the motion of us having sex, so we were both excited about the whole notion. We tried just as we planned, but we were unsuccessful in making it happen. I was disappointed, but Benny just said, "Don't worry. We'll just have to keep trying until it happens."

Later that night, Dad came home and forced me to have sex with him. During the torture session, I began to feel that sensation to pee again. I silently prayed to God to make it go away. I didn't want to have my first real orgasm with my daddy. I didn't want to have *any* orgasm with my daddy. I cried as the feeling grew more intense, silently begging for God to make it stop.

Please God, just make it stop. I don't care if I ever have an orgasm—not even with Benny. Please, just turn it off. Just like that, as soon as it had started, it stopped. I don't know if Dad knew what was going on or not, but when it was over, he asked me if I had felt anything different while he was doing it to me. I lied and told him no.

After he left, I cried out of both relief and sadness. I wanted to have sex because I *wanted to*—not because my father forced me. What the other girls in the locker room were laughing and squealing about was something that I didn't want my body to feel. If that happened while I was with my daddy, I was sure that I would lose what I had left of my mind. Life just wasn't fair.

* * * * *

Dolly seemed to calm down and came to my house less and less, but my drinking was at an all-time high. It was getting harder and harder for me to go through the motions of being normal. I tried to smile and act as if everything was all right, but I was slowly dying and no one noticed. Every time Dad violated me, he killed a piece of my soul. The little girl in me who had hopes and dreams died, and I saw her take her last breath.

Around me, everyone was developing a routine. By this time, Dad and Benny worked for two or three hours in the garage before Dad went to Christie's and left me alone with Benny. Benny and I would have sex before Dad came home for the night; then Dad would have sex with me upon coming home and some mornings again before he left for work.

Everything came to a screeching halt one Sunday morning when Sammie made all of us breakfast. She was cooking bacon, one of my favorites, but the smell made me sick. I got up from the table, ran to the bathroom, and vomited. When I came back, no one said a word, but I noticed them exchanging strange looks. I decided not to eat breakfast. Later that afternoon, Dad called me to the basement.

"When was the last time you had your monthly?" he asked.

"I don't know," I said. "It has never been regular."

"Well, when was the last one?" he asked again in a louder tone.

I explained what had happened in November, and he asked me if my breasts were sore.

"Yeah, they have been a little sore," I said, "but Benny said that my body is just getting used to being sexually active."

Ignoring my reply, he said, "You're not going to school tomorrow. I'm going to have someone take you to the doctor. Now, get out of here."

I didn't mind not going to school, but I knew that going to the doctor was a waste of time. Being pregnant never crossed my mind. I guess the idea should have occurred to me, but I felt confident in the answers that Benny gave me. After all, I didn't know the symptoms of pregnancy. None of my friends had ever been pregnant for me to know the signs.

The next day, Benny's sister Amy picked me up in her Lincoln to take me to the doctor's office. She stayed in the room with me while the nurse asked me if there was a chance that I was pregnant. I told her no. I told her my symptoms, but I reassured her that I wasn't pregnant. I told her that my boyfriend said that my body was just going through some changes because I had just started having sex.

"Well, hopefully you're right, but I need you to take a pregnancy test just to make sure." Then, she handed me a cup. "Fill this up to the line."

After I came back to the room with the cup full of urine, I sat in the room with Amy. "What are you going to do with a baby if you're pregnant?" she asked.

"Nothing, because I ain't pregnant," I replied matter-of-factly.

Just then, the nurse walked in, took my hands, and told me that the test was positive. I just smiled and said, "Oh good."

She looked directly in the eye and said, "Dorthea, you did hear me, didn't you?"

I repeated what she had told me. "Yes. You said the test was positive. Positive means that I am not pregnant."

The nurse, who had known me all my life, who had given me my annual physical, who had given me all my shots, gasped and hugged me. "No, honey, positive means that you are pregnant."

I didn't know what to do or think. How could this be happening? How could I be pregnant? I had just turned fourteen in October! What was everyone going to think about me? I was too numb to even cry.

Amy and I drove in silence to Kewanee Corporation. I asked her to pull up to the lunchroom doors while I went in and asked for my daddy. When Dad came over to the doors, he didn't even say hello. "What did they say?" he demanded.

"I'm pregnant."

"Fine. I'll call Christie. She'll take you to get rid of it."

Then, he turned around and returned to work. He never even asked me what I wanted to do or how I felt. As Dad walked away, I yelled, "Can I talk to Benny?"

He didn't say anything, but I continued to stand there, and a few minutes later, I saw Benny walking toward me. When I saw the look on Benny's face, I knew Dad must have already told him. He came up to me with tears in his eyes.

"Don't worry about it, sugar. I take care of my other children, and I'll take care of this one, too. Did the doctor say how far along you are?"

"Twelve weeks," I said numbly.

"Okay. We'll talk about it more when I get off work."

Amy drove me back to my house. After I got out of the car, I stood there, stunned. I didn't know what to do. Should I go into the house or keep walking? I didn't want to be pregnant, but I didn't want to get rid of my baby either. Sammie noticed me outside standing in the snow and called for me to come in out of the cold.

* * * * *

That night, Dad dropped Benny off at our house and went straight to Christie's house. Benny came in with an attitude and took it out on me. When I asked him what the problem was, he started screaming. "I don't want to kill my baby. I just don't understand why yo' daddy thinks you're too good to have my baby. You ain't the first fourteen-year-old to get pregnant, and you sho' won't be the last."

Seeing how badly he wanted to have a baby with me, I told him that if he wanted to have the baby, we could, but I wasn't staying in Kewanee where everyone would talk about me. Hearing my feelings about the subject, he seemed to calm down and decided that he would do some checking to see if his momma would help us if we kept the baby.

Long after Benny had left for the evening, Dad came to bed in the basement that we shared as a bedroom. Again, he demanded sex from me. "Dad, I've had a hard day. Please, don't make me do this tonight. I just found out that I'm pregnant, and I'm only fourteen!"

"The damage is already done now. Your hard day don't have nothing to do with my needs," he said.

* * * * *

The next day, I didn't go to school. After work, Dad and Benny came to the house, and Dad called Christie. She told Dad that she wasn't able to get me an appointment for two more weeks. She said that it might be too late by then. Dad was obviously upset, but Benny and I were secretly happy about this turn of events. For the next two weeks, Benny made plans to take me away. Several times, I tried to talk Dad into allowing me to keep the baby, but he said that there was no way that he'd allow me to keep the baby and stay in Kewanee.

The two weeks passed quickly, and I was supposed to go to the clinic to see if they'd perform the procedure. The night before, Christie called in order to prepare me for what was going to take place at the clinic. After she explained what they'd do during the abortion, I told her that I wanted to keep the baby and raise it with Benny. I told her not to tell Dad, but later that night, Christie called Dad and gave away my secret. She warned him that if I went into the appointment and told them that I didn't want the procedure done, then they definitely wouldn't do it. She told him that if I was hesitant about it, then they would make me wait and reschedule. She feared that I wouldn't be able to have the abortion if they made me reschedule, since I was already cutting the time down to the wire.

Dad waited until Benny left to assault me with words. "If you don't have this abortion, I'll see to it that Benny goes to jail for the rest of his life."

"Why do you want me to have an abortion so bad?" I asked him.

"If you have this baby, then you'll be ruining your life," he replied.

"Well, it's my life to ruin, and I want to keep my baby."

"How in the hell are you going to raise a baby?"

"Benny's family will help me raise the baby. He's already asked them."

"Oh, you've got it all figured out, huh? Well, if Benny goes to jail for the rest of his life, it'll be because of you, and I guarantee you that they won't help you raise it then. They might even trick you into going to Kentucky so Dolly can get at you. Besides, even if Benny does get out of jail, he'll resent you for being the reason he got put in there in the first place. Jail's a hard place, and bad things happen to men who go to jail, so when he gets out, he'll hate you for making him go through that. Maybe you need to think about all of that."

* * * * *

On the morning of the appointment, Christie picked me up, and we drove me to Peoria, Illinois, to have the procedure. All the way there, I was scared of what they would do to me. I was scared of what would happen to Benny if they weren't able to perform the procedure. I was scared of the sin of killing my baby. I tried to tell myself that the sin was not mine, that it was my daddy's because he was forcing me to do this.

Within an hour, we were back on the road heading home to Kewanee. They weren't able to perform the procedure—I was too far along. They gave Christie pamphlets about a place in Missouri that would perform the procedure up until twenty-four weeks. The sonogram had determined I was over fourteen weeks. On the drive home, I was both secretly excited and scared. Maybe, I would finally be allowed to leave with Benny and begin a life without my daddy. On the other hand, I wondered if he would really let me go. Would he have Benny arrested? I rode home in silence while Christie worried aloud if my daddy would find some way to blame her for things not going according to plan today.

That evening, after Dad found out that I didn't have the procedure, he had a meeting with Benny outside in the garage without me. When Benny came into the house, Dad didn't come with him. Dad went to Christie's house. Benny came into the house very drunk and began cursing my daddy, calling him the devil. Benny ranted and raved about how my daddy had talked to him like he was "nobody." I tried to calm him down and reassure him that soon we would be long gone—living together in Kentucky with his momma where my daddy couldn't bother us again. He grabbed both of my wrists.

"There's not going to be any baby," he yelled. "Your daddy told me that he wants you to go to St. Louis to have an abortion, and he said if you didn't go through with it, then he's going to put me in jail. He's sending you to stay with your sister until you get the abortion. Not only that, but he said that your sister would probably try to talk you into having the baby. He threatened me. He said that I have to convince you that having the abortion is the right thing to do—or he'll press charges against me!"

"What about our plan?" I cried. "We can still go to Kentucky and raise the baby together!"

"I can't afford to go to jail. If I'm in jail, who's gonna take care of Dolly and the kids?"

"But you said that even if you go to jail, your momma would help," I wailed.

"Well, your daddy said that he would press charges against anyone who helps us, including my mother. You're still a minor, so he's right. If you go to my mother's house, then she'll get in trouble for keeping you. I can't do that to my momma. She shouldn't suffer for my mistakes." Though he was still screaming, tears streamed down his face.

As I listened to him, it all sank in—Dad was determined to make sure that I didn't have this baby, even if he had to turn Benny against me to accomplish it. I cried harder when Benny's voice softened.

"I don't have the right to ruin your life. After you have the abortion, I'm going to leave you alone and go back to Dolly and the kids."

I cried and begged him not to leave me.

"Your daddy has a point. You need to finish school. You're young. In four years, when you graduate, if you still want to be with me, then we can be together without your daddy getting involved."

I grabbed him as he tried to walk out the back door. I ran after him, screaming that I couldn't live without him. I told him that I loved him, but he kept walking, pushing me away from him. I threw myself down at his feet and begged him not to leave me. Benny reached down to the floor and touched my cheek. "I love you too, but I can't deal with your daddy. This was the last straw."

Benny didn't even wait for Dad to get back to give him a ride home. After he left, I felt so alone. What was I going to do now that Benny had left me? How could I live with myself if I went through with the abortion?

* * * * *

The next morning, Dad woke me to tell me to be ready when he got off work. He informed me that he would be taking me to Missouri to stay with my sister Angel until the abortion was complete.

"I don't want it," I said quietly. "It's a sin to kill my child. It's bad enough that you've turned me into your girlfriend, but now you're making me a murderer."

"It's a sin to sleep with a married man."

Ignoring his reply, I said, "Why do I have to have the abortion?"

"Are you crazy? You'll have that baby over my dead body. I ain't going to jail."

I thought he meant that he might go to jail for allowing me to be with Benny. Then it began to register—he must believe the baby was his.

"You think this might be your baby? No, no, no. I know it's Benny's baby," I said quickly.

He was quiet for a moment, and then he asked, "How can you be sure that it's Benny's?"

"Two times, the condom broke."

"Why didn't you ever tell me that? I told you to explain to me everything that happened between the two of you!"

"It makes me uncomfortable talking to you about that stuff."

For a moment, he relaxed. "I guess if you're sure that it's Benny's baby, then you can have it, but you're still not living in this house. You'll have to get out of my house if you're going to have this baby."

Secretly, I shouted with joy. There was nothing I wanted more than to get out of this house. Just when I relaxed and began to think everything would be fine, the phone rang. It was Angel. She told Dad that she had secured me an appointment the first part of the next week. She wanted to make sure I was truly coming to stay with her. I waited for him to tell her that he had changed his mind, but he assured her that I would be there.

I waited all the next day, thinking he would change his mind and not make me go to my sister's, but when he came home after work, he told me to get ready, and after he went to get fuel, he'd be back to get me.

"Where's Benny?" I asked. "I'm not going without Benny."

"Benny don't need to go. I told Benny to go back to his wife and to leave you alone."

"If Benny went back to his wife, then there's no reason for me to come back here after the abortion. If I don't have Benny anymore, then I'm just going to stay at Angel's house in St. Louis. I'll go, but I'm not coming back!"

"Into the basement—now! We need to have a serious talk," he yelled.

I was scared to go to the basement with him, but I hid my fear and defiantly replied, "No. My legs hurt. I can't go down those stairs."

"Fine, but let me tell you this. I don't care if you come back or not, but you're going to have this abortion. If you don't have the abortion, I'm going to do what I said I'd do. I'll have Benny arrested. In fact, I'll take you up to the police station right now. If that is Benny's baby, then he is going to jail tonight." I grew scared because Dad, who usually screamed at us, was not screaming. He was speaking slowly and deliberately. "Get your coat on. We're going to the police station right now. I'm tired of this shit!"

When I didn't move, he marched over to me and pulled my arm. I still wouldn't move, so he slapped me. I screamed, "Dad I'm pregnant. You can't hit me while I'm pregnant!"

"I don't care about that bastard you're carrying. I wish the both of you would die!"

Maybe it was his words or maybe it was the way he said it, but I knew he meant it. I dialed back my attitude, and in a calm voice, I said, "I'll have the abortion if you let Benny ride to St. Louis with me."

Without another word, he turned and walked away from me.

* * * * *

When Benny walked into our house, he was already drunk. He staggered into the house and snapped at everyone who tried to speak to him, even me. I needed him to love me and give me moral support, but he only thought about himself. On the road, he didn't speak to me at all. He slept and looked out the window. Whenever he was awake and we were driving through a town that had streetlights, I saw tears running down his face. When I tried to reach out to him to comfort him, he pushed me away from him and took another drink from the bottle that Dad had brought for the trip.

We had arranged to meet Angel's husband at Uncle Andre's house, and then we would follow him to Angel's house. When we arrived, it was late, and Uncle Andre didn't know we were coming. "Hey, everybody. Come on in! What ya'll doing out so late? Ace, why didn't you call me and tell me ya'll was coming?"

As we all entered the house quietly, trying not to disturb anyone, we could hear Uncle Andre calling out to Aunt Grace that we were at their house. We could hear them whispering about what would make us travel so late at night. Within moments of the whispering, Aunt Grace stood before us. She was her usual cheerful self—offering everyone coffee and something to eat. Everyone but Dad declined.

While Dad ate, Benny wandered off into the front room of their house. I followed him. I needed him to talk to me. I needed to hear him tell me that he loved me and wouldn't leave me once this was all over. I guess he had sobered up, because he held me and told me that he was so sorry for messing up my life. I reassured him that he hadn't messed up my life like my daddy kept telling him. I told him that my life was messed up the day I was born. This made him laugh, and he kissed me.

Just then, my aunt walked into the room and saw us.

"Child, is this man your boyfriend?" she asked incredulously.

"Yes," I replied proudly.

"Does your daddy know about the two of you?"

We both nodded.

"Why are you here—and not in school?

"Um—I'm coming to spend the week with Angel."

She sat with us a little while longer before she exited just as quietly as she had entered. Benny and I picked up where we had left off, and we became so lost in kissing each other that we didn't hear the arguing at first. Then the screaming grew louder.

"How dare you bring this man up into this house with Dorthea!" my uncle screamed. "You ain't ever been no good, and something tells me that you're trying to involve me in something that ain't right—something that's very wrong."

"It's not anything you need to worry about. I'm not involving you in nothing. We just need to wait here till Angel's husband gets here. We're going to follow him to their house."

"If you didn't have Dorthea here, I'd put you and that *man* out right now. I don't know exactly what's going on here, but I'm not stupid, and I think I've got a few things figured out."

"You're overreacting. Take it down a notch or two, Andre."

Uncle Andre excused himself, saying that he had to get up in the morning for work. Aunt Grace and Dad sat in the kitchen and talked while we continued to wait.

Benny and I talked about why my uncle was so upset with my father. How dare he pass judgment on anything I did! He didn't even know me or anything I had been through. The last time I had seen him, I was ten years old at a family reunion.

Luckily, it wasn't long before Luis, Angel's husband, arrived. We followed him home and went into their apartment. As soon as we got into the apartment, Dad said, "Okay, now that she's here, Benny and I have to go. We've got to get on the road because we gotta work in the morning. Benny, go get her bags, and let's hit the road."

After Benny took my bags in, he kissed me and held me so tightly that I thought he would never let me go. He began to say, "Maybe I could—" Then he stopped and just turned around and walked back out the door. I began to run down the stairs, calling out to him. "Benny, what did you mean, 'maybe I could'?" He continued walking behind Dad as if he did not hear me calling out to him. I had to know what he was going to say to me, so I followed behind him.

I began to run faster, trying to reach him before he got into the car with Dad. I knew whatever he had to say, he would not say it in front of Dad. When I reached the bottom floor and looked outside, Benny was only a few steps from me. I hollered out to him, "Benny, what did you mean when you said, 'Maybe I could'?"

He had begun to walk back toward me when Dad stopped walking and turned around to watch us. Just as Benny began to climb the stairs to the entrance to the apartment building to explain to me his answer, Dad called out to him. "Benny, we don't have time for you to talk to Dorthea. We need to get back on the highway."

Benny stopped climbing the stairs toward me and looked at me for a few moments before turning around and walking back toward Dad. I began to walk down the stairs toward him, calling out to him. When he turned to me, he said, "Dorthea, go back in the building. You don't have no business out here."

"But I want to know what you were going to say to me!"

Benny began to open the door to the car, but before he disappeared into the car, he turned and looked back at me. "I'll call you," he yelled. Then he was gone. I stood there in disbelief for a moment before I realized I was outside by myself, and then I turned and went back into the building.

Luis left and escorted them to the interstate. When he returned he was quiet, but after a while he could not contain himself any longer and blurted out a question: "What is going on between you and that old man?" When I told him, he asked me why I was at his house and why my dad had given him an envelope of money to give his wife. I thought he knew why I was there, but when I figured out he didn't know, I told him the truth. He sat there with tears in his eyes while he listened to me. Under his breath, I heard him ask himself what had happened to my dad's mind. He retired to his room to wait for my sister to come home from work in the morning.

The next morning, I was awakened by my sister and her husband arguing over the situation that Dad had dumped in their laps. Angel kept telling him that I was her baby sister and that she would do anything to stop me from ruining my life. Luis just questioned her about why Dad had allowed a grown, married man to sleep with his fourteen-year-old daughter. My sister just kept saying that she didn't know what Dad was thinking, but if her daddy asked for her help, she was going to help him. I lay there for a while and pretended that I was still sleep until I heard the door close as Luis left.

My sister came out of the only bedroom in their apartment and poked my shoulder. I didn't want her to know I was awake, so I waited until she had poked it a couple of more times before I pretended to be waking for the first time. She wanted to know what had happened and why Dad was allowing me to date this man. She told me how she had agreed to help, but she said that it was causing trouble between her and her husband, and she had a right to know what was going on in Kewanee.

I gave her a limited version of the story in order to not cause any more trouble for Benny or myself. "Okay," she said with a heavy sigh. "I made you an appointment on Monday afternoon. According to Dad, you're pretty far along, so you've got to have this done as soon as possible." Then she left to take a shower.

When she got out of the shower, she called me into their bedroom to talk to me. "While I was in the shower, I had an idea," she said. "You can have the baby and give it to me and Luis to raise."

"No way," I said. "I can't just give my baby to you. Besides, how will I explain to Dad and Benny that I didn't have the abortion?"

"All you have to do is tell Dad that the doctor said you're having a reaction to the abortion and that you need some time to rest. You can stay here, have the baby, and nobody will have to know—not Dad and not Benny. I can come get you sometime, and when you visit, you can see the baby."

Sitting there silently, I wondered if her proposition would work. Maybe, I could secretly tell Benny that I had the baby, and everything would be all right between us again. Then my heart sank. "This won't work. Dad will never let me stay here long enough to have the baby."

"Yeah, he will. He won't mind. I talked to him on the phone this morning, and he said that he wanted you away from Benny."

"What? He told you that this morning?"

"Yeah. I called him. I told him that the only way I'd help you out of this was if he assured me that he wouldn't let it happen again. Abortion is not a form of birth control. I know the psychological effects of doing this, and I don't want to be a part of it this time, much less again. I told Dad that. Dad said that he was just going along with you by letting Benny come with you to St. Louis until you got the abortion. He said that he already told Benny that he ain't going to let him see you again. Benny knew that when he left here last night."

"I don't believe you. He would've told me. He acted like everything was normal between us. I need to talk to him."

"That's what Dad said. If you want to know for sure, call Benny and ask him."

I called the pay phone at Benny's job and asked for him, but instead of him coming to the phone, Dad came to the phone. "Where's Benny?" I asked.

"He's busy. What do you want?"

"I want to talk to Benny."

"I'll tell him to call you." Then, Dad hung up the phone.

I cried off and on all that day, but whenever I called and asked for Benny, Dad would come to the phone and tell me the same thing. Seeing me crying, Angel came and put a hand on my shoulder. "Dad's not going to let you talk to him. He's trying to make sure that the two of you stay apart."

Maybe I could trust my sister. Maybe I could stay here forever. Maybe I could even tell her what Dad was doing to me and why he was so insistent that I have an abortion. She did my hair that night, and we rented a bunch of movies. She was being so nice to me, and she kept telling me that she would spoil me the whole time I was pregnant. "I'll spoil that baby too. Because it's your baby, I'll spoil it to death," she said.

By evening, Luis had joined in, and he was nice to me as well. He told me that he did not believe in abortion and would let me stay with them and keep my baby. He told me that St. Louis was big enough that if I chose to keep the baby, they could hide from Dad and he would never find me. I began to believe that I could have a life in St. Louis. Maybe Benny could save enough money to come for me, and then we could live in St. Louis with our baby.

* * * * *

I woke up Sunday with my mind made up that I was going to stay in St. Louis and keep the baby. I just needed to talk it over with Benny to make the decision final. Sunday night, when my sister left for work, Luis came into the den where I sat watching TV and asked me what I had decided. I told him that I had decided not to go to the appointment on Monday afternoon, but that I just wanted to talk it over with Benny on Monday morning. I told him how Dad was blocking my phone calls from getting through to Benny and asked him to help me get Benny on the phone. In an instant, Luis jumped out of his seat. "Wait a minute. No one is supposed to know. Everyone's supposed to think you had the abortion—including Benny. This deal is only on if Benny is out of the picture completely. This man is just using you, and I'm not going to help you if you don't give up on this."

When I started to cry, he walked out of the room and went to his bedroom. I didn't see him anymore that night. Angel called me that night to check on me because she was bored at work. She wanted to know if I was still leaning toward staying with her and keeping the baby. I told her that I didn't know because Luis had told me that I had to give up Benny in order to get any help from either of them. She was furious and asked me where he was. I told her that he was in bed. "Okay, don't tell him I called." Then, she hung up the phone.

The next morning, I awoke to go to the restroom. While I was in the restroom, I heard my sister come home. Immediately, she and Luis began to argue. I pressed my ear against the door to listen.

"Do you want to be with my sister? I can't think of any other reason why you're trying to come between me and my family!" she yelled.

"I just don't agree with her continuing a relationship with that man. He is way too old for her, and he's just using her for sex."

It was hard to make out all of the words, so I slinked into the kitchen to listen better. My sister sounded furious. She bellowed, "Well, why you always bending over backward to make sure she eats?"

"Are you crazy? I would feed any pregnant person. Dorthea is like my little sister."

"I cook for her every day, and if she's hungry enough, she'll eat my food. You ain't got to go get her more food. You going outta your way to do stuff for her."

"I don't see what the big deal is. So what if I went out and grabbed her a couple of meals? She's family. Why are you freaking out like this?"

"I just don't know why you're so concerned with what she's eating. She ain't carrying your baby."

"You better watch how you talk to me."

"Are you trying to keep Benny away from her so you can get into her pants? Is that it? It's pretty obvious that Dad is raising a little whore, if she got pregnant at fourteen by a married man."

Just then, Luis saw me standing in the kitchen listening to them. He told my sister to shut her mouth and walked out of the apartment. Angel then turned on me.

"You're trying to cause problems in my house. Don't even say anything. If you make me any madder, then I'll put you out on the streets right now."

I didn't know what to do, so I walked through her bedroom, went into the living room, lay down on the couch, and cried.

"And stop crying too, before I put you out," I heard her holler at me.

I made up my mind right then and there. I would have to have the abortion and return to 909 Denton Avenue. It was obvious that I didn't have anywhere else to go. Shortly after that, my sister yelled out again. "I'm going to sleep. Be ready to go to the clinic at four when I wake up." She slammed the door to her bedroom.

Dad called my sister's house at lunchtime. He just wanted to make sure that I was still going to go through with the procedure. I told him that I would, but I also told him that I wanted to stay in St. Louis with my aunt and uncle. After a moment of silence, he said, "Why do you want to stay there with them?"

"You know why," I said.

"Tell me. Tell me why, exactly."

"You know why."

"Is your sister home?"

"Yes."

He got quiet again. "If you have this procedure, then I won't ever force you to make any deals again. I just want you to get it done, come home, and go back to school."

"Can I just ask them if I can stay with them?"

"Look, you need to come home anyway. Benny's been moping around here all depressed. He almost lost his job this morning because he was too drunk to come to work. You need to get everything taken care of there so you can get home and make things right here."

Hearing how badly Benny was dealing with things, I told him that I would get it done and come home. About that time, my sister came out of her room. "Are you having the procedure?" she asked.

"Yes," I replied.

"Look, I'm sorry for the way I acted. I was just tired from working all night, and I took it out on you." She promised me that it would never happen again, but how could I trust her after what I had heard her say about me?

* * * * *

At the clinic, they called my name, and Angel went back with me. She paid the money and filled out the paperwork. When they did my sonogram and counseled me, she kept asking them all sorts of questions. She wanted to know the sex of the baby. Because I had confided in her that I sometimes felt butterflies in my stomach, she asked the nurse to tell me what that meant. The nurse ignored my sister's questions and began to exit the room, but then she came back into the room, took a deep breath, and slowly began to speak to my sister. "I do not think it is productive for your sister or you to bother yourselves with such questions, and in light of the situation, I find the questions to be unnecessary and burdensome." With that being said, the nurse turned and exited the room, leaving my sister dumbfounded at her response.

"I don't really think that was necessary. She did not have to act like that. All I asked her was a few questions. I bet if I told her boss she treated you like that, she would get fired." I sat there quietly and thought to myself that I wasn't angry with the nurse. I was relieved she had gotten my sister to stop with the questions.

The nurse stepped out while I got dressed. I was not scheduled to have the procedure until later that evening. Because of the length of my pregnancy, the procedure would be done in two steps. I would come back that evening for the first step and then come back the following night for the second step. They explained what would take place during both steps.

On the way home, my sister said, "That fluttering in your stomach is the baby moving around. You're carrying a four-month-old boy."

"How do you know what it was? The nurse didn't tell us that it was a boy."

"I saw the male parts. Plus, the nurse wrote it on the chart. I saw her."

I don't know why, but I screamed at her to shut up. I couldn't stop. I screamed at the top of my lungs. She kept threatening to put me out of her car if I didn't stop, but I couldn't. It was as if there were two of me. There was the one of me that was watching me act like this—wishing I would stop—and there was the other one of me that couldn't. When we pulled up in front of her apartment building, she got out of the car and left me sitting there screaming. After a while, I calmed down and got out of the car.

As it began to sink in that I did not remember which building my sister lived in, I began to get nervous. I looked back and forth from building entrance to entrance, trying to remember something that would trigger a memory in my mind, a memory that would indicate which entrance belonged to the my sister's building. As I realized they all looked the same, the panic inside me began to rise. I could fill the pounding of my heart increase in speed. What was I going to do? I realized I couldn't just start knocking on doors until I found her. What if I knocked on the wrong door and someone snatched me inside? The fear began to take hold of me, and I could fill myself becoming light-headed. I looked around for somewhere to throw up and heard the entrance to one of the apartment buildings open and close. Just as I looked up to see if I needed to run for cover, I saw my sister walking toward me. Without saying a word, she climbed into the car. I got back in too, and we went back to the clinic.

When we arrived, my sister pulled up in front instead of parking. I asked her if she was getting out and coming in with me. "I don't have time to be seen with crazy people. You obviously need help, and I'm not the one to help you."

As I got out of the car, I wanted to beg her to come in with me—anyone would be better than facing this alone. Before I could ask her, she hit the gas and pulled away. I was still holding onto the door as she drove away, and I stood there startled as the car pulled me forward.

I entered the building and realized that I didn't even know her phone number to call for a ride when I was done. I couldn't worry about that right now. I had to get enough courage to walk through the doors. I knew my mother lived in St. Louis somewhere, but would she take me in? I doubted it. She didn't want me—let alone me and a baby. I didn't have any other choice but to go through the doors and face what was on the other side.

Once I was inside with the other women who had come to terminate their pregnancies, it all became real. I had to strip down to my undergarments in a locker room of sorts and place my garments inside a locker. I looked around, and it appeared that I was the youngest girl there until a girl who appeared to be around nine or ten arrived.

When a nurse called my name, I followed her into one of the back rooms. She busily explained the procedure to me while instructing me to sign here, sign here, and initial here. When I hesitated, she stopped and looked directly at me. In a stern voice, she asked, "Do you want to do this or not? The doctor is running behind schedule, and if you don't hurry up and make a decision, then you're going to have to reschedule."

Whatever haze I was in, I snapped out of it and nodded my head. She opened a door and told me to climb up onto the bed and to put my feet in the stirrups. Once on the table, she hurriedly placed straps on my legs and extended them out and up in the air. As if I wasn't scared enough, having my legs in the stirrups frightened me more.

The doctor came in, and immediately I tried to close my legs, but they wouldn't budge.

"Open your legs wide," he said. He wasn't at all like my doctor at home who called me by name and asked me how my day was going. I tried to lie back and relax while he inserted instruments into my body. I tried to remember what they said was going to happen. I vaguely remembered: slight discomfort, light bleeding, and minimal recovery. That didn't sound that serious, so I began to relax.

I pulled the sheet up over my head to hide my embarrassment at the doctor seeing my private parts. When the doctor finished, he informed me that I needed to make sure to return the next night to complete the process.

"What happens if I change my mind?" I asked.

"It's too late for that. If you try to carry the baby to term now, you could bleed to death, which would also kill the fetus," he said roughly.

Surprisingly, when the procedure was done, I found my sister sitting alone in the waiting room area. When she saw me, she picked up her keys and walked toward the exit. I went back to my sister's apartment and went straight to bed on her couch. I didn't feel like eating or talking to anyone. My sister had to work that night, so she decided to get a nap before she went to work. The lights stayed off, and I fell asleep quickly.

* * * * *

Sometime in the middle of the night, I awoke to a sharp cramp. I called out to Luis, and he woke up and came to see what the matter was. I told him about the cramping, and he immediately called my sister at work and handed me the phone. She told me that everything was going to be all right and that the cramping was to be expected. They had told me that I would feel some slight cramping and might experience some bleeding, but I didn't know it would be this severe.

I slept pretty much most of the next day until it was evening and time to return for the second step of the procedure. On the way there, my sister finally spoke to me. She told me that she had spoken to a friend of hers who told her it wasn't too late—I could still carry the baby. She told me that all I had to do was stay on bed rest for the rest of my pregnancy and there was a good chance that I could carry the baby for another two or three months.

I told her what the doctor had told me about dying if I tried to carry the baby to term. She reassured me that St. Louis had the best doctors, and they could save both the baby and me with no problem. I thought about it, and then I remembered how she had treated me and wondered if she had my best interests at heart. I told her no, that it was too late. We continued the drive in silence. Again, she dropped me off in silence, and I walked into the building, knowing that this time when I exited the building, I would no longer be pregnant.

This time, when the nurse opened the back door, she didn't move as fast. She seemed calmer tonight. Again, she informed me to sign here, sign here, and initial here. Then we walked down the corridor.

In the examination room, I climbed onto the table and tried to pretend I wasn't there. I didn't ask any questions. I cried through the procedure. I heard a sucking noise, and it scared me. I wondered what they were doing to me, as I felt heaving in my stomach. Just when I thought I would faint from the pain, I smelled a strange odor that made me nauseous. It was too much for me to deal with. I pulled the sheet up over my head and tried to pretend I was somewhere else, but no matter how much I tried, the smell wouldn't let me forget. It was if the smell wanted me to remember the horrible thing that

I was allowing to be done. No matter how hard I tried, I couldn't imagine away the smell.

As I exited the building, I felt more alone than I had ever felt in my entire life. I walked slowly down the corridor. I dressed in slow motion. I walked out into the area where my sister sat waiting for me. I didn't hear her as she talked nonstop all the way back to her apartment. I didn't feel the snow as it hit my face while I walked to the apartment building. As I climbed the steps to Angel's apartment, I didn't wonder why I felt so cold.

When I took off my boots, I finally wondered why I didn't feel the snow on my hands. Feeling nauseous, I ran to the bathroom. Sitting on the toilet, I quickly checked my undergarments. I saw blood, and I smelled that same strong odor. Again, the smell took hold of me and made me sick. I moved slowly through the fog. The fog was a gift to silence my inner cries—the tears that no one saw because no one cared. At that moment, I felt as if I had died and that this person who slowly walked through Angel's apartment was someone else. When I lay my head on the pillow, I knew that anywhere was better than where I was. I just wanted to escape into the fog—the fog that cloaked the part of me that had died with my baby. They hadn't just sucked my baby out of me—they had taken my soul with it.

* * * * *

The next day, I slept. My sister kept waking me up to make me go to the bathroom to make sure that everything was all right, but as soon as I lay down, I fell back asleep. I don't know if I was actually sleepy or just tired of my life. I liked the way the sleep carried me away. While I slept, I didn't have to deal with my life. I could get lost in my dreams. My dreams concealed me from a life that, so far, had dealt me only pain. I had a grip on sleep that wouldn't loosen. The only time I let go of sleep was when Angel told me that Dad was on the phone and wanted to speak to me. He wanted to let me know that he would be leaving tomorrow as soon as he got off work to come get me. I asked him if he was bringing Benny, and he said yes. I gave the phone back to my sister without even saying good-bye.

The next morning, I awoke, bathed, did my hair, and waited for Dad and Benny to arrive. Luis and my sister whispered that it was not normal the way I just snapped out of the fog as if nothing had happened. They both watched me and whispered all day. My sister kept asking me if I was sure I was ready to go home. I told her no, but that I was going anyway. My sister even asked her husband to speak with me to see if I was all right, but I merely smiled at him and told him I was fine. They kept trying to think of excuses for me to stay longer.

Dad arrived late that evening to pick me up, and I was shocked to see that Benny was not with him. I asked him where Benny was, and he told me that Benny wanted to spend some time with me by himself to get things straight. On the way home, I listened as Dad spoke. "I asked Benny to come with me, but he said that he was too busy. I think you should know, while you were gone, I went over to Benny's house and found him in bed with Dolly. He got back with her. I know how much he means to you, but it's time that you leave Benny in your past and start over."

Tears streamed down my face as I heard the news, but Dad continued talking. "I'm sorry for everything I've done to you, and I'm sorry for allowing Benny to use you. When we get home, things are going to be different. You can get back in school and get your life back on track, and I promise, I won't ever do anything inappropriate to you again."

My mind was reeling. Benny had left me! Benny was back with Dolly? As I looked over at Dad, I saw tears running down his face as he continuously promised me that this time, things would be different. I was devastated by Benny, but Dad's promises gave me hope.

After everything I had been through, maybe something good would come out of it—maybe I'd finally have freedom from Dad. While Dad drove down the highway, I fantasized about what my life could be like if I were a normal girl. Things would be different, and I would be successful. As the car raced down the highway, I decided to focus on the positives that were about to happen in my life. I promised myself that I would leave all my miseries behind me in St. Louis. I would forget about the past and focus on my new future—a brighter future where I could be happy.

God's choice

A sound in the kitchen jolted me back to reality. Dad was watching TV intently again, unaware of my mental visit to the past.

I thought back over the years. Upon returning home from St. Louis, I found I could not function like other children. It was probably a matter of days before I quit school again. It wasn't official, but I quit just the same. If I thought it was bad before, now it was even worse, because I had to deal with the longing for a child I would never know.

If only I had stayed in St. Louis and had my baby. Then I wouldn't have been tormented by regret and the little boy I never got to hold. Even today, whenever I see someone around the age he would be, I often wonder what he would have been like. Would he have had the best qualities of his father and I—would he have been like my oldest living child, his younger sister, who is such a go-getter? Would he have had the muscular build of this father? Would he have been hard-working and honest? Or would he have inherited our worst traits: would he be a heartless liar or womanizer? I'll never know.

How naïve I had been to believe Dad would keep his promise to me. I soon learned he would have promised me both the moon and stars if I had asked for it—anything to make sure I didn't tell anyone about his activities in St. Louis. I also learned over the years there were reasons he and his family weren't close, and had I have spoken out, things may have turned out differently. After all, they knew their brother before I did. He continued to molest me until I finally broke free from his grasp at twenty years of age.

In the meantime, at age seventeen, an acquaintance from school began to come around who liked to smoke weed, and for a time, I did too. But after a while, it no longer dulled the pain anymore, so I finally left the drugs alone. During this time, I not only did drugs, but I also sold them. I was a major part of the one the biggest drug circles in the state of Illinois. In fact, my dad was arrested for being a drug kingpin, when in all honesty his only crime was sleeping with the women who were addicted to cocaine and needed money. Dad had no interest in the business end of operations, so that left me to do all the business transactions. My sole interest was gaining financial freedom from both Benny and my dad. But when Dad was arrested, it all ended as quickly as it began, and the money and my opportunity for escape were gone.

Benny and I continued to see each other. However, due to my growing up and recognizing he was just using me, the dynamics of our relationship changed. He still continued to give me money, but he also began to have affairs with other women. On one of the occasions I tried to break free of him, he deliberately sought to get me pregnant, and he was successful. I gave birth to Latae, my oldest living child, three months short of turning twenty-one.

I had thought Benny would have been a wonderful father to our daughter, but it was quite the opposite. Hurt by his mistreatment of my child, I tried again to break free from him, yet I still didn't feel I could go it alone. So at age twenty-two, I got married to another man as a result of a business agreement. He was about to come into a substantial amount of money, and he promised to let me control it if we got married. At the time, I was suffering from a clinical diagnosis of chronic depression with post-traumatic stress disorder, which was particularly bad that winter, so it sounded like a good plan to me.

I am not proud of my decision to marry my first husband, but to be honest, I got what I deserved. Once winter ended, I started to come out of my haze and realized I was married to a man I didn't even like. From then on, it was a constant battle to gain my freedom. There was a great deal of domestic violence throughout this marriage, and I am ashamed to admit that I was the aggressor most of the time. At the end of that marriage, I gained my freedom and another beautiful baby girl.

Ironically, Benny was the one who helped me gain my freedom from that first marriage, as he still considered me to be his property. While I continued to lean on him, his indifference toward our daughter was still a major turn off and caused me to continue to look elsewhere.

A few months after my divorce was finalized, I met DeAnte, and six weeks later to the day, we were married. I am not going to say it has been perfect, because it hasn't. We've had our share of ups and downs, but through it all we have managed to collectively raise five children. On our wedding day—April 7, 1995—we joined his son and my two girls together as a family. Over the years we added two additional sons to the mixture we call our family.

I had finally gotten free from my dad, and I had a family who loved me. Why did I want to stir up the past? What made me think anything had changed? Just as I was about to tell my dad I needed to get home, I remembered why I was here—and that night at the revival of my former church, Bethel COGIC, three years ago, when I returned to my first love.

* * * * *

At that time, my husband DeAnte and I were separated as a result of domestic violence, I was pregnant with my youngest child, and I could no longer understand why my life was constantly filled with disappointment and pain. My church was preparing to host a week-long revival, and the pastor had told us to fast during the revival and to come to church every night expecting God to show up and show out on our behalf. I had gone to the revival every night expecting something to happen. One night I watched as my cousin was filled with the precious gift of the Holy Spirit. Although I was happy for her, I was sad that nothing in particular had happened for me.

As the week came to a close, my godmother called and asked if I would be attending church that night. I told her that I did not think I would be going. She must have heard something negative in my voice, because she said, "Now, now, Sister Dorthea; don't be acting like that. You have got to have faith. You need to get dressed and come on out tonight and see what the Lord has for you." I told her I'd try to make it, but as I hung up the phone I knew I had no intention of really going. It had been a long week of dragging all three children out every night just to be disappointed again and again. I lay there and tried to settle in to watch some television, but I just couldn't seem to get comfortable. I kept thinking to myself, *What if tonight is the night I am going to get my blessing? If I don't go, I will miss my blessing.* I continued to lay there until about thirty minutes before the service was scheduled to begin, and then I jumped up from the couch as if I were on fire. I called out to my children, "Get ready! We are going to church."

The service was supposed to be special tonight, because Missionary Bell, a prophetic speaker from Peoria, Illinois, was the guest speaker, and everyone knew she was truly anointed by the Lord. She started by asking if anyone needed something special prayed about. I wanted to run to the altar, but at that time I was still unsure of myself and did not feel worthy. I sat in my seat and held my breath as she moved around the church, calling on different people to give them special words from the Lord, until the service was almost over. Even though she hadn't called on me, it was an awesome experience. From time to time she would look over at me, but then call on someone else to my right or left. So when she called out the next time and looked in my direction, I assumed she again was speaking to someone else. But lo and behold, when I turned around to see who she was speaking to, she told me to stop turning around and get up and come to the front of the church!

I almost did not get up. I was so shocked: what could she possibly want with me? As I made my way to the front, I tried not to look at anyone. I wanted to turn around and look back, but I wanted to hear what the Lord had to say to me even more, so I continued to walk up the aisle, eyes forward, until I was standing in front of Missionary Bell. At first she just stood there looking at me, not saying anything. She just smiled. She stood there for what was probably all of thirty seconds, but to me it felt like forever. I kept fighting the urge to run back to my seat.

Finally she spoke: "Daughter, God is telling me to hug you. He said to tell you he loves you." Before I could do anything, she reached out and grabbed me—and hugged me. It felt awkward, but I stood there and allowed this woman whom I did not know to hug me. I did not hug her back. I stood there motionless with both my arms at my sides, not knowing how I was supposed to respond.

When she let me go and stood back, she spoke again. "Daughter, I have to be obedient. You just don't know how much God loves you!" She approached me and hugged me again. This time I felt something as she hugged me, but I did not know what it was, so again I stood there motionless. This time when she stood back, she just looked at me for a few seconds before she spoke yet again. "Daughter, the Lord said to tell you he heard your cries when you were a little girl, and you thought he didn't hear you. He said to tell you he loves you so much and that he did not want for you to hurt, but you had to go through it because there is a ministry in your belly."

Before I could do anything, she reached out and planted her hand on my belly and spoke again. "You have to forgive him before you will be made whole. You know what I'm talking about, don't you?" I nodded yes, and my eyes began to fill with tears. She then told me, "God said, 'One more time!'" and she hugged me again. This time as she hugged me I felt a dam break in my heart, and the tears began to flow. This time I received her hug by placing my arms around her. She held me and whispered in my ear, "Baby, there is a ministry in you. God didn't keep you so that you would keep it to yourself. Baby, God said, 'Get ready to share your story, so many women and children will be delivered through you.' God said he chose you to deliver this important message. God said he loves you and you are important to him."

For the first time in my life, I began to feel like my life had meaning. I held onto her, crying, not wanting to let go. As I walked back to my seat, I continued to cry. It felt like I was shedding all the years of self-hate, oppression, or whatever else had held me back from letting go of the pain and allowing myself to move on.

That night changed the course of my life forever. God had made his choice to begin a new work in me—one that would give me the strength to return to college and not get one degree but three. One that would allow me to share my testimony with others who have suffered hurt and pain at the hands of a loved one. One that would allow me to return to my first love, Jesus, who helped me make peace with the daddy in my nightmares I had buried long ago. Where there was nothing but hurt, pain, and confusion, God would replace it with forgiveness, compassion, and love.

The next day I awoke with a determined mind. I would call my dad and forgive him. I was scared to call: what if he cussed me out? I decided I would ask for his forgiveness first, hoping that he would do the same. I lifted the handset and dialed his number—all the while hoping he would not answer the phone. But he did.

I began by apologizing for not being the daughter he wanted me to be, but it didn't go as I planned. He became angry and began to scream at me, "You needed to apologize a long time ago. If I had left you like your momma did, what would have happened to you?" He continued to inform me, "Your momma didn't want you. I didn't have to stay with y'all. I should have done what my momma told me to do. I should have left y'all with the police and caught a plane to El Salvador." I held the phone and began to cry. Why did I listen to Missionary Bell? She didn't know me; she didn't know my dad! Tears continued to run down my face. Then I began to relive the events of last night and remembered what she had told me. There was no way she could have made that stuff up. She *didn't* know anything about me. The message from God had to be real.

I wanted to scream at him, *Yes, you should have left us! Maybe then your children wouldn't be all messed up. Maybe we would have had a better chance at life living with strangers!* I wanted to slam down the phone and never speak to him again. But I didn't. Instead I listened as he told me how his children would have had pretty hair and speak another language if he had listened to his mother, but instead he got stuck with good-for-nothing children who were never going to be nothing because of our no-good momma. When he realized I was not going to say anything back to him, he stopped yelling at me and hung up the phone.

I sat in disbelief, holding the phone for a while, not knowing what to do or where to go from there. How was I going to forgive him if he wouldn't ask for forgiveness? Well, I would have to try again, but only after I had a chance to speak with my pastor later in the week, after Friday's service.

However, before I had the chance to do that, later that afternoon my sister Angel called and told me that Dad had sent for her to come get my three children and take them home with her to Davenport, Iowa. Since I was seven months pregnant, he thought I could use some time to get some rest and get ready for the baby.

I did not know what to think. Maybe it was the Lord's plan for us to speak again so I could forgive him. I didn't like the idea of sending my children home with the same sister who had been mean to me so often when I was a child, but I decided to play along and go to my dad's house so I could continue to talk to him. Maybe the Lord was working on him: surely he had to be, since Dad had even offered to pay my sister to care for my small children to give me a break.

I waited until DeAnte arrived home from work, and he, the children, and I all loaded up and went to my dad's house. Once we arrived, DeAnte quickly walked across the street to the long-term care facility where his good friend was living. I hated that DeAnte always had a way of leaving me alone when I needed him the most. I watched as he crossed the street, smoking his cigarette, never even glancing back over his shoulder to make sure we were all right. The children and I entered into the garage and walked through the house where everyone sat waiting for us to arrive. My youngest brother Jake, his girlfriend Kayla, Angel, and Benny all sat around my dad, talking. Kayla had always been there for my children and me whenever my dad did something particularly cruel. Now, because she had taken up with my brother, my fight was no longer her fight. She chose to be entertained by my dad's treatment of me instead of repulsed. As soon as my children walked out onto the back patio, my dad sent both Jake and Kayla to KFC to get some chicken for my children before they hit the highway.

While I sat there waiting for the chicken dinner to return, I tried to think up excuses for why my children could not return to Davenport, Iowa, with my sister. My dad sat and made jokes about his children while everyone sat and laughed. Today, the jokes were on my two oldest brothers Andre and David, mainly David. I tried to be grateful he had decided to not pick on me. However, the longer I sat there listening to everyone laugh while he picked on my brother, I became furious. Before I could stop myself, I confronted him: "Maybe if we had a better father, we would have all turned out better!"

"You know, if that's how you feel you can leave my house!"

"I sure can, but before I go, what type of man destroys his children and then sits around and makes fun of the way they turned out? I bet you think you are so smart!"

"Smart enough that I can pay my own bills and I don't have to live in the projects!" he screamed at me.

I was so furious when I looked around the yard and saw everyone laughing— including Benny, who was almost as much to blame as my dad for the issues I struggled with every day. He had used me from the age of thirteen to twenty-three—how dare he laugh? I looked at Kayla, who had taken care of my girls when I had to be hospitalized due to a nervous breakdown a little over a year ago. I looked at Angel, who sat and agreed with my dad, and hung on to every word his cruel mouth uttered.

"Daddy, don't do nothing for her!" Angel said. "I swear, I don't know what is wrong with my little brothers and sisters. Daddy, they're going to learn one day how cruel this world is and wish they had you to turn to. Boy, I learned my lesson. They just are so ungrateful. Don't worry about them, Daddy!"

I looked at everyone, and before I knew it I opened my mouth and nothing but hurt and pain escaped. "I guess I should have been grateful to my dad for climbing into my bed every night and forcing me to do the things only a woman should be doing?" Everyone stopped laughing and began to look around at each other. "Yes, Dad, you were so smart that the only person you could get to have sex with you was your eight-year-old little girl. You were so smart you couldn't figure out I was your child!"

I knew everyone was listening in shock, but I couldn't stop myself. It felt good to say it out loud. "What, no one's laughing now? You guys thought it was so funny when he just sat there and picked on his children, but you all want to play deaf when I talk!"

Angel screamed at me, "Stop lying on my daddy! You are sick! Why would you scream that outside in front of everyone?"

"Shut up talking to me! This does not have anything to do with you!" I screamed back at her.

My dad yelled at me, "Shut up before I bust you in the mouth!"

"Oh wow, if having sex with me as a child was not enough, now you want to hit me when I'm seven months pregnant? Wow, you are really bad. Just try it, old man—I'm not a little girl anymore!"

My dad ran toward me, and I ran toward him.

Angel intercepted us and kicked me in the side of my stomach. I felt a sharp pain as liquid began to travel down my legs. Just as I was about to fight her back, DeAnte grabbed my arms and began to pull me backwards. As my husband led me to the truck, my dad ran at me with his broken hand lifted in the air. The same hand he had broken at work when I was a child, supporting his family, was now used as a tool to bring about pain. Too many times I had been smacked with that hand. I screamed out, "You better not hit me!"

DeAnte stopped walking and turned toward my dad. "I been turning my head long enough. I don't understand why anyone puts up with you. But now this affects my unborn child. If you lay one hand on her, I will knock you out right here, old man!" That must have done the trick, because no one came after me from that point on. Just as we were leaving, the police pulled up into the yard and began to ask questions. Once DeAnte began to explain the situation, they told him to get me to the hospital immediately.

The hospital treated me and sent me home. Apparently my water had not broken; Angel's kick was to my bladder, which caused a spasm. I gave birth to a healthy eight-and-a-half-pound son two months later.

I stayed away for about eighteen months until we tried again. We had an anniversary barbecue for myself and DeAnte at Dad's house to try to mend the fences between the three of us. However, Daddy was upset because DeAnte had allowed my daughter Latae to ride his 350 Warrior, and Dad had threatened to blow DeAnte's brains out if she got hurt, causing everyone to make their excuses and leave. This time the argument did not end with a physical altercation, but it was very much verbal.

That's when I decided I just couldn't do it anymore. I had made up my mind that in order for me to be happy and healthy, I had to distance myself from him and all negative people, no matter what their relationship was supposed to mean.

Three years passed. Even when I had been told over and over that Dad had cancer and "this was it," I never returned. But one night, as I was working on my homework for my human resources bachelor's degree, I received yet another phone call from Angel about Dad, and this time felt different. I wasn't sure what to do, so I called my pastor for counsel. He informed me it was time to forgive my dad. I asked him, "But what if it's like all the other times, and he picks a fight? I haven't spoken to him since the big fight in his yard three years ago."

"Daughter, listen to what I tell you! The Lord said it is time for you to go! Your dad needs this just as much as you do. You need to forgive him so you can began to heal and be the mighty woman of God that he created you to be."

"Can I wait until tomorrow? Can you come with me to Kewanee?"

"Daughter, if you want me to I will, but you don't need me. The Lord has already worked it out."

My pastor prayed with me, and we hung up the phone. I sat at my desk, trying to complete my homework, and before I realized what I was doing, I had put on my coat and shoes and found myself standing at the front door of my dad's house.

I snapped back to the present moment. I tried to fight back the tears. Yes, I knew I had to at least try to forgive him. Even if he would not do it for me, I had to do it for both of us. We both needed to release each other. I just kept reminding myself that God loved me and this too he would see me through. I looked over at my dad and smiled.

A commercial came on, and Dad briefly turned to look at me, causing me to become restless all over again. That's the thing about self-doubt; it is always waiting in the wings to take hold of your mind and heart again if you allow it.

No. I had come here for a reason. I had to accomplish what I set out to do. I had to do it now. I held my breath, and the burdens began to shake loose, making my body feel lighter. I exhaled before I spoke. “Dad, I forgive you,” I whispered.

FOR THE DEVELOPING WORLD
LIBRARY
FOR ALL
DIGITAL LIBRARY

www.ingramcontent.com/pod-product-compliance
Lightning Source LLC
Jackson TN
JSHW021411170426
101040JS00013B/197